ESSENTIALS OF TEAM BUILDING

Principles and Practices

Daniel W. Midura, MEd

Roseville Area Schools
Roseville, Minnesota

Donald R. Glover, MEd

University of Wisconsin, River Falls

Human Kinetics

Library of Congress Cataloging-in-Publication Data

Midura, Daniel W., 1948-
  Essentials of team building: principles and practices / Daniel W. Midura, Donald R. Glover.
    p. cm.
  Includes bibliographical references.
  ISBN 0-7360-5088-4 (soft cover)
  1. Teamwork (Sports)--Study and teaching. I. Glover, Donald R. II. Title.
  GV706.8.M52 2005
  796.07--dc22   2004030396

ISBN-10: 0-7360-5088-4
ISBN-13: 978-0-7360-5088-3

The Web addresses cited in this text were current as of April 26, 2005, unless otherwise noted.

Safety Reminder: The reasonable risks present in the challenges and activities in this book could result in physical harm, but can be minimized by following the safety suggestions in chapter 4 and the specific instructions for each activity. The authors and publisher do not assume responsibility for the use of information offered in this book either written or implied.

Acquisitions Editor: Gayle Kassing, PhD; **Developmental Editor:** R. Chris Johns; **Assistant Editor:** Michelle M. Rivera; **Copyeditor:** Bob Replinger; **Proofreader:** Ann Augspurger; **Permission Manager:** Dalene Reeder; **Graphic Designer:** Fred Starbird; **Graphic Artist:** Yvonne Griffith; **Photo Manager:** Kelly J. Huff; **Cover Designer:** Keith Blomberg; **Photographer (cover):** Kelly J. Huff; **Photographer (interior):** © Human Kinetics, unless otherwise noted; **Art Manager:** Kelly Hendren; **Illustrator:** Craig Newsom; **Printer:** Sheridan Books

We thank Roseville Area Schools in Minnesota for assistance in providing the location of Falcon Heights Elementary School for the photo shoot for this book. We also thank Gopher Sport for providing images for this book. Contact: Gopher, P.O. Box 998, Owatonna, MN 55060 (phone number 800-533-0446)

Printed in the United States of America   10 9 8 7 6 5 4 3

Human Kinetics
Web site: www.HumanKinetics.com

United States: Human Kinetics
P.O. Box 5076
Champaign, IL 61825-5076
800-747-4457
e-mail: humank@hkusa.com

Canada: Human Kinetics
475 Devonshire Road, Unit 100
Windsor, ON N8Y 2L5
800-465-7301 (in Canada only)
e-mail: info@hkcanada.com

Europe: Human Kinetics
107 Bradford Road
Stanningley
Leeds LS28 6AT, United Kingdom
+44 (0)113 255 5665
e-mail: hk@hkeurope.com

Australia: Human Kinetics
57A Price Avenue
Lower Mitcham, South Australia 5062
08 8372 0999
e-mail: info@hkaustralia.com

New Zealand: Human Kinetics
Division of Sports Distributors NZ Ltd.
P.O. Box 300 226 Albany
North Shore City, Auckland
0064 9 448 1207
e-mail: info@humankinetics.co.nz

To my wife, Carol, thanks for all of your support. I love you.

Don

To my parents, Walter and Alexa Midura, and to Jack and Ann Cook, my father-in-law and mother-in-law, thank you for your example and spiritual leadership in our lives. To my sons, Luke and Seth, I love you guys. To Shirley, I could not do any of this without you. I look forward to another 35 years together.

Dan

Contents

Preface

Helping people become respectful competitors, cooperative team members, and community leaders is a goal that educators, coaches, and recreation and community leaders alike deem worthwhile. Going hand in hand with this idea is the goal of developing good character traits in our citizens. Despite the importance they place on these goals, however, few teachers, coaches, and recreation and community leaders develop specific strategies for achieving and assessing progress toward achieving them. Team building, adventure education, and character education are ideal vehicles for meeting this challenge.

Team building provides individuals and teams physical, social, and emotional challenges. Moreover, team building is the conduit by which people achieve these challenges. Specifically, team building is the strategy of facilitating the creation of a team through a series of purposeful activities and then assigning the team carefully constructed physical challenges to overcome. The people on the team must work together to develop and implement a strategy for achieving their objective. Team building allows participants to find out for themselves that the process of achieving a goal is what's important and that the outcome follows the process. This is an extremely valuable lesson. In addition, team building provides an environment that helps participants understand that failure is only temporary. When one fails, he or she needs to reorganize and try again, and in doing so, travel a much sweeter path to success.

Team building addresses several specific skills:

- Problem solving
- Appropriate risk taking
- Building working relationships
- Cooperation
- Leadership and communication
- Creative thinking
- Building trust
- Making decisions
- Setting goals
- Developing physical skills

We have learned firsthand the value of team building during the nearly 30 years since we first started using what we then called group tasks or problem-solving activities. In just the past decade we've witnessed the excitement and success enjoyed by the thousands of people who have attended our classes and workshops. But the value of and the results gained from team building have certainly not been limited to the children, young adults, and adults with whom we've worked. Here is a small sampling of team-building successes:

- The United States improved its medal count at the 2002 Winter Olympics by 161%, hauling in 34 total medals. United States Olympic Committee president Sandy Baldwin credited the USOC's summit program, which brought together potential Olympians with former medalists for a retreat and team building (Metcalfe 2002).

- Gordon French, director of executive development at Cox Enterprises (Atlanta, Georgia), has had 140 managers successfully participate in a version of team building. He said, "The program shows a significant impact on the variables we are measuring, including behavioral change, measured by 360-degree reviews, and several million dollars of business impact" (North Carolina Outward Bound School n.d.).

- The Odyssey School (www.odysseydenver. org), a public school chartered by Denver Public Schools, has shown significant improvement in standardized test scores in a study five years after implementing an expeditionary learning Outward Bound program. Outward Bound programs include adventure education and many physical and mental challenges that encourage students to cooperate to solve them. Outward Bound programs use team-building principles but take place almost exclusively outdoors.

These are just a few positive examples of what can happen when teachers and leaders deliberately plan to teach respectful competition, teamwork, selflessness, and character through team building. Unfortunately, many examples show what can result from not addressing these issues. Many factors contribute to the flourishing of gangs in our communities, not the least of which is that kids want to belong to something. Instead of joining gangs, kids should be participating in youth sports and learning how to be good teammates and respectful competitors. The many arguments and occurrences of poor sportsmanship at youth sports events, by both players and parents, are painful examples of the result of not addressing respectful competition, teamwork, selflessness, and character.

The purpose of this book is to provide you with both the principles and practices of effective team building. We use these terms together because they are closely related. We explore this relationship in chapter 1 and explain why it's an effective strategy and how it can work in a variety of school, recreation, community, and business settings. In chapter 2, we help you organize your team-building program and detail effective teaching and leadership styles. In chapter 3, we discuss a vital aspect of successful team building—the assessment process. This process includes personal reflection, group discussion, and structured debriefing activities. In this chapter, we also introduce student portfolios and show you how to use this effective evaluation tool with your team-building class. In chapter 4, we show the safety considerations and equipment needed to promote a positive team-building atmosphere and minimize the risk factors of these activities. In chapter 5, we provide a sample design for a semester team-building course that includes 36 day-by-day lessons plans.

In chapters 6 through 10, we provide a wealth of activities and challenges that have proved successful with a variety of participants and environments. Each activity presented includes all the information you need to lead it, including the following:

- Setup. This information gives you correct distances, heights, mat placements, and other specific information that you need to set up the challenge properly.
- Rules. The rules tell you exactly what participants may or may not do during a challenge. The rules also tell you what penalties the team may have to pay if it breaks a rule.
- Equipment. This section will tell you what equipment you need to set up the challenge.
- Variations. You can make modifications to every challenge to offer a slightly different version. For instance, you may want to time a challenge and set time records, or you may want to change a challenge to make it easier for younger children or more difficult for older students.

Finally, we provide an appendix that includes challenge and organizer cards. These cards give the teams all the information they need to get started on the challenges. Please see chapter 2 for further explanation on how to use these challenge and organizer cards. We also include answer keys for some of the challenges and directions for constructing some of the equipment for specific challenges.

Whether you are a teacher, coach, business executive, recreation or community leader, you will find this book a complete source of information on helping your students, players, employees, or children and young adults learn to become respectful competitors, valuable team members, problem solvers, leaders, and selfless, high-character members of school, team, company, or community.

How to Use the DVD

DVD icons have been placed throughout the book to indicate which team-building challenges are demonstrated on the DVD. You can view the video clips to get a sense of how the challenges are performed, or show them to students to see how others have successfully completed the challenges. DVD icons are also used throughout the book to indicate challenge and organizer cards that can be reproduced from PDF files on the DVD.

You can view the video content either on a television set with a DVD player or on a computer with a DVD-ROM drive. The reproducible challenge and organizer cards can only be accessed through the DVD-ROM on your computer (see further instructions at the end of this section).

The DVD includes a main menu where you can select team-building activities. After you have viewed a challenge, the DVD will automatically return to the main menu.

To use the DVD, place it in your DVD player or DVD-ROM drive. A title screen will welcome you to the program. The main menu will then appear with buttons for each category of challenge activities. When you click on one of the buttons, the video will play.

To access challenge and organizer cards from Windows®:

1. Insert the DVD into your DVD-ROM drive.
2. Access Windows Explorer.

3. Click on the DVD-ROM drive icon.
4. Select the PDF file you want to view.

To access challenge and organizer cards on a Macintosh computer:

1. Insert the DVD into your DVD-ROM drive.
2. Double-click on the "TEAM BUILDING" DVD icon on your desktop.
3. Select the PDF file you want to view.

Note: If your DVD viewing program is set to automatically launch, the video content will automatically run. You will need to close out of the DVD viewing program before accessing the PDF files.

You will need Adobe Reader to view the PDF files. If you do not already have Adobe Reader installed on your computer, go to www.adobe.com to download the free software.

Select the HK Running Man logo on the main menu to access information on contacting Human Kinetics to order other products and to view production credits.

Essentials of Team Building
DVD Menu

Acknowledgments

We would like to acknowledge Leigh Anderson. Leigh is the co-author of *Character Education* (Glover and Anderson 2003) and is an expert in the area of assessment. Without Leigh our assessment chapter would not be nearly as complete as it is.

We would also like to acknowledge James Tangen-Foster and Susan Tarr. Both are professors at the University of Wisconsin-River Falls and both contributed to this book. James teaches outdoor education and Susan teaches curriculum and instruction in the physical education department. Jean Berube, an assistant professor at Gallaudet University, and Tom Heck, the "Teach Me Teamwork" coach, gave us invaluable suggestions and input in the area of safety and spotting.

CHAPTER 1

Introduction to Team Building

Team building is the cooperative process that a group of individuals uses to solve both physical and mental challenges. While using this process and solving the challenges, the group learns how to share ideas, how to praise and encourage one another, how to support one another physically and emotionally, and how to start becoming a team.

Team building was introduced into the physical education world in Minnesota in 1972. The basic philosophy behind this concept is that kids need to learn how to be good teammates while struggling to solve a challenge. Team building forces students to exchange ideas and work together to solve a problem. They learn to listen to one another, to deal with failures, and to persevere as a team. While being a member of a team, kids learn that the best way to solve a challenge is to cooperate and offer one another both physical and emotional support. Throughout each challenge, kids learn to value teamwork. They learn to brainstorm solutions, develop a plan of attack, and praise and encourage teammates along the way. Team building provides kids with a connection to a team—a connection that many of us can remember from our early athletic experiences.

The skills that students learn from team building are important components of personal and group development. They are the necessary components for positive action by people, both as individuals and as members of teams, in everyday life, work, and community. Team building has rapidly gained acknowledgment by various disciplines in higher education as a valuable experience and as an attribute of personal and group development.

BENEFITS OF TEAM BUILDING

The many benefits of team building provide a rationale for its importance and inclusion as a learning component in a variety of disciplines and settings. Team building is a concept that supports an array of activities and programs in many settings. We believe that the space, equipment, and curriculum of the physical education setting offer the best support for team building and the challenges included in this book. The challenges offered in physical education can teach students to take the next step and solve the problems and trials that adventure education offers.

As we will show later in this chapter, team building has been proven to enhance the self-confidence of participants. Everyone who participates in team building has an opportunity to practice a leadership role. We believe that this practice will enhance leadership traits. Team building is community building. Each participant will feel that he or she is part of the team, and a sense of community will evolve. Team building also provides opportunities for character education. Teammates learn how to care for and support one another. This learning is a basic building block of character education.

Team building is more than just doing cooperative activities. The focus of team building is teaching kids how to become good teammates. Discussions about how to be an effective teammate and how to support teammates during failure and reorganization must precede any attempts at solving team-building challenges. We feel that the discussions before the challenges and the debriefings after the challenges are as important as the challenges themselves. Setting up challenges in a gym and allowing teams a chance to solve them without having any discussion before or after reduces the effectiveness of team building as a teaching tool. Chapter 3 provides specific examples of prebriefing and debriefing discussions.

Acquiring Leadership Skills

All students involved in team building have the opportunity to develop leadership skills. As you start getting more involved in the team-building curriculum, you will notice that students may start to offer suggestions about how to solve challenges. Trying to influence the direction of a team involves taking a risk. In their book, *Effective Leadership in Adventure Programming,* Priest and Gass (1997) define leadership as a process of influence. In most informal group settings, people who become leaders influence other group members to create, identify, work toward, achieve, and share mutually acceptable goals. The process of learning how to become a leader is a long and sometimes difficult road for many. To be an effective leader, one must

- take the risk of expressing an opinion in front of a group and be able to communicate that opinion effectively,

- become organized to facilitate the needs of a group,
- be able to foster group trust and communication,
- know the strengths and weaknesses of the group and be able to apply those strengths and weaknesses toward group success, and
- be able to praise and encourage others, a difficult skill that many students acquire only by having the opportunity to learn how to encourage others and then practice the skill of encouragement.

Many of these skills associated with leadership suddenly appear or become easier to acquire as we become mature adults. But for some, leadership skills will always be difficult to achieve. Team building can help foster leadership skills that are needed in physical education, adventure education, and community building. The process of team building requires several unique roles, including organizer, encourager, praiser, and summarizer. These roles should rotate among team members with every challenge. Chapter 3 describes these roles in depth. By having children fill these roles and practice the related skills, team building offers all children a chance to become effective leaders.

Team-building activities reinforce positive encouragement among students.

Developing Self-Confidence

Becoming an effective group member and, especially, becoming an effective leader, requires confidence in one's abilities. During our years as team-building instructors we have always believed that team building enhances personal and team self-confidence. In 1992, we wrote that a student's self-confidence grows as teams successfully master challenges, and we assumed that this statement was true when we wrote it. In 1998, a study by Vicki Ebbeck and Sandra Gibbons, published in the *Journal of Sport and Exercise Physiology,* investigated the effectiveness of a program of team building through physical challenges on the self-conceptions of physical education students in grades six and seven. The treatment group performed one team-building activity every second week for eight months, whereas the control group completed the regular physical education curriculum without any team-building activities. The results were convincing and revealed that both male and female students in the team-building group were significantly higher on perceptions of self-worth, athletic competence, physical appearance, and social acceptance than were those in the control group. Female students in the team-building group were also significantly higher on perceptions of scholastic competence and behavioral conduct than were female students in the control group. The original statement published in 1992 was proved accurate in 1998. Students were starting to connect to team building.

Earning Self-Esteem

One reason that team building has become such a useful tool in building self-esteem is that children are not handed success; they have to earn it. The challenges become increasingly more difficult as the team moves through the sequence of introductory to advanced challenges. More often than not a team will fail in its pursuit of a solution. Frustration may start to show up in various team members. For example, many of the challenges require the team to start over if it breaks a rule. Team members must reorganize, try new solutions, support one another, and eventually solve the challenge. Students learn that failure and struggle only make the eventual victory sweeter. Sometimes students need to fail in order to learn. Repeated failures sometimes lead us to greater exaltation when we eventually succeed.

Lillian Katz, professor of early childhood education at the University of Illinois and former president of the National Association for the Education of Young Children, seems to agree. In her article "All About Me" (1993) in *American Educator* magazine, she describes the importance of young children developing a positive self-image. In particular, the following passages from her article support team building.

> "Self-esteem is likely to be fostered when children have challenging opportunities to build self-confidence and esteem through effort, persistence and the gradual accrual of skills, knowledge, and appropriate behavior."

> "Cheap success in a succession of trivial tasks most likely will not foster self-esteem. Young children are more apt to benefit from real challenges and hard work than from frivolous one shot activities."

> "When children are engaged in challenging and significant activities, they are bound to experience some failures, reverses, and rebuffs. Children are able to cope with rebuffs, disappointments, and failures when adults acknowledge and accept their feelings of discouragement and at the same time tell children they can try another time."

> "Learning to deal with setbacks and maintaining the persistence and optimism necessary for childhood's long and gradual road to mastery: these are the real foundations of lasting self-esteem."

Thus, the team-building philosophy follows Ms. Katz's philosophy. It strengthens the need for physical educators to embrace team building as one way to get students to earn their self-esteem, gain confidence, and further connect with physical education.

COMMUNITY BUILDING AND TEAM BUILDING

Community building in the academic classroom is an important component within the educational setting. We believe that everyone wants to belong to something. It is human nature to want to belong, to fit in, to be noticed, to contribute, and to help others. When a group of people feels this way and establishes goals and visions and then works together to achieve its visions, a community is born.

The Community Toolbox (http://ctb.ku.edu), an online community-building resource, defines community building as "a group process where participants experience and practice communication skills that create the possibility for a deeper human connection." Individuals come to know themselves and others in new ways. Differences still exist, but they are transcended and celebrated. As group members work together, they become characterized by a sense of profound respect, appreciation, and joy. Practicing team building in school gives students concrete, practical experience for community building within society later in life.

The Community Toolbox talks about how to build strong communities within our society. One method is to build strong teams. The Community Toolbox explains further that a team is a group of people who function as a single unit and that team members who work well together can accomplish more than individual members working alone, because each member's work supports and complements the work of others. Team building in schools enhances community building in one other important area, which is communication.

The difference between team building and other cooperative programs, such as those offered by Terry Orlick (1982) in *The Second Cooperative Sports and Games Book*, is that team-building teams must pay a price if they fail. The price may be starting over from the beginning or having one or two members of the team start over. A team that fails has two options: reorganize and begin again or quit. A team that has pride won't quit. In our combined 60 years of team-building experience, we have noticed that few teams give up when the going gets tough. Team building teaches a community, a family, a workforce, and a sports team to reorganize and persevere. As students go through life and join communities and neighborhoods, the pride they felt during team building will manifest itself as they accomplish goals set forth by their communities.

ADVENTURE EDUCATION AND TEAM BUILDING

How does team building relate to adventure education? Are the two disciplines more alike than different? Can team building in the physical education classroom enhance outdoor education or experiential education? Will the lessons that children learn in physical education team building raise their self-esteem and improve their ability to make leadership decisions in outdoor education? In their book, *Effective Leadership in Adventure Programming,* Priest and Gass (1997) describe adventure education as a "process that involves the use of adventurous activities that provide a group or an individual with compelling tasks to accomplish. These tasks often involve group problem solving, usually requiring decision making, judgment, cooperation, and trust."

Many believe that adventure education greatly enhances students' self-confidence as they take risks and accomplish things in the outdoors like rock climbing or kayaking. In 1997, Hattie, Marsh, Neill, and Richards did an analysis of 96 Outward Bound studies published between 1968 and 1994. The analysis concluded that Outward Bound programs stimulate the development of interpersonal competencies, enhance leadership skills, and have a positive effect on adolescents' sense of empowerment, self-control, independence, self-understanding, assertiveness, and decision-making skills. Team building and adventure education thus appear to be closely linked, and both have a powerful influence on the social and emotional lives of students. Both programs offer much in the areas of leadership, group support, self-esteem, and confidence.

Adventure education leaders are similar to physical education teachers who lead a team-building unit. Priest and Gass (1997) give the following guidelines for leaders in adventure education. Comparing these guidelines to our suggestions for leading a school team-building unit, we find the following similarities:

- "Unless safety is an issue, allow clients to take as much responsibility as possible to solve problems for themselves." We suggest that teachers should not be quick to help. Allow teams to struggle and allow failure. When teams finally succeed, the success will be much sweeter.

- Encourage "challenge by choice." Forcing people to perform or get involved in an adventure education program can reduce or even eliminate their perceived freedom of choice. We believe that students need to support the choices of their teammates by honoring their decision to participate or not. If a student decides not to participate physically, he or she can still contribute to the team intellectually and emotionally (by offering encouragement).

- Adapt adventure experiences to suit the varying levels and needs of all members.
- Deal in perceived risk with acceptable or recoverable outcomes.
- Create conditions that appear risky but keep real dangers low by using correct safety procedures.
- Create a situation in which the consequences (positive or negative) are natural outcomes of the client's actions. Learning from mistakes can provide valuable information.

Team building offers introductory, intermediate, and advanced challenges so that students can gradually transform beginning success to increasingly more difficult choices. Team building can be made much more fun by creating a story line to add excitement. For example, having students climb under an electric fence in a rainstorm to get back to camp or cross a raging river filled with alligators adds much to the excitement of a challenge, but each challenge should be made as safe as possible.

An entire chapter of this book is devoted to safety. As mentioned earlier, we have a list of rules and consequences. If a team breaks a rule, it may have to start over. This affords the team members the possibility to learn from their mistakes and chart a new path to success.

Team building and adventure education are closely linked. Both help develop communication and relationships within teams. Team building in school can help students with adventure education by giving them practice in relating effectively to the team during a challenge. This skill is important when participating in adventure education.

TEAM BUILDING AND CHARACTER EDUCATION

We believe that the development of good character is one of the most important by-products of team building, adventure education, and community building. Character education is becoming entrenched in the curriculum of an increasing number of schools. Team building, community building, and adventure education are teaching character education by the very nature of the

activity. The physical education classroom is a model resource for the development of good character. Competitive situations are abundant; these situations often test the patience and character of our students. When students participate in a character education program enhanced through team building and adventure education, they learn to become respectful competitors and cooperative teammates.

Through team building, adventure education, and community building, students understand and incorporate into their lives the values and behaviors that reflect good character. We believe that some of those values and behaviors are caring about and supporting others, and having pride in one's life, school, and community. Showing evidence of good character means showing respect for others. This behavior is evident in a close-knit team or community. If they show respect and cooperation, students are more likely to engage in cooperative and competitive activities.

The Character Education Partnership (CEP) Web site, www.character.org/principles, provides 11 principles that a school can use to plan a character education effort (Lickona, Schaps, and Lewis 2003). One of these principles is that students need opportunities for moral action. In other words, instead of talking about character education values, we need to give students a chance to practice them. Team building gives them that practice; adventure education gives them that practice. Team building and adventure education present activities that promote team unity, team respect, and team support.

SUMMARY

Without a doubt, a student pursuing a major or minor in physical education, outdoor education, or recreation can gain many new skills through team building and adventure education activities. From an individual perspective, people can always refine skills such as communication, cooperation, risk taking, active listening, and leadership. From a group perspective, it is never too late to learn or hone skills such as setting team goals, developing and implementing a team plan to reach goals, and providing encouragement to team members. University faculty, however, sometimes assume that their students know these skills and are able to use them appropriately when performing team activities.

CHAPTER 2

The Process
of Team Building

Team building in the physical education setting gives all students a chance to be supportive and be supported by teammates, regardless of their athletic skill, inclination, or age.

Many physical education, outdoor education, and recreation students are skillful and knowledgeable in their favorite activities or sports, but they may lack effective ways to communicate and cooperate. Faculty need to introduce or reintroduce these basic skills to students, provide them with opportunities to use these skills within their peer groups, and encourage them to use these skills with others in their communities. Team building is one way to provide communication and cooperation practice.

PREPARING
FOR TEAM BUILDING

Team building is the one method used in physical education today that comes closest to providing a nonthreatening, peer-supportive environment for students. Some of us were fortunate enough to be on a supportive athletic team while growing up. One of the rewards of being on a team was the memories that the experience created—the struggles, failures, and eventual success brought a lot of satisfaction to our lives.

Team building is the cooperative process that individuals in a group use to solve physical and mental challenges. While using this process and solving the challenges, group members learn how to share ideas, praise and encourage one another, support one another physically and emotionally, and slowly start becoming a team.

Negative Social Behaviors

We cannot assume that our students know what makes an effective team member. If we are preparing students to be leaders in our society, they need to know what positive skills to include within an effective team and what negative behaviors to eliminate. Start with a classroom discussion. Ask students what types of behaviors negatively affect the performance of a team. As they respond with ideas, write them down on the board. Someone will say that put-downs are a negative behavior. Ask the class to define a put-down before you give the dictionary definition. The dictionary defines a put-down as a criticism or insult. Ask students to give examples of put-downs. Ask them if they have ever received a put-down or if they have ever insulted or criticized a teammate. Talk about feelings. Did receiving a put-down make them angry? Did it make them want to try harder, or did it make them want to be less determined? Does giving a put-down make a person stronger?

Someone may say that negative pressure is detrimental. Again, ask students what they think negative pressure is before you tell them. Then give examples of body language that creates negative pressure—rolling the eyes, angry looks, shaking one's head in disbelief over a teammate's error. Write the examples on the board and ask students to think of times that they have seen or experienced negative pressure.

How does negative pressure differ from sarcasm? What may seem like a funny remark to some may be hurtful to others. This classroom discussion is important because it highlights and records social behaviors that weaken teams and bring about bad feelings. Record and discuss as many negative team behaviors as the class can uncover. Here are some examples if the class draws a blank:

Put-downs

Negative pressure

Boastfulness

Inability to listen

Cliques

Me-first attitude

Sarcasm

Low tolerance of team-mates' poor physical skills

Impatience

Being thin skinned, feeling insulted if ideas are not accepted

Positive Social Behaviors

After the discussion on negative social behaviors, start a discussion on behaviors that make the team stronger. Follow the same discussion format as you did for negative behaviors. When students introduce praise and encouragement to the discussion, explain to the class that although we are always practicing our physical skills, we should practice our social skills as well. The following discussion is a good way to identify and practice positive team behaviors.

Reinforcing Praise and Encouragement

At a conference on facilitating responsibility through physical activity, Debbie Vigil, winner of the 1994 NASPE (National Association of Sports and Physical Education) Elementary Physical Education Teacher of the Year, demonstrated an excellent technique to teach praise and encouragement. With it, she reinforced our belief that you cannot just tell students to praise and encourage one another. You must teach them what praise and encouragement are and then give them practice situations in which they can use their new skills. Starting the year with this lesson may be an effective introductory technique to get children to understand what kind of place the gym environment is. With your large group, pose the following question: "What is praise, and when would you use it?" On a large chart, write the heading "Praise" in big letters and beneath it write two subheadings, "See" and "Hear." Ask the students to give examples of praise that one can hear. List these under the "Hear" column. Follow this by asking students to give examples of praise that one can see. List their responses under the "See" column. Duplicate this process by using the encouragement chart (see figure 2.1). Some of the

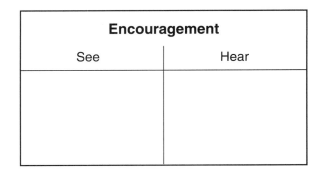

Figure 2.1 Encouragement chart.

Reprinted, by permission, from D. Glover and L. Anderson, 2003, *Character education* (Champaign, IL: Human Kinetics), 36.

responses for encouragement that one can hear might be the following:

- Way to go.
- You can do it.
- Try again.
- Good effort.

Some examples of encouragement that one can see might be the following:

- Thumbs up
- Pat on the back
- Clapping
- Okay sign

Praise and Encouragement Practice

When your students finish giving examples of encouragement that they can hear or see, give them the opportunity to practice using these terms in a physical activity. The following activity is a great way to practice giving praise and encouragement. Each group practices the rope-jumping skill called the Egg Beater. Four students turn the ropes, one student is the jumper, and the sixth student is the recorder. Provide a worksheet, pencil, and clipboard for the recorder. The turners and jumper rotate positions so that all turners get a chance to jump. The recorder does not have to rotate. Students can add the advanced skill of jumping a short rope inside the egg beater as well.

Although both the turners and the jumper practice their skills, only the turners practice their praise and encouragement skills. The

Social Skills Observation Sheet

Name	See	Hear

Figure 2.2 Social skills observation sheet.

Reprinted, by permission, from D. Glover and L. Anderson, 2003, *Character education* (Champaign, IL: Human Kinetics), 38.

recorder then records the responses of the jumping team on a social skills observation sheet (see figure 2.2). After the students have had time to practice the physical skill of jumping rope, bring them back into a large group for discussion. The recorders can now give the class information on their observations. Reporting to the large group not only gives students recognition for their social skills but also allows the class to evaluate what has occurred. Additionally, you may pose some questions to the class at this time.

- Were any put-downs or criticisms used?
- How did receiving praise make you feel?
- How were you encouraged?
- Is it difficult to praise or encourage another person?
- Was it difficult to receive praise or encouragement?

Ms. Vigil's lesson is one way to use praise and encouragement in an activity lesson. Students need to practice and reinforce these social skills just as they practice and reinforce physical skills.

FORMING TEAMS

We have worked with groups as small as 7 and as large as 150. More commonly, however, we tend to see groups the size of an average-sized school class, 24 to 32. Our experience has shown that grouping students into teams of 7 to 9 gives the optimum number of participants for team-building challenges. Groups of fewer than 7 tend to experience less struggle in achieving success in many of the challenges, although a group of 6 will work, whereas groups larger than 9 simply have too much waiting time involved in the group activity.

When working with school classes or teams in which you have a knowledge of the participants, we recommend setting up the groups to create an even distribution of various factors such as gender, physical size, physical attributes (such as having a physically flexible person on each team), and varying temperaments. If you have two students in class who have significant conflicts, you may wish to place them in different groups so that you do not have to monitor their relationship continually. Conversely, you may choose to place those students in the same group so that they have to work together and may possibly reconcile their differences.

We have occasionally had to form groups randomly in just a few minutes or someone may have randomly set up groups for us before our coming to the activity setting. In either case, we have had successful and enjoyable sessions. Random assignment may work for your needs as well, but if you have the opportunity, creating groups ahead of time allows for better organization and use of time.

Selecting Team Names

A suggestion that we have given at most of our workshops and conferences and one we frequently use in our own teaching is to have the groups create or choose team names for the time they spend solving challenges. A name can give a group a certain identity, and in choosing a name, group members begin the process of listening to one another's suggestions and coming to a consensus as a team. Some suggestions for choosing a name include the following:

- The team chooses a name with three or fewer terms.
- The name should relate to the brain, the mind, or creative thinking skills.
- The name should be positive or neutral in nature (that means no negative names).
- The name can be humorous.
- The name can relate to terms studied in academic units or may possibly have a geographic relationship to the group.

Examples of acceptable names are the Mind Masters, the Walking Encyclopedias, the Brainy Bunch, the Einsteins, the Dynamic Dendrite, and Minnesota Mentors. Examples of names we have vetoed are Mega Brain Death, the No Minds, the Dweebs, Dumb and Dumber, and the Brain Tumors. Although team names are not crucial to team building, they can add to the fun of being on a team as well as develop group identity.

Constructing a Team Pact

The next activity for teams is to plan how they are going to be successful. They should do this activity before starting the challenges. From these guidelines, the teacher could highlight consistencies among teams and post them as "Our Class SOP" (standard operating procedures).

The teacher may say, "Your team needs to come up with guidelines to ensure success. What needs to happen with each teammate for your team to function as positively and productively as possible? Think about what we have talked about. What did you learn about the characteristics of a good team member? With these questions in mind, go ahead and determine your guidelines. These guidelines are going to be called your team pact. Once you have finalized your team pact and everyone agrees on it, each team member needs to sign it. Determine a fair way to designate who will be the recorder for your team." Each team could then be responsible for coming up with eight guidelines. The following is an example of what a team may come up with as it determines a team pact (see figure 2.3).

We decided that to achieve the results we were looking for in team building, we would have to teach skills to meet that outcome. If we wanted to have our students speak respectfully, we needed to provide and use a vocabulary of positive praise phrases, encouragement, and positive adjectives. In addition, as we considered building accountability features into team building, we saw the need to create clear, simple, and succinct rules to govern the challenges. We wanted students to be inventive, creative, imaginative, clever, and helpful as they solved the challenges that we created or accumulated. But we don't allow the team members to do just anything; they must solve the challenges within a framework that uses skills to find solutions without breaking the rules of the challenge. Although several solutions to the challenges may be correct, not everything is acceptable.

To achieve these results, we found several ways to approach the outcome. One way is to get right into team building. Give your participants the chance to solve some introductory challenges right away. As they go through the experiences of working together for a team goal, they can put into practice some simple methods of encouraging and praising one another by assigning roles for team members.

Student Roles in Team Building

We have felt the need to increase some specific roles for team members. These roles should rotate among teammates during the challenges to create situations in which teammates deliberately attempt to encourage, praise, and support one another. The student roles that we feel are important to the team-

Team Pact

for_____
Team Name

For our team to be successful, all members will adhere to the following guidelines (Be specific. If you say that everyone needs to respect each other, what does that mean? What behaviors show respect?):

- Don't use put-downs.
- Encourage teammates when they make a mistake, when they are down about something, and when they are doing something that is hard.
- Praise teammates when they do something good.
- Listen to whoever is talking and don't interrupt.
- Don't always just sit by friends in huddle activities.
- Include everyone on the team and be nice to him or her.
- Always high-five each other after class.
- Don't always be the one who has to go first.
- Find a fair way to make decisions.
- Help teammates solve problems.

Figure 2.3 Team pact.

Reprinted, by permission, from D. Glover and L. Anderson, 2003, *Character education* (Champaign, IL: Human Kinetics), 39-40.

building process are the organizer, encourager, praiser, summarizer, and recorder.

Organizer

Many of us have had an opportunity to be leaders during our journeys to adulthood. Opportunities to practice leadership during team building are plentiful. One of these opportunities is the role of organizer. This role should rotate among team members, thereby giving everyone a chance to lead. When the team approaches a challenge, they will see two cards—a challenge card and an organizer card. You may want to photocopy and laminate these cards and place them by the appropriate challenge. The organizer card (shown on page 12) includes a series of questions designed to help group members understand what was read to them on the challenge card (shown on the same page). All challenge and organizer cards can be found in the appendix and on the DVD-ROM.

Group members should come to a consensus that they understand the answer to each question. We use the organizer cards to check for understanding by having the organizer call the teacher to the group. The teacher randomly asks each group member one of the questions. Team members may not volunteer answers; they must wait for the teacher to call on them. If a group member incorrectly answers a question, we leave the group for at least a minute and a half (an eternity for students who want to become engaged in the activity). A good organizer does not chastise the group if its members cannot answer all the questions, and he or she should communicate the challenge to the group again. The organizer must then review whatever parts of the challenge card need clarification. Once this step is complete, the group may then begin to solve the challenge. One reason for using this element in preparation is to help the group focus clearly on the rules and sacrifices. It is quite discouraging for a group to begin its

CHALLENGE CARD:

Lifeline

Equipment

One tire, one tug-of-war rope, and two scooters.

Starting Position

The group starts on one side of the swamp with only one scooter. One scooter is inside the tire. The tug-of-war rope is across the swamp.

Our Challenge

The group completes the task when all group members cross the swamp without touching the swamp (floor).

Rules and Sacrifices

1. No one may touch the floor with any part of his or her body or clothes.
2. No one may stand on a scooter.
3. No one may call others by their last names or use put-downs.
4. If a group member breaks a rule, that person and one successful person (or the person who has advanced the farthest) must go back to the starting line. They may not take a scooter back with them unless it was the first scooter that the group used.

ORGANIZER CARD:

Lifeline

Questions

1. What are the boundaries of the swamp?
2. What equipment do we get?
3. What happens if a group member touches the swamp?
4. Where will we be when we complete the task?
5. Can you think of any safety issues that we should discuss?

process of solving the challenge and then be held accountable for information that it should have processed. The instructor should not be solely responsible for enforcing the rules of a challenge. A group should have the integrity to acknowledge or recognize when it must give up a sacrifice for breaking a rule during the challenge.

A group may occasionally become stumped in its efforts. The organizer should be the person who asks the instructor for help or tips. We recommend that instructors give as little help as possible during these activities, because the struggle involved in the process of success is of great value. Helping the group solve the challenge defeats the purpose of team building.

The organizer reads the challenge card to the team or passes it to someone else if he or she feels uncomfortable reading. This act of decision making puts the organizer in a leadership position. If the organizer decides to read the card to the team, the leadership role expands. Talking to the team and attempting to explain a challenge through these cards is a leadership experience that team building provides. This experience will be extremely helpful during adventure education. Leadership roles are often given to people based on traits demonstrated in previous situations, such as the most verbal person, the best athlete, or the class clown. By rotating each person into the role of organizer, you might see other students blossom or demonstrate qualities that their group members may have never seen.

A sacrifice is the penalty or consequence for breaking one of the rules within that challenge. For example, if a group member breaks a rule, the entire team must start the challenge over from the beginning. Alternatively, the person breaking a rule must start over and take a successful teammate back with him or her to the starting position.

Encourager

By definition, to encourage is to give others courage. The role of encourager is, in our opinion, an important role. We hope that all group members will eventually take this role without it being assigned. An encourager's job is to find positive words to inspire teammates while the group is attempting the challenge. As you begin the challenges, you might describe the function of the encourager as one of offering specific encouraging phrases to one or two specific teammates. Another way might be to challenge the encour-

ager to offer a word of encouragement to each group member before the group completes the task. The role of encourager is ongoing throughout the task.

Praiser

The praiser should find at least one specific act to praise before the completion of the challenge. For example, if a teammate makes a good suggestion or helps another student balance, the praiser should acknowledge that act. A good praiser will be sincere when praising someone, not phony. The roles of praiser and encourager should rotate as the team moves through the challenges. Ideally, everyone will start praising and encouraging before long, allowing the elimination of the roles of praiser and encourager.

The roles of praiser and encourager offer another opportunity to experience leadership. Some students must learn to praise because not all students acquire this skill easily. In offering praise and encouragement, a student must decide to take a risk. Quiet, shy students may learn to offer praise only when the instructor assigns them the task of praiser. The act of praising or encouraging a peer makes the person being praised feel good and elevates the status of the praiser. Certainly, praise can elevate the self-esteem of team members and inspire the team to attempt challenges that are more difficult.

Again, we hope that this role becomes a natural outcome of the group's developing a sense of team camaraderie. To begin with, however, the assigned role of the praiser is to find specific acts to praise. These acts will be identified when the group has successfully completed a task. If needed, you can supply a list of praise phrases to the team or the praiser to help prompt the use of respectful or honorable terms.

Summarizer

You can give the role of summarizer to an individual, or summarizing can become a group activity. If an individual provides the summary, he or she can give the instructor an account of how the team solved the challenge, what some of the fun elements of the task were, what was hard or frustrating, what the key elements were to achieving success, and how group members helped one another. The summarizer can be given a team report card (see example in chapter 3). You can modify the team report card to meet the needs of your group or to achieve a desired scope of discussion.

Recorder

The recorder highlights, for the instructor or the full class, specific praises and encouragement that the group used during the challenge. The recorder could be given a recording sheet similar to the one used in the Debbie Vigil lesson. By reporting to the class specific encouraging phrases and praise phrases, the reporter keeps the limelight on the importance of supporting teammates with words. After doing the reporting following a series of challenges, this job can end because, ideally, the students will realize the importance of praising and encouraging. The recorder can give the recording sheets to the teacher after reporting, and the teacher can put them on the bulletin board. This further emphasizes the importance of this skill.

Positive Adjectives

We have been using positive adjectives as long as we have been doing team building. We feel it is a very important and worthwhile activity. At the completion of the team building unit have the teams sit in a semicircle with one team member sitting in front facing their teammates. Each team member should have a copy of the positive adjectives (see figure 2.4).

One by one, teammates pick three positive adjectives that best describe the person sitting in front of them. This may produce giggles at first as it is not easy to say something nice to someone else when you are in middle school. It is also hard to receive praise from so many people at once—especially when you are sitting in front of them. This activity will foster closer relationships between team members and after using it for 30 years we are convinced of its importance.

After all teammates have had a turn describing the teammate in front of them, the team rotates and a new member sits in front of the semicircle. Remind the students to look at the student being described, say their name, and use only the terms on the sheet. They are not allowed to embellish or add new terms. The same terms can be used by more than one teammate. After one person uses three positive adjectives the person in front shall say "thank you" prior to the next person speaking.

Positive Adjectives

Kind	Organized	Convincing
Strong	Courageous	Content
Nice	Honest	Sensible
Happy	Clever	Creative
Active	Inventive	Independent
Cheerful	Imaginative	Determined
Courteous	Enthusiastic	Humorous
Intelligent	Helpful	Pleasant
Polite	Aggressive	Delightful
Friendly	Bright	Confident
Energetic	Thoughtful	Daring

Figure 2.4   Positive adjectives.

Reprinted, by permission, from D. Glover and L. Anderson, 2003, *Character education* (Champaign, IL: Human Kinetics), 108.

Instructor's Role in Team Building

The instructor needs to avoid solving the challenges for the groups. Although it can be tempting to offer help to teams, especially those experiencing frustration, discouragement, or failure, teams should work through the difficult aspects of solving challenges. Teams must learn how to function when things become difficult. Allow team members to fail. This approach does not mean that you abandon them. Be a good observer, encourager, and praiser. Point out the success of the good ideas that they have already demonstrated. Do everything you can to eliminate negative team pressure.

When preparing the challenges for participation, be sure that you have set out the correct equipment for the teams. Look over all safety concerns and arrangements. Examine the figures in the book, read the challenge descriptions to ensure that you place the equipment in the correct or suitable places. Discourage unsafe or silly behavior.

SETTING UP ACTIVITY SPACES AND EQUIPMENT

After the teams have been established, you may choose to have group members involve themselves with icebreakers or communication activities, or you may have them begin a team-building challenge. We recommend setting up the gym or activity space so that you have more stations available than you have participating groups. When working in a school setting in which we have three or four groups in a class, we set up one more station activity than we have groups. That way, if one group finishes a challenge, it will have an open station to which it can go to start a new challenge. This in turn allows another group to rotate to the station used by the first team to finish. Depending on how long your groups meet, as an instructor you are not constantly setting up new or different challenges. Of course, as all groups complete certain challenges, you will replace them with new tasks.

As we developed challenges over the years, we attempted to create them with equipment that was either readily available or economical to procure. As you look through the challenges presented in this book, we feel confident that you will be able to obtain most of the items without difficulty.

Our experience as physical education teachers has logically resulted in our using gymnasium space for conducting team-building activities. However, as we have conducted workshops or special event activities for groups in team building, we have used spaces such as lunchrooms, classrooms, outdoor playground areas, meeting rooms in motel or hotel facilities, sanctuaries of churches, ballrooms and hallways in casinos, stage areas, beaches, and other spaces where we simply moved out tables, chairs, and other equipment to create a large open space.

Gymnasium space usually provides the most straightforward venue for the administration of the challenges that we are presenting in this book, but with a little creativity you can modify any challenge to meet your needs. For example, for the Black Hole challenge you can easily suspend a hula hoop from a basketball hoop. If you are in a space that does not have a basketball hoop, you may have to suspend the hoop from a ceiling structure or an overhead beam or railing. If you do this task outdoors, suspend it from a structure such as a football goal post or playground equipment such as a swing set.

Most challenges that we are presenting simply need adequate room for travel or movement. The ceiling need not be as high as that of a gymnasium. A large open room such as a recreation hall, lunchroom, or dance floor offers the same functionality as a basketball court. Keep in mind that the size of your group will determine how many challenges you set up at one time. Additionally, some challenges require very little room to conduct. We have observed classroom teachers move all desks to the perimeter of a classroom and set up Stepping-Stones I and II, the Maze, Construction Zone, and Building Blocks. Hallways of buildings can accommodate challenges such as Tire Bridge and Lifeline, which require long, narrow working areas.

While the learners are developing team skills, the instructor should create an environment in which each student feels the same, both physically and emotionally. To create a safe environment, the instructor could include the individual connection between teacher and student. As learners enter the play space, the teacher can welcome students to class and let them know just how good it is to have them in class. This simple act can mean the world to the student. Often times students do not hear this sort of appreciation enough or even at all during the day.

SELECTING AN ACTIVITY OR CHALLENGE

As the instructor prepares the environment, she or he must also select activities. The books *Team Building Through Physical Challenges, More Team Building Challenges,* and *Character Education* provide a variety of challenges at introductory, intermediate, and advanced levels. Additionally, you may select activities presented at conferences or workshops. Just as we want our students to select the most developmentally appropriate activity for their students, we must do the same at the college level. To do so, we must first identify the goal that we want students to accomplish through the team challenge. For example, if the goal is to develop group cohesiveness with a focus on communication, the Great Communicator team-building activity would be perfect. Each group member must actively listen to the person selected as the Great Communicator while attempting to reproduce the object that is described. The Great Communicator must also refine his or her communication skills so that team members can experience success. Regardless of the source of the activity, you must determine how you will use it with your students in your environment. Feel free to modify the activity to meet your students' performance or behavioral needs.

In discussions, people often ask why all groups should not do the same challenges at the same time. The main reason is simply that you are not likely to have enough of the same equipment to set up three or more similar stations at one time. A more practical approach is to set up a few challenges of equal difficulty. As an example, in the first few meetings of your teams, they may all attempt introductory challenges. Prior to starting introductory challenges you should introduce a few ice breakers from chapter 6. We have not set up the individual challenges in a sequential order. Instead, we have grouped the challenges into three levels of difficulty: introductory, intermediate, and advanced. The beginning challenges do not require nearly as much physical support among teammates or as much planning and problem solving as the intermediate and advanced challenges do. We suggest choosing a number of challenges by level as you prepare your groups for their tasks. In addition, the equipment that you have at your disposal will dictate the challenges that you present to your participants.

SUMMARY

Teaching students and adults how to be good teammates by helping them discover what makes a team stronger or weaker is of monumental importance. You must teach them about encouragement and praise and then give them a chance to practice using those skills before they actually solve challenges. Jumping into team-building activities without teaching about praise and encouragement beforehand will prevent students from gaining the greatest benefit from the challenges. Letting team members decide on a team name and letting them construct a team pact are two community-building activities that will start bringing the team together. These two activities are useful in teaching social skills to students and helping them begin to bond as a team.

Setting up the environment with one or two more challenges than there are teams will allow the teams to rotate among the challenges and stay busy. The teacher will simply move around the gym and watch the teams attempt to solve the challenges. The teacher must enforce any rules and make the teams start over if necessary.

Teaching social skills and putting a priority on them, letting students take some ownership in construction of the rules, and showing them that you are glad they are involved in the team-building unit by greeting and acknowledging them will go a long way in the development of good character. By involving them as a team in solving challenges, you will give students more opportunities to practice the social skills that you have highlighted. Team building offers a chance to practice moral behavior!

Assessment Tools

Assessment is not a separate entity in the teaching and learning process. It is an important concept in creating a safe atmosphere and promoting continued interest in team building. To make physical education a brain-friendly place that inspires students to exercise, we must change traditional assessment techniques. Many of these techniques, such as testing students in physical activities in which they have no interest, only turn them further away from activity. Assessment means different things to each teacher. We need to find assessment techniques that inspire critical thinking as much as team building does.

DEVELOPING A SUCCESSFUL ASSESSMENT PROGRAM

We are going to look at many different assessment techniques as they relate to team-building activities. Our goal as physical education teachers has been to keep our students active. We have observed in both practice and philosophy that many, if not most, of our colleagues feel that we would rather have our students be active than take the time to administer tests or use assessment tools. So one of our challenges as instructors is to view assessment as an integral part of the teaching and learning process. Assessment should relate to the concept of creating a safe learning atmosphere and promoting interest in physical education.

In this chapter, we will look at the topics of grades and testing. We are interested in finding the best way to assess our students. Is traditional physical education testing the best way to give a grade in physical education? We don't think so. For that reason we are going to look at incorporating team-building portfolios into the assessment pro-

cess. We will also look at getting students involved in the assessment process as reflective learners rather than as memory robots. We will be asking participants to respond to higher-level thinking skills rather than to memorize lists. This type of assessment will focus on the process of learning and problem solving. We believe that this type of assessment will alleviate much assessment anxiety.

Numerous books and publications address the subject of assessment. In *Character Education* (Glover and Anderson 2003), we acknowledged that assessment is a complex issue being faced by educators. As seen in many books, articles, and professional publications, debate continues regarding the best way to assess performance or knowledge. What we are trying to assess and how we recognize growth as students are learning are two of the most important aspects of assessment that we explore.

Grading and Testing Team Performance

Marking a grade or placing a check mark on a report card seems like a simple way of grading a student's performance. But more and more people are asking what a particular grade means or what is being assessed. Do all those who give marks use the same definition or standard for a letter or number grade? How important are these assessment tools? Do these assessment procedures offer the students or participants any incentives for improving their team-building skills?

Many educators say that assessment is the measurement of a student's growth over a period of time. But what is the growth? How do you compare the growth of one person to another if they begin at different levels or if they bring different levels of experience or ability into the class? Do points earned in a class constitute learning or growth? We are not saying that points earned cannot reflect that learning has taken place. We ask the question to examine what we should consider when defining assessment.

Most of us have experienced the following situation. Lindsay comes to physical education class as a student-athlete. She loves sports and demonstrates a high level of performance. She has a wonderful attitude, treats others with respect, and is a joy to have as a student. Sean, on the other hand, is uncoordinated, performs his skills at a low level, and looks out of place in team game activities. He does, however, get along with his classmates and tries hard. By the end of the semester Sean has shown a great deal of improvement but at best demonstrates only average motor skills. Lindsay, working just as hard as Sean does, finishes the course at the same high level of ability that she began the course with. Lindsay receives an A for the course, and Sean gets a B. Why is this? Most likely, Lindsay is rewarded for her genetic makeup in the motor skills area as well as the excellent attitude that she brings into the class. So here the grades do not measure growth. On the other hand, do we consider giving Lindsay a lower grade because she didn't show much improvement, although she performed at a higher level than most of her classmates?

Developing a consistent reporting system has always been a challenge for educators. Developing a consistent assessment tool or program becomes the current challenge for all those working with any type of group. In school settings, the purpose of grades varies greatly. Often, grades are simply a judgment call made by an instructor, and we hope that they are not just a system of rewards and punishments.

Testing is one way to determine what students have learned. But testing is often overemphasized, and many consider it a method that does not measure creativity and higher-level thinking skills. In 1995, an *Odyssey of the Mind* newsletter published a list of the top 13 skills desired by Fortune 500 companies. Here are the top 10:

1. Teamwork
2. Problem-solving skills
3. Interpersonal skills
4. Oral communication
5. Listening
6. Personal and career development
7. Creative thinking
8. Leadership
9. Goal setting and motivation
10. Writing

The most desired trait was teamwork, the ability to work as a member of a team. Do not misunderstand us; testing for facts has a valid place. As an example, we want an electrician to have complete understanding of electric circuitry and building codes when working in our homes. Deciding how many outlets or light fixtures to install on a circuit should not involve guesswork or an attitude of "This feels okay." We want an anesthesiologist to know correct formulas when putting us under for surgery. Feeling good about yourself is fine, but we want these people to know the correct answer to the existing situation. Testing for facts or specific knowledge has a place in the process of evaluation.

Colleges and universities place incredible emphasis on entrance exams such as the ACT and SAT and school grade point averages. Because of the pressure exerted by these tools for college entrance, our educational system increases the pressure for high school students to be prepared for these examinations. The pressure extends to the middle school and then to the elementary school. Higher test scores surely mean that students are better prepared for college, right?

How interesting it is that the skill most desired in the workplace according to the Fortune 500 survey is not how much you know but how well you work with other people. We would like to have someone to blame for all our testing woes—the government, the educational system, local school boards, or taxpayers. We recognize that state legislatures are looking for ways to account for spending on education. Educational administrators need to show their constituents that learning is taking place. Taxpayers want to feel that their dollars are being used well. So that leaves the teacher, instructor, or evaluator in the role of teaching, motivating, and producing balanced, knowledgeable students. We will not even try to discuss all the variables that students bring into the classroom or learning environment.

Higher-Order Thinking Skills

Few teachers have not heard of Bloom's taxonomy. His work has been in the world of education since the 1950s and has been used in countless, if not nearly all, teacher training programs in U.S. colleges and universities. His practices also support use of student portfolios. Bloom (1956) contends that knowledge-based questions given in the form of true–false or multiple-choice tests require the least amount of brainpower, whereas evaluation and synthesis questions require the greatest use of brainpower. Memorization, direct recall, reciting, definitions, and so on are what students do in typical knowledge-based tests. Often, they lose the information they learned for the test after they take the test. Students set aside higher-level thinking skills to memorize facts. Possibly, teachers use these types of tests because they are easier to give and easier to score or grade. For information to be stored in the brain, it must have application to our lives.

We do not want to mislead anyone into thinking that memorization is not important. Memorization is essential when reciting a poem, singing a song, learning a piano piece, performing a gymnastics routine, or executing a play in a ball game. In these instances, what the person is learning (memorizing) connects to delivery of the performance.

Synthesis and Evaluation

To enable greater understanding, instructors need to help students reach a synthesis and evaluation level, allowing them to use higher-order thinking skills. Developing opinions, judgments, or decisions are examples of thinking about content and its relationship to life applications rather than just memorizing a list of facts. These types of questions create a problem. How can teachers or instructors effectively measure someone else's opinions and judgments? Realistically, measuring opinion is not possible; therefore, teachers do not ask these questions because they are too hard to score, grade, or quantify. With this in mind, we might ask, why do teachers need to put a score on everything? Maybe we should create a climate or environment in which students can ask questions or give opinions without the apprehension of being judged or graded.

Examples of synthesis and evaluation-based questions include the following:

- Do you agree that . . . ?
- What do you think about . . . ?
- What is most important . . . ?
- How would you put the following in order of importance . . . ?
- What responses did you observe . . . ?
- How would you assess . . . ?

Let's say that a student group completed a team-building challenge or a series of group problem-solving activities. How might you test the students on the information they learned? Would you give them a test? How might they demonstrate what they learned specifically about the activities, or how might they express the learning that occurred during the time they spent with their group? Quite possibly, if an emotional connection has developed within the group as its members solve these challenges together, a series of questions might generate a discussion that evokes a better demonstration of learning than a test could produce. Some questions that include synthesis and evaluation as they apply to team building include the following:

- How did the rules of the challenge influence your group's solution?
- If you could change a rule, what would it be? How would this rule change affect the solution to the challenge?
- What did you like about the challenge?
- What caused your group difficulty during the challenge?
- How did the group handle various suggestions?
- Did you feel that members listened to your suggestions?
- Did the information that you read about the challenge give you a clear sense of what you had to do to solve the challenge?

In this assessment of the challenge, group members have to make judgments and express opinions, leading to the development of higher-level thinking skills. Many people might look at these questions and say that there is no way that they can assess all students' opinions and evaluations of the activities in which they just participated. This judgment would be true, yet a teacher should be able to discern if learning was taking place by the quality of discussion and by expression of opinions offered. Allowing students to discuss, compare, judge, and even dispute their methods of teamwork will, we hope, motivate them to progress toward the joy of learning and applying their learning to the challenges they encounter.

Student Discussion

Permitting students to discuss issues by listening to others' thoughts and offering their own ideas creates a nonthreatening, enriching atmosphere.

William Glasser (1998) has stated that we generally learn

- 10% of what we read,
- 20% of what we hear,
- 30% of what we see,
- 50% of what we see and hear,
- 70% of what we discussed with others,
- 80% of what we experience personally, and
- 95% of what we teach to someone else.

If we accept these statistics as reasonable, then it follows that students are more likely to remember and apply what they have learned by discussion and by working together than by working on their own. For some teachers, the hardest part of giving this control over to the students is giving up the notion that the power belongs to the teacher. The more that students see the teacher is on their side and is helping to facilitate learning, the more likely it is that they will exceed expectations rather than take advantage of the freedom to direct their own learning.

PORTFOLIOS

Portfolios can be defined as a collection of work or performance data that illustrates effort, growth, and achievement. The collection of this work could include assessment and evaluation samples, sharing of personal interests or observations, opinions of activities, or critiques of projects. "Students must be involved in selecting and judging the quality of their own work, including self reflection. With portfolios, traditional teaching roles may not work. Teachers need to facilitate, guide, and offer choices rather than inform, direct and predetermine priorities. Partnerships are established among teacher, students and parents" (Melograno 1998).

The key to a successful portfolio is that it must show growth. Many use it simply as a scrapbook, collecting various pieces of work along the unit of study. A key factor in communicating that growth, is including a baseline before each unit of study. A baseline will show students what they know or what they can do at the start of a unit of study. You cannot tell how far you have come if you do not know where you started.

Student portfolios have become popular during the past decade. They have proved to be both effective and meaningful. We have been using portfolio evaluations for nearly 20 years while teaching team-building activities. One purpose of using this assessment tool is to help students move beyond memorizing rules and statistics, and move toward analyzing their level of effectiveness on a team. In addition, portfolio evaluations allow students to increase their involvement in personal practice plans, fitness plans, and analysis of each unit activity in which they participate. Giving students a voice in their education is invaluable. Furthermore, we have observed that students are more likely to discuss their portfolio evaluations with their parents than discuss a particular letter or number grade.

Benefits

As teachers we have been using student portfolios for many years. We started using them as a way to communicate with parents about the activities that their children experienced in physical education class. The use of portfolios encourages student-led goal setting and helps students track their progress as they strive toward meaningful goals. Portfolios also become a vehicle for students to verbalize what they were experiencing in class, thus allowing them to identify their strengths and deficiencies more accurately. In addition, students become more reflective in their responses. They think about what they have done, what they are doing, and what they might do next. Using questions with portfolio evaluations can cause students to think more deeply about how they see themselves performing and what goals or expectations for improvement are realistic. Here are some examples of questions to include on your evaluations:

What did I do?

How or why did I do it?

What did I do well?

How can I improve?

Portfolios cause students to focus more on their own abilities and growth as opposed to their ranking among others or exclusive concentration on the final product. Finally, portfolios help students assess themselves and provide a sense of ownership in their performance. By evaluating their work or performance, students can develop personal plans for improvement.

Additionally, evaluation develops an emotional connection about how physical education (or in this case, team building) relates to lifelong learning or lifelong appreciation of becoming physically educated. We feel that students benefit far more by portfolio evaluation than they do by looking at a letter, number, or percentage grade and wondering how they received that grade or how they could improve it.

Creating a Portfolio

Portfolios should have examples of students' work, thoughts, and opinions. Portfolios should include other basic elements. The personal reflection of the student is one of these elements. This reflection can show how the student felt about the team-building activity, perhaps how he or she felt about the team, and any other thoughts about the experience of team building that impressed the student. The student should include a self-evaluation as well as assessments of how he or she feels that the team performed in solving a challenge. Peer evaluations—a short reflection by another team member about how the student worked within the team—can also be beneficial. Students can also include behavior goals in their portfolio, such as "I would like to encourage more" or "I need to offer more suggestions to our team." At the beginning of a portfolio, the student should prepare a personal introduction page that includes some biographical information. This could lead into gathering some information from the parents. The teacher could send home a parent survey that could help with the evaluation of the student as a team member. Some examples of parent survey questions will be shown later in this chapter.

Student Evaluation and Assessments

As mentioned earlier, to reach a higher level of understanding, students should regularly have opportunities to evaluate their actions, behaviors, and attitudes. When students engage in these exercises, they learn more about themselves and how they've learned through the experiences that we provided for them. An example of a student evaluation that we have used with our students is shown on page 22.

If students are old enough or mature enough, you might challenge them to construct their own evaluation form under your direction. As an example, you might say to the class, "Please answer the following questions, and I will use the information to create an evaluation for the course. List five rules that everyone should follow during team building." Another question you might ask is, "What are the three most important elements of being a good team member?" Here are some additional questions to consider when creating a portfolio evaluation form or questionnaire.

- Thinking back on this unit, what grade would you give yourself and why?
- What did you like about the team-building challenges?
- What did you dislike about the team-building challenges?
- What was the most important thing you learned during this unit?
- How would describe your attitude during team building?
- Did you feel that you were a good teammate? Why or why not?
- What hurt your team during the challenges?
- What did you enjoy during team building?
- What three things that you observed helped make your team more successful?
- If you were to teach this unit, what would you tell people were the five most important things they needed to know about team building?

Another assessment tool that you can use to evaluate the team-building experience is the evaluation questionnaire (shown on page 23), which allows teammates to measure their own teamwork and sportsmanship.

You may also decide to survey or assess student knowledge or opinions on safety or equipment usage during the team-building unit. As you will see in chapter 4, "Safety Strategies," we feel that providing plans, procedures, and preparation for safety is essential for a good team-building unit. Assessing student knowledge, understanding, or attitudes toward this issue may provide valuable information to you as an instructor if indeed these preparations translate into safe practices by the team-building participants. Understanding why a team uses equipment in certain ways may be as important as knowing how a team uses the equipment to solve the challenge.

Student Evaluation

Name_____ Class_____

Note to parents: During the fall, students have been involved in a series of problem-solving activities in physical education. The students are usually in groups of seven to nine members. They must solve numerous problems using a limited amount of equipment, and all students must be successful for the group to be considered successful. Meeting this goal requires that teammates help one another in a variety of ways.

The name of our group is _____

The members of my group include

_____   _____   _____
_____   _____   _____
_____   _____   _____

We successfully completed the following challenges (the ones I have circled):

The Bridge	Swamp Machine	The Whole World in Their Hands
River Crossing	Teamwork Walk	Riverboat
Human Billboard	Plunger Ball	The Maze
Lifeline	Stepping-Stones I	Bridge Over The Raging River

My three favorite challenges were

1. _____   2. _____   3. _____

Three positive adjectives that my group members used to identify me were that I am

_____, I am _____, and I am _____.

I would like to do more group tasks? (circle answer)   Yes   No

My favorite task was _____ Why?_____ .

The hardest task was _____ because _____ .

One of the best things I liked during group tasks was _____ .

I thought the _____(name of task) was the most fun.

The best thing about my group was _____ .

A mistake my group made was _____ .

One of the most interesting problems we solved was _____ .

One idea I gave my group was _____ .

I am rating my group with this number (circle one number):

10   9   8   7   6   5   4   3   2   1
Outstanding   Average   Poor

From *Essentials of Team Building* by Daniel W. Midura and Donald R. Glover, 2005, Champaign, IL: Human Kinetics.

Evaluation Questionnaire

Directions: Students, circle the word that best describes you. Teachers, circle the word that best describes the student.

1. I was able to talk through any disagreements in a fair and kind manner.

    No   Sometimes   Usually   Yes

2. I argued about decisions that my teammates made.

    No   Sometimes   Usually   Yes

3. I practiced good teamwork by accepting or taking a specific role on the team.

    No   Sometimes   Usually   Yes

4. I made excuses or blamed someone if I made a mistake.

    No   Sometimes   Usually   Yes

5. I was kind or encouraging to my teammates when they made a mistake.

    No   Sometimes   Usually   Yes

6. I enjoyed working on _____ (name of a specific task) even if we were not successful.   Yes   No

7. If my teammates made a mistake, I gave them a nasty look or questioned their effort.

    No   Sometimes   Usually   Yes

8. My teammates would want me to be on their team again.

    No   Probably not   Probably yes   Yes

Additional Questions: What Is Teamwork?

1. Three important qualities to have in order to work well in a group are

    • _____
    • _____
    • _____

2. The definition of teamwork is _____.

3. Three characteristics that could hurt a team are _____.

4. Activities I do outside of physical education that require teamwork are _____

    _____.

5. Five activities or jobs that I may have in the future that require teamwork are_____

    _____.

Adapted, by permission, from D. Glover and L. Anderson, 2003, *Character education* (Champaign, IL: Human Kinetics), 180.

From *Essentials of Team Building* by Daniel W. Midura and Donald R. Glover, 2005, Champaign, IL: Human Kinetics.

Peer Evaluation

Peer evaluation is similar to a reciprocal teaching style in which students carry out roles such as partner observer and evaluator. This person could discuss with a partner how the partner feels about team building and how the partner thinks he or she performed as a team member. Students assess their peers' performance based on previously stated criteria. In evaluating others, students are compelled to think deeply about what they are evaluating, thereby making the skill or behavior more meaningful or significant to them in the process. Students may learn as much from watching, observing, and evaluating their teammates during team building as from participating in the activities. Coaches often film games and practices so that athletes can watch their own performances as well as those of their teammates. By seeing what they did right or wrong, teammates can develop a better understanding of what is necessary for improvement. This type of tool can be effective in other disciplines of learning as well.

Peer evaluation can be a compelling learning tool. As stated earlier in this chapter, William Glasser (1998) asserts we learn 95% of what we teach to someone else. Although peer evaluation may not specifically be defined as teaching, peers must take a deeper look at the skills or responses to teamwork and provide feedback to teammates in a manner that allows the observer to see what learning or improvements are taking place within the structure of the team. We often see things from a different perspective than other people do. The feedback that we give to others or that we receive is one more tool to help us improve our performance. Disagreeing with the feedback might cause some interesting debate, but disagreement can be a helpful step in the process of evaluation.

Peer evaluation can enrich student learning by guiding the participants to interact meaningfully with their teammates. Instructors should encourage students to be fair and accurate with their peer evaluations. Peer evaluations develop problem-solving and communication skills. An essential component of both team building and peer evaluation is trust.

The class should thoughtfully review the responsibilities of evaluating someone else's performance. Peer evaluation is not simply an exercise in judgment. The following are examples of questions that you can pose to your evaluators before the peer evaluation assessment:

- What is the purpose of peer evaluation? Why should you evaluate someone else's performance?
- Do you think that peer evaluations are fair?
- What do think might be a benefit of this type of evaluation?
- What could be a problem with peer evaluation?
- How do you think others might feel if they know that you are evaluating them?
- How might you feel if you know that someone is evaluating you?
- What might you learn from someone's evaluation of your performance?

Because peer evaluation could threaten some students, teachers should discuss ahead of time what peer evaluations should accomplish and how they can benefit the class. Again, evaluations are not simply a vehicle for negative criticism but are a tool for growth.

Personal Introduction Page

A personal introduction might be a written page describing personal characteristics, areas of interest, and recognition of personal strengths, or it could be a picture, collage, or drawing to serve as a cover to the team-building portfolio. This assignment could take place later in the unit. Students could link specific activities in which they have participated to the design of the portfolio page or folder cover.

Parent Feedback

Portfolios are an excellent way to communicate with parents. First, a portfolio gives parents a clear picture of what their children are actually doing in class. In this respect, it offers much more than a grade does. Using the evaluation example that we provided earlier, parents can see who was in their child's group, what activities their child attempted, what others said about their child, how their child evaluated the group, what some of the observations made during the unit were, and what strengths and weaknesses of the group were recognized during the challenges. We have found that when parents read the portfolio evaluations, they are likely to comment on the uniqueness of the team names (they often want to know why a name was chosen and sometimes what the name means). Parents often express curiosity regarding the names of the challenges. Asking a student to describe how to do Lifeline evokes greater discussion than asking what the student did in school today.

To increase the likelihood that parents communicate with you, the teacher or instructor, you may wish to develop a simple feedback form for the parent to return to you. Questions could include the following:

- What did you learn about team building from reading the portfolio evaluation?
- What surprised you the most?
- Could you tell what level of interest your child had with this activity?
- What did you find that made you proud of your child?
- Was your child able to articulate or describe elements of teamwork because of participating in team-building activities?

We get more feedback from parents during this unit activity than from any other activity we have taught during our entire teaching careers.

Special Assignments and Final Projects

In our experience of teaching in public schools and colleges, in both undergraduate and graduate courses, and in conducting seminars and workshops, we included final projects when we had the opportunity. Time is a factor when deciding whether to include projects in your course. As an example, if you have an elementary or middle school class that meets only a few times per week or if your unit lasts only 7 to 10 days, you might not even consider including a project. If you do add a project, you might use a simple one such as giving a group a specific challenge and asking the students to modify it and present the modification either in writing to you or possibly as a demonstration to the other class members. If your class meets for a semester or for a summer course every day of the week for several hours, the project could be to create a new group task or challenge and present it to the entire class.

Over the years, when we have taught classes on team building to teacher groups or graduate course participants, we have put class members into small groups of two or three. We give these groups time to create a new group challenge, present the challenge to the other course participants (usually asking six or seven people to perform the challenge), and then discuss, critique, and make

practical modifications to the challenge. A number of challenges presented in this book, such as the Maze, Indiana's Challenge, Building Blocks, and Knights of the Around Table, are a result of this process. In our first book, *Team Building Through Physical Challenges,* Tarzan of the Jungle was a challenge partly created by a group of sixth graders after they received some guidelines and ideas for a new task.

If you have some interesting equipment, you may consider asking groups to develop a challenge centered on the specific use of that equipment. A group of students in one of our summer courses created the challenge Meteor Shower. We specifically asked them to engineer a challenge using balls. They did so and included scooters as well, because using scooters in other challenges was so much fun that they wanted to do more with them! If you give class projects such as these, you must allow enough time for practice, demonstration, and discussion. On numerous occasions, intense critiquing after the presentation and discussion of a challenge has produced modifications that made the new challenge more effective or focused it on a specific age group or population of students.

When giving challenge creation assignments, we recommend that you give students a form or outline (shown on page 26). This way you receive sufficient information for all aspects of the challenge as demonstrated by the descriptions and information that we provide in the challenges in this book: name of the challenge, description, success criteria, equipment needed, setup, rules and sacrifices, possible solutions, conclusion of the task, additions and variations, and safety concerns.

We advise the students to present a solution that works. We had one group present a challenge called Human Pegs. This challenge was a modification of a children's game that uses marbles, or golf tees as pegs. As they presented the challenge, we discovered that the solution they thought would work was impossible to accomplish using the rules that they created. We liked the idea enough to work on the rules and came up with solutions that worked. We should mention that having groups modify existing challenges as a project may be helpful to your administering the challenges to participants. Having groups modify challenges may also reduce the time necessary to complete a project. Creating brand new challenges can be time consuming.

Team-Building Outline

Location _____   Date _____

Group members:

    1.   6.

    2.   7.

    3.   8.

    4.   9.

    5.   10.

Name of our new challenge _____

    I. Description:

    II. Success criteria:

    III. Equipment needed:

    IV. Setup:

    V. Rules and sacrifices:

    VI. Possible solutions:

    VII. Conclusion of the task:

    VIII. Additions and variations:

Any additional information:

From *Essentials of Team Building* by Daniel W. Midura and Donald R. Glover, 2005, Champaign, IL: Human Kinetics.

RECORD KEEPING FOR TEAMS

Keeping records of team accomplishments or achievements can be simple. Records can provide a basis of discussion about the success of groups as well as the frustrations and difficulties they experience while solving problems. When administering a team-building unit, you may find it valuable to keep a visible record of team accomplishments. One method of record keeping is to make a list of accomplishments (as shown on page 28) that all classes can use. You can display the list on posters in your work space, such as a gymnasium.

A simple method of keeping records is to have team members sign their names on a line beneath their team name. As groups solve challenges, the instructor can circle the challenge solved, initial it, and possibly note the date on which the group solved the challenge. As the unit ends, this record can serve as resource for the groups when they fill out their team-building portfolio evaluation forms.

TEAM REPORT CARD

One of the first tools we used in team building was the team report card. We used it first as means to deal with teams that were having difficulty solving challenges or had team members who were creating problems for the team. At times we witnessed teams struggling with a team member's behavior. The other team members were usually reluctant to confront this person, or the person was a domi-

nant or aggressive leader. We used the team report card as a strategy to allow team members to voice their concerns or observations in a controlled, disciplined manner. The team report card (as shown on page 29) offers a structured but simple format for discussion to take place.

Although the team report card may not be an integral part of assessment, it can help groups generate discussions as well as help groups or individuals within a group work together for the good of the team. The purpose of team building is to have team members work together to solve challenges. The team report card can help a team get back on track if it loses its focus. An effective team can use the team report card to verbalize the positive strengths evidenced during team-building activities.

SUMMARY

The assessment process can be as important to the development of a student's intrinsic motivation as doing the actual challenges. Assessment techniques that actually promote critical thinking in the area of team building will contribute to the student becoming a better teammate. Developing opinions and judgments, as well as making informed decisions, is going to be as beneficial to a student's development as memorizing facts. Using portfolios that include student assessment show individual growth, involve the student fully, and communicate activities to parents.

Team Accomplishments

Class _____   Grade _____

You can add as many challenges to this list as you think necessary or supply blank lines on which you can write challenges attempted.

Team name	Team name	Team name
_____	_____	_____

Team members	Team members	Team members
_____	_____	_____
_____	_____	_____
_____	_____	_____
_____	_____	_____
_____	_____	_____
_____	_____	_____
_____	_____	_____

Tire Bridge	Tire Bridge	Tire Bridge
Lifeline	Lifeline	Lifeline
Swamp Machine	Swamp Machine	Swamp Machine
Construction Zone	Construction Zone	Construction Zone
Stepping-Stones I	Stepping-Stones I	Stepping-Stones I
Riverboat	Riverboat	Riverboat
Indiana's Challenge	Indiana's Challenge	Indiana's Challenge

From *Essentials of Team Building* by Daniel W. Midura and Donald R. Glover, 2005, Champaign, IL: Human Kinetics.

Team Report Card

1. How did our team involve everyone in solving the challenge?

2. Did our team use negative pressure or put-downs during the challenge?

3. Did we listen to one another or use ideas that we shared?

4. How many and which team members used praise phrases and positive encouragement?

5. What were some of the praise phrases used?

Reprinted, by permission, from D. Glover and D. Midura, 1992, *Team building through physical challenges* (Champaign, IL: Human Kinetics), Appendix.

From *Essentials of Team Building* by Daniel W. Midura and Donald R. Glover, 2005, Champaign, IL: Human Kinetics.

Safety Strategies

The issue of safety must always be part of planning for motor activities. Those of us who have spent years in the field of physical education or recreation should always have safety on our minds. The range of safety issues is virtually endless. It can include teaching children to move safely in the gym without falling or running into others; using a type of ball that has good texture, weight, and visibility and can therefore be easily caught without jamming a finger; teaching children how to dismount from a set of horizontal climbing ladders on a playground; teaching participants how to support the legs of a partner who is doing curl-ups or crunches; or preparing mats under a cargo net or climbing ropes before participants climb the apparatus.

Possibly the best advice we can offer is to think safety. No matter what activity we present, we can reinforce or teach methods of participation that reduce the risk factors of that particular activity. In this chapter, you will learn about general safety issues and guidelines relevant to team building and safety rules for specific tasks.

GENERAL RULES

In the challenges that we present in this book, we deal with safety suggestions for each task. So rather than list each safety precaution we will present some general safety rules or recommendations related specifically to team-building activities. These include the following:

- Make sure that all participants understand the need and importance of physical support during many of the challenges.
- The instructor should be aware of the physical limitations of all participants in the class. If some of the participants cannot physically accomplish a task, the instructor should make or offer adaptations.

- As the instructor, you should pay close attention to activities that could potentially injure the head or neck. Make students aware of the possibility of injury if they attempt to solve the challenge while disregarding safety practices. Point out the potential for injury for each challenge that contains elements of risk.
- Participants will be lifting objects such as tires, mats, other teammates, and so on. Discuss safety practices for lifting. Participants should lift by using the legs rather than the back.
- Before doing any challenges, the teams should always address safety concerns. One question the instructor can ask of a team is, "Have you thought of any potential safety issues that this challenge might present?" Other questions could focus on equipment: "How can we safely transfer a scooter? Could we get our fingers pinched using a scooter? How can we avoid a sore back from lifting tires?"

Besides offering these general rules, we list some safety concerns for each challenge as part of the description and administration of challenges found in chapters 6 though 10.

In their book, *Effective Leadership in Adventure Programming*, Simon Priest and Michael A. Gass write substantively about safety skills, accident theory, risk management, and legal liability. We think that their text and other resources effectively present a substantial resource base for outdoor adventure education, indoor wall climbing, and related activities. We therefore do not intend to duplicate their information, and we encourage readers to access the resources they have already provided. Keep in mind that the activities presented in advanced outdoor adventure education and indoor wall-climbing curricula usually present a much greater physical risk than the risk involved in the activities that we are presenting. Even so, those participating in team-building challenges must be firmly committed to safety. We strongly advocate that you prepare your activities in the safest manner possible to avoid any type of accident or injury. As we mentioned earlier, we have divided our challenges into introductory, intermediate, and advanced levels. In the introductory challenges, risk factors are minimal but nonetheless important.

SPOTTERS AND SPOTTING

We have found that two types of spotting are needed to ensure safety and success in team building. The first type is the general concern that one teammate has for another. This awareness may consist of offering one's hand to help a teammate maintain balance or giving someone a boost or helping hand to complete a challenge. This type of support shows care and concern for others. We hope that this type of help and support becomes second nature to everyone involved in team building.

The second type of spotting requires participants to protect teammates from injury. This type of spotting means that teammates must trust one another. Without trust, members may not try challenges such as the Black Hole, which requires participants to lift and pass teammates through a hoop. To build that trust among participants, the teacher must convey the importance of spotting and impress upon teammates that fooling around during a difficult challenge diminishes trust among one another. The teacher must teach students how to lift and how to protect a teammate's head and neck so that everyone is safe.

Establishing trust in team-building activities requires emotional and physical support from all team members.

Teaching Spotting

Spotting is an art. Know how and what to do in different situations to make the participants as safe as possible and have fun at the same time. Take an entire class period to practice these skills before the group goes into events where people may be catching or lifting each other. Often this one class really helps bring the group together. As the instructor, you set the tone. If you make safety and proper spotting a priority, the participants will quickly follow your example. In those cases in which you do not have enough spotters for an event or for a particular person, postpone doing that event until you do have adequate help. This is another way to emphasize the importance of participants' safety.

Tom Heck, the "Teach Me Teamwork" coach (www.teachmeteamwork.com), developed the following pointers for teaching spotting:

- Explain the concept and meaning of spotting.
- Practice spotting with participants before they need to use the skill in an activity.
- Promote the attitude that teasing and joking about not catching someone has no place in your program.
- Supervise spotters closely.
- The leader must model spotting.
- A good spotter shares the responsibility of spotting equally. Working as a team when spotting is easier and safer.
- Spotters should stand in a balanced position, holding hands up in a ready position, or as some say, "Bumpers up." Spotters should focus on the participant.
- Spotters should cushion a fall, not catch and hold, and should move with the direction of force.

Courtesy of Tom Heck the "Teach Me Teamwork" coach on www.teachmeteamwork.com.

Spotting Guidelines

By Jean Berube

Team-building challenges take place while participants are standing on the ground, falling to the ground, swinging or transferring in the air, or using equipment. Each of these environments has some similar yet specific criteria for spotting a participant.

Before describing the specific spotting needs for each environment, some general rules apply:

1. Always protect the head and neck of the person you are spotting.
2. While spotting, stand in a stride position.
3. Participants and spotters should remove jewelry and watches as well as belts with large buckles.

On-the-Ground Spotting

The catcher absorbs a backward or forward fall by meeting the falling person with his or her arms extended and then bending the arms halfway as contact is made.

While spotting someone who is falling backward, spot the shoulder blades with open hands and bend your arms slightly to absorb the fall before returning the person to a balanced position.

While spotting someone who is falling forward, catch the upper arms of the faller (whose arms are crossed) and bend your arms slightly upon making contact. Return the person to a balanced position. This sequence reverses when putting the person back into balance.

In a circle while performing a trust pass (involving external locus of control) or a trust circle (involving internal locus of control), participants and spotters have different requirements. In a trust pass, the person in the middle should lean from the ankles, and the body should be stiff; the arms should be folded across the chest. Catchers (spotters) stand in stride position in the circle. Hands of the catchers should be in front of the body to support the person in the middle. The person is then passed gently around the circle in a continuous flow.

During a trust circle the person in the circle makes the decision to fall and in which direction to fall. In this challenge, two or more catchers accept the person falling on the shoulder blades or upper arms and return the person to a standing position. It is *not* the job of the catchers to push the falling person across the circle unless that technique is being used to teach a special lesson. If the catchers are to push the person, they must be very careful because the person in the middle could easily be dropped if the group members are not alert or willing to accept responsibility for another person. It is often difficult to regain a person's trust if he or she is dropped. In a trust circle, there should be at least four hands on the person at any one time.

Note: Sometimes the group includes people of varying heights, such as a 6-footer and a 4-footer as catchers. In circle formations, the tall people should stand at different places around the circle so the person in the center who is falling is always protected. When a short adult or child is in the center, tall people should kneel so they can catch the faller more easily and not injure their own lower backs by leaning over to do the catching.

Off-the-Ground Spotting

If a person is off the ground, a minimum of two people should spot that person at all times. There should never be a situation in which there are fewer than three people involved in an off-the-ground challenge.

Spotters and catchers stand in stride position; their hands are up and ready to catch, and the elbows are slightly flexed. Two people spot the catcher and the faller. Catchers and spotters work together when a person falls. The following is a description of several off-the-ground situations:

- If the person starts to fall, try to help them regain balance. When trying to push the person back to center, if the person is slightly above the catcher, spot at the hips. Never go below the hips because the center of gravity for the falling person will be higher than the catcher and both the faller and the catcher could fall.
- If you cannot put the person back into a balanced state, catch him or her at the hips and try to bring the person down to the ground.
- If the person's weight is going over the catcher's head, the catcher should back up and bring his or her arms up and under the person's armpits. The catcher continues to back up while the feet of the person falling come down until the faller's legs can get under his or her body and can regain balance. In this situation, both the falling person and the catcher should be spotted.

Hoop and Swing Spotting

When spotting such activities as the Black Hole, in which people go through a hanging hoop, "spirit spotters" do the following:

- Spot the head and neck of the person going through.
- Stay close to the person going through. The hoop might bump the spotters, but it won't hurt if the spotters stay close.
- Have their hands ready to catch or give support if the person going through needs protection.
- Keep their knees bent and move with the person going through and near the hoop.

Spotting people on a swinging event such as Grand Canyon, in which people must get across a "canyon" via a hanging rope in the middle of the river, "spirit spotters" must do the following:

- Stay focused on the person attempting the challenge.
- Stay close to the moving object so the spotter can avoid receiving a hard hit from the object and be in a position to protect the person who is going across.
- Have hands ready to catch or spot, bend knees, and have feet in a stride position.

Note: Many people do not have the upper-body strength to swing across an area by only holding onto a rope; or on the first try, they might hold the rope incorrectly and fall off. To protect the person trying to swing across, lay a two-inch-thick tumbling mat across the canyon to soften the landing if spotters are unable to break the fall.

If participants swing on a rope or walk across a balance beam, spotters should do the following:

- Stay close to the rope or beam.
- Focus on the person crossing.
- Have the hands ready to catch the person.

Note: By staying close to the rope or beam, spotters may get bumped, but that is minor compared to being a couple of feet or more from the swinging rope when it hits them.

Lifting From and Lowering to the Ground

To lift a person in a supine (faceup) position from the ground, spotters kneel while facing each other on opposite sides, close to the person. They sit back over the heels and keep their backs straight. Spotters follow these steps:

1. Slide hands under the supine person.
2. On a given count, lift the person waist high.
3. Shift the body weight from over the heels to directly over the knees.
4. Place one foot on the floor.
5. On a given signal, everyone stands up together and places both feet on the floor.
6. Keep back straight and knees bent.

Note: Reverse the procedure when going down to the ground. Four to six people are required for people under 5 feet, 6 inches tall; six to eight people are required for people up to 7 feet tall. The number of spotters required is also influenced by a person's weight: The heavier the person is, the more people are needed.

When lifting upward and overhead, spotters should do the following:

- On a given count, arms raise the person to shoulder level.
- On another count, the group lifts the person overhead.
- The group turns to face in the same direction while supporting the supine person overhead.
- Arms lock and the hands spread out to support the entire body.
- Spotters must give special support to the head, neck, shoulders, hips, and legs.

Note: Reverse these steps when bringing the person down.

Standing on Another Person's Back

The person kneeling on the ground should have his or her knees under the hips and the arms directly under the shoulders. The back should be concave (arched downward).

The person standing on another person's back should have assistance in getting on and off. The feet should be placed over the hips and shoulders of the kneeling person. The standing person should never place a foot on the lower back. This is the weakest part of the person's body. The standing person never should jump off the back because that would cause the kneeler to fall over and the jumper to lose her balance and fall.

We have made every effort to anticipate a variety of solutions to every challenge and to address safety issues. There is always a chance that a group can come up with a different solution, so the leader should keep safety in mind at all times.

Learning how to spot reinforces the belief among teammates that they must help protect and support their teammates. The instructor must emphasize the skill of spotting and teach students to lift with their legs, not their backs, and always be on the lookout for potential danger.

EQUIPMENT SAFETY

The first realm of concern is the equipment itself. Most of the equipment used for team building will already be in your storage room or can be easily obtained. Be sure to inspect the equipment for any safety issues (i.e., frayed ropes, poor wheels on scooters, or tires with exposed steel belts).

Remember to periodically inspect the equipment and store it safely.

Tires

In many challenges we use automobile tires. You can obtain them free of charge at virtually any establishment that sells or services tires. Additionally, you can recycle your own tires into your inventory of equipment and thus avoid paying the recycling fee attached to each purchase of a new tire. Be aware of exposed steel belts. Do not use any tire with exposed metal material (steel belts) that can cause a cut. We recommend washing used tires with soap and water both inside and out and then wiping off the tire with a car-care cleaning product such as Armor All. This process leaves the tires clean and usable so that they will not mark the floor, cause marks on clothes, or leave dirty hands. Smaller tires less than 13 inches (33 centimeters) in diameter are harder to find. We recommend looking for boat trailer or utility trailer tires at marine centers or auto centers that sell trailers. Some radial belt tires in these sizes still come without steel belts.

Ropes

In a number of our challenges we use jump ropes in various ways. Our recommendation here is to use sash cord rope (the old-fashioned jump ropes). Many hardware stores, full-service home or lumber stores, and canvas warehouses carry this type of rope in 100-foot (30-meter) lengths (called hanks). These ropes are durable. Segmented ropes or the licorice-type jump rope (also called speed ropes) may break if used for pulling teammates or equipment. If participants step on a rope, the rope could roll, causing them to twist an ankle.

Scooters

We use scooters in some challenges. We tend to use the standard 12-inch (30-centimeter) square scooter for most school-age students and the 16-inch (40-centimeter) square scooter for adults and students with special needs.

Each year, manufacturers seem to be making better wheels that allow users to travel farther with less effort, usually a desired outcome. But this may not be what we want for our purpose. Before we discuss the travel issue, we caution you to forbid participants from standing on scooters at any time, even if the students are certified skate board professionals. Scooters are not made to be

16-inch scooter from Gopher Sport.

12-inch scooter from Gopher Sport.

stood upon. Standing on scooters can lead to a variety of safety problems that you do not need to experience. Standing on them is forbidden, period! We have found that using older scooters that do not roll quite as easily as newer ones do cause participants to work harder or find more ways to assist one another. This struggle, from our perspective, is desirable in team-building challenges.

The misuse of scooters can include running over one's own fingers or the fingers of others, being pushed off the scooter and landing unsafely on the floor (both forward and backward), and being pushed too fast or too far. Over the many years that we have used or bought scooters, we have not seen safety standards for their use. Therefore, we recommend that you create a list of prudent safety items related to the careful use of this piece of equipment.

A few of our challenges that specify the use of scooters require, as part of the solution, the transfer of scooters from one student to another or from one group to another group. Students must demonstrate safe ways to transfer the scooter. As

an example, if a student pushes the scooter as though he or she were delivering a curling stone, it would probably arrive safely at the intended destination. If a student called out a teammate's name and pushed the scooter directly toward that student, it should also arrive in a responsible manner. On the other hand, if a student carelessly flings the scooter across an open space, it could interfere with another group or strike a student who may not be watching the action. We recommend a clear discussion concerning the responsible transferring of scooters. We have found that students are excited about using scooters, and we have not witnessed accidents, but that favorable circumstance may be because we insist that users follow safety rules and suggestions.

Cage Balls

Another piece of equipment that we regularly use is a large inflatable cage ball. Generally, we use a 48-inch or 60-inch (120-centimeter or 150-centimeter) diameter ball. The appearance of a large ball of this nature elicits some overwhelming desires. First, students are tempted to run up and kick the ball, an action that in a learning environment might be more disruptive than it is harmful or dangerous. The second temptation is to run, jump on the ball, and roll over, an exploit that can result in the student's landing on his or her head, which is generally not recognized as a safe maneuver or strategy. No matter what activity or lesson you teach, you will eventually find yourself in a situation that you never anticipated. We had a student whose method of moving the cage ball was to hold the laces with his teeth and try to carry it across a long space. This method did not seem conducive to healthy teeth (you can bet that another person was just itching to kick the ball). To say the least, this way of using the ball is not acceptable, although it may be a clever solution to a challenge.

Poly Spots and Vinyl Bases

Vinyl bases or poly spots are other items that we use in a few challenges. To keep them from moving or slipping out from under the participants' feet, we recommend cutting strips of mat tape, folding them over, and placing them underneath the base to create a sticky bond from the base to the floor. Mat tape is usually sold in rolls that are 3 or 4 inches (8 or 10 centimeters) wide. The primary use of mat tape is to repair wrestling or tumbling mats or to tape them together. This type of tape is usually a thick, clear vinyl product. Most sporting-goods catalogs carry this product.

Wooden Boards

Some challenges use wooden boards, such as two-by-fours (boards about 3.8 centimeters thick and 9.0 centimeters wide) that are 8 feet (2.5 meters) long. For participants of any age we suggest that a discussion take place regarding common sense when transferring equipment. As an example, this discussion could cover the hazard of stepping on one end of a board that is unsupported at the other end. This action could cause the board to flip up and lead to an uncomfortable and embarrassing event. Allowing a board to fall from a vertical position could cause someone to be hurt. Turning quickly while holding a board in a horizontal position could cause the board to hit another person. Covering the edges of the board with duct tape will eliminate the possibility that a sliver will catch someone in the hand.

Plungers

In some challenges, we use plungers—yes, the old-fashioned rubber toilet plunger. In our challenges, participants use plungers primarily as a pushing device or to manipulate a ball. No matter what the age of your participants, an overwhelming desire develops to place the plunger on another person's head, to stab the plunger to the ground so that the suction cup sticks there, or to throw the plunger to the ceiling to see if it can be stuck there. You must discourage all of these incorrect uses. Probably the best approach is to describe or pretend to show the participants in a humorous way what you are thinking. If you do not address the issue right away, you will have some equipment problems. Plungers that are stuck to the ground, for instance, usually are pulled up quickly by the person who jammed the plunger down, often causing damage to the threads inside the plunger, thus reducing its effectiveness as a tool for your challenge.

Cargo Nets

We have a few challenges that make use of a cargo net. Should you have access to one, you would be prudent to have a periodic safety inspection by yourself and a representative of the organization that owns the facility in which you use the apparatus. Be sure that a sufficient number of crash pads or tumbling mats are beneath the cargo net. We also recommend that you give participants a set of safety instructions that include disallowing climbers from climbing over the top bar or top of the net. Instruct participants to climb no higher than what feels comfortable to them. You should demonstrate how to get off the net safely without simply jumping or dropping off the net. Encourage students to help each other onto and off of the cargo nets. In addition, you should give instruction about how climbers can avoid stepping on the hands or heads of teammates as they travel up and down the cargo net.

Tug-of-War Ropes

A few challenges use tug-of-war ropes. These ropes are generally heavy but usually do not pose a great safety risk. Some cheap manila ropes have fibers that break off like tiny slivers. Avoid using these ropes. If participants swing a rope in a careless or lasso fashion, they may strike another person, who probably will not feel happy about the experience.

Blindfolds

We have used blindfolds in a number of our challenges. We have also noted with interest that many of our students and workshop participants like to add handicapping conditions as variations to many of the challenges that we do or that they create. Having teammates give up their sight is usually the first idea presented. We have some definite observations about the use of blindfolds. First, participants who choose to wear the blindfolds need to make a commitment that they will not wander away from the group when blindfolded. Group members can trip on objects or teammates, run into objects such as walls, or accidentally strike another person with a piece of equipment that they may handle during the challenge. Sighted teammates need to monitor their blindfolded team members to ensure their safety.

SAFETY ISSUES WITH SPECIFIC CHALLENGES

As we noted earlier, we will include specific safety concerns for each challenge as they appear in the book. But some safety issues are important enough to be considered in a general discussion on safety. By highlighting these issues for a few specific challenges, we believe that you will have greater inclination to think about safety for every challenge you present to your participants.

Black Hole

In one of the advanced challenges, the Black Hole, we use a hula hoop suspended from a basketball hoop. We recommend attaching the hoop to a jump rope using a piece of masking tape.

If a student should fall or put too much pressure on the hoop during this challenge, the tape will quickly snap and the hoop will fall. This setup prevents a participant from falling onto the hoop and finding himself or herself suspended on the hoop or falling hard to the ground. This circumstance could occur if the hoop is attached directly to the rope. In addition, we recommend that sufficient padding, in the way of crash pads or tumbling mats beneath the hoop, always be in place to break the fall of anyone who loses his or her balance or is dropped by the group.

During this challenge, participants lift their teammates. Remind the group to lift safely and correctly (using their legs). Some students have

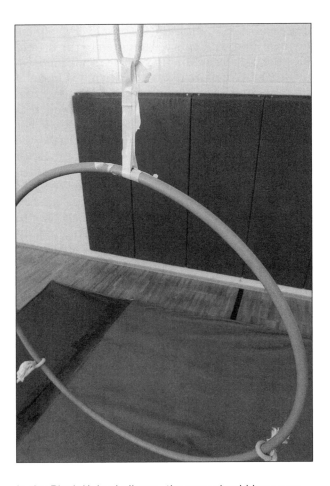

In the Black Hole challenge, the rope should loop over the basketball hoop and the hanging ends should be tied together. Attaching tape between the hanging rope and the hula hoop will allow it to suspend.

an overwhelming desire to dive headfirst through the hoop. Do not allow this action to be part of the solution. Other teammates may suggest that the group throw someone through the hoop, or a student may volunteer to be thrown through the hoop; this technique is not safe either. Make sure that this challenge has a crash pad as a base for proper standing support.

Electric Fence

Electric Fence is an advanced challenge in which participants cross a high balance beam to the other end by going under a net that is hanging above and touching the beam. You should consider having participants wear long-sleeve shirts and long pants because they may obtain bruises and burns from attempting to get on top of the balance beam. Make sure that plenty of mats are on the floor. Keep the balance beam as low as possible while having enough room for participants to hang under the beam without touching the floor.

Knights of the Around Table

Knights of the Around Table is an advanced challenge that requires the group to transfer all members over and under a table without touching the floor. Do not allow team members to go feet first around the table because doing so puts their heads in an unsafe position. Also, be certain that the table you use is extremely sturdy.

Bridge Over the Raging River

This intermediate challenge requires all group members to cross a distance using four automobile tires, two 8-foot-long (2.5-meter-long) boards, and two ropes. Participants must use caution when moving the two-by-four boards. In addition, the group must be aware that the board could flip up if someone steps on one end of the board without having the other end supported. They also must be careful when lifting and moving tires.

We hope that this discussion of safety issues for a few challenges will prompt you to think about safety concerns when administering the challenges. The challenges are fun and motivating. Our own students and workshop participants continually challenge us to think about safety. If we do not point out safety concerns, we will have someone come up with a dangerous way of solving a challenge or circumventing a rule.

CREATIVE WAYS TO OBTAIN EQUIPMENT

Having been public school teachers for over 30 years, we have spent our careers with limited budgets, living within frugal means, and making the best of whatever equipment we could accumulate. Most teachers understand this all too well. When we began creating team-building challenges, we looked at the equipment and supplies we had in our storerooms and asked, "How can we use what we have or what we can get?" We were not entrepreneurs looking to manufacture products to sell. We were painfully pragmatic. As we stated previously, you can collect automobile or trailer tires free of charge from your own home, friends, tire stores, or service stations. You should not

have to spend a dime to get decent tires. Remember to clean the tires before using them. Wooden boards used in challenges are available at reasonable prices at any lumber store. If you work for an educational or parochial institution, you can ask a contractor or carpenter to donate materials and perhaps gain a tax deduction. You can buy sash cord rope from a hardware store or full-service lumber store at reasonable cost. Some items, such as plungers and highway-type cones, can be found in liquidation stores or unclaimed freight stores. Certain items that we use, such as scooters, cage balls, poly spots, vinyl bases, tug-of-war ropes, cones, and deck tennis rings, are available from sporting-goods suppliers such as Gopher Sport of Owatonna, Minnesota.

If you have virtually no money in a budget, you may wonder what you can do to obtain equipment. Here are a few suggestions. If you work in a school situation, you can always request assistance from a parent–teacher organization such as PTA, PTO, or PTSA for funds or a grant. In many communities, organizations that deal with charitable gambling or pull-tabs must donate, by law, a percentage of their earnings to educational or charitable organizations. You could contact a group like your local VFW or Lions Club and inquire about their grant policies. If your school or group administers Jump Rope for Heart or Hoops for Heart events, you may qualify for a grant through your state AAHPERD organization. Companies such as Campbell's Soup (Labels for Education) and General Mills sponsor label and point programs that are designed to exchange product proofs of purchase for athletic or physical education equipment.

We recommend that you buy safety equipment such as tumbling mats or crash pads from a reputable company or manufacturer. Likewise, you should buy items such as balance beams, cargo nets, and climbing ropes through a commercial enterprise. Making your own gymnastics equipment could open you up to legal and liability issues.

One of our challenges, Toxic Waste Transfer, uses a 5-gallon (20-liter) paint bucket or sheetrock joint compound bucket. You should always be able to find this item free. In the bucket, you use packing peanuts, a product that you should also be able to save or find without cost. Just ask friends, family, or neighbors to save packing peanuts for you. Poles such as those used in Plunger Ball can be found in the plumbing section of any home store. PVC plumbing pipe in 8- or 10-foot (2.5- to 3-meter) sections is inexpensive. We still use thick bamboo poles, which used to be available from carpet companies, who used them inside the carpet rolls. If you cannot afford vinyl bases or poly spots, you could use carpet sample pieces. Asking a carpet establishment for discontinued samples is the simplest way to obtain these items.

Our intention here is to show you that you do not need a great deal of money to use the challenges we have written or to create your own challenges. When we have conducted team-building classes and have assigned our students the task of creating their own challenges, we often find that they come up with ideas from the equipment that we have on hand or from items that they find in their own homes. An example of this is Great Balls of Color, a challenge that is now being sold in catalogs. Our challenge designers simply took a sheet sized for a single bed, cut five holes, used five different colored markers to outline the holes, and used five colored softball-sized Wiffle balls to create a challenge that they called Hole in the Bucket. This group created a challenge that cost them nothing except the resources that they found

in their own homes or garages. Practical use of existing equipment and materials and a mind-set of safety will take you a long way in creating an inventory of team-building supplies.

As team building has become popular over the past number of years, more sporting-goods companies are carrying inventories of equipment needed for team-building activities. Many companies are encouraging teachers and instructors to invent new challenges based on creative equipment uses and designs. We will be including a few of these challenges in the next few chapters.

SUMMARY

Using good judgment and common sense is no different for team building than for any other physical activity. Be sure the equipment is safe, that floor areas are properly matted, and that participants understand that horseplay can result in unsafe conditions or injuries.

Team-Building
Sample Course Outline

Now that you have an understanding of the major concepts of team building, safety strategies, and assessment of participants using portfolios, we present a sample outline for a semester team-building course. The authors and Jim Tangen-Foster, an outdoor adventure educator at the University of Wisconsin-River Falls and an expert at coordinating team-building activities with outdoor adventure experiences, developed this course outline. The outline is based on a 12-week semester with 50-minute class periods, meeting three times a week for a total of 36 classes. Chapters 6 through 10 in this book contain specific instructions for icebreaker activities and all challenges used in this sample course. Please refer to the table of contents to locate each activity referenced in the class plans. The authors would like to emphasize that this is only a suggested course outline, a guide for you if you are interested in developing such a course. Please add or modify additional course assessments and activities that might be more appropriate for your equipment, facilities, and age groups.

Keys to team-building success include good communication and organization of all activities.

Class 1

A. Introductions. Each student tells his or her major, hometown, and motivation for taking the class.

B. Course expectations

1. The instructor states expectations and how course grades will be given. The following criteria are required for this course:

    a. Notebook portfolio. The portfolio must include the following:

       (1) All handouts received from the instructor.

       (2) You must research and include additional materials pertaining to course subject matter. The additional materials should include at least 10 pages of articles from outside class.

       (3) The portfolio should include a minimum of one typed page of reflection of six class meetings. This reflection must include several elements:

           (a) Date

           (b) Description of activity

           (c) Opinion about the purpose of the activity

           (d) Additions or variations to this activity or opinion about the value the activity has to learning

    b. You must attend the overnight canoe field trip. You must type and include a two-page paper about your experiences. The paper should discuss how this field trip affected your learning experience, which activities on the trip were most beneficial, and which activities were not useful. Also, touch on how your team performed during the trip.

    c. Your team must become involved in one community project. The minimum length of your volunteer activity must be three hours, and your team must do the project as a group. Some suggestions are the following:

       (1) Food Shelf

       (2) Toys for Tots

       (3) Habitat for Humanity

       (4) Mentoring

       (5) Volunteering in any other community project

       (6) Creating a community-building project

You must include in your portfolio a reflection about your experience. This item must be at least two typed pages long. Touch on how your team worked together on this experience. Do this outside the classroom and describe it completely in your portfolio.

    d. Complete one team report card and include it in your portfolio. Do this assessment at the completion of the team-building challenges.

    e. Complete an evaluation questionnaire and include it in your portfolio. The instructor will provide all of these assessment sheets. These assessment sheets can be found in chapter 3.

    f. Complete a student evaluation sheet and include it in your portfolio.

    g. The notebook portfolio must be neat and organized. The organizational structure is up to you.

    h. Design and implement a team-building challenge with your team. The other teams in the class will attempt to solve your challenge. A template will be provided. Use the team-building outline to write your challenge and provide everyone in the class with a copy. (The outline can be found in chapter 3.) This is a team effort.

Point Values for Class Requirements (total = 100 points)

1. Notebook portfolio = 25 points
2. Field trip and paper = 25 points
3. Presentation of team challenge = 25 points
4. Volunteer community-building activity = 25 points

First Activity

- Divide the class into teams of six to eight, depending on the number of students. Four teams would be ideal. For this book, we will use four teams of six.

- Put the newly formed teams in a circle. Give them the job of coming up with a team name and getting to know one another better.

Class 2

A. Discuss the importance of teamwork.

You may want to ask these questions:

1. Can you give me examples of effective teamwork situations that you have experienced?

2. What types of skills must a good teammate have? Someone will say, "The ability to encour-

age." Discuss the meaning of encouragement (it means to give others courage). Ask the class to give examples of encouraging things that you can see, such as the following:

- Thumbs-up
- High five
- Pat on the back
- Clapping
- Smiling

Ask the class for examples of encouraging things that you can hear, such as the following:

- "Try again."
- "You can do it."
- "Don't give up."
- "Now you are getting it."

  3. Discuss behaviors that disrupt a team and cause it to malfunction. Explain how sarcasm, negative pressure, or outright put-downs affect team performance. Give examples of each.

B. Each team should now sit in a circle and create a team pact. This pact will contain rules for conflict resolution and rules for working together to solve challenges.

C. First team icebreaker—Moving Team Juggle
- Equipment: three foam playground balls per group.
- Large area such as a gym.
- Time: 10 to 15 minutes.
- Objectives:
  - To learn teammates' names
  - To learn support and encouragement
  - To have fun
  - Directions: See specific activity instructions in chapter 6.

D. Second team icebreaker—Group Construction
- Equipment: 10 toothpicks per class member.
- Time: 15 to 20 minutes.
- Objective: improvement of skills in listening and giving directions to a group.
- Directions: See specific activity instructions in chapter 6.

You will not have enough time to allow everyone a chance to be a construction manager. Explain to the students that they will continue this or a similar icebreaker during the next class period.

Class 3

A. Continue with Group Construction for 15 minutes. At the end of 15 minutes, give those who were not construction managers a chance to be the Great Communicator, which is the next activity.

B. Third team icebreaker—The Great Communicator
- Equipment: paper and pencil for each student.
- Keys: Refer to the Great Communicator in chapter 6.
- Time: 15 to 20 minutes.
- Objective: As in the toothpick activity, students will learn to listen and give directions to a group.
- Directions: Refer to the Great Communicator in chapter 6.

C. You may want to use these discussion questions at the conclusion of these activities:
  1. Did you enjoy these activities?
     - Moving Team Juggle?
     - Group Construction?
     - The Great Communicator?
  2. Can anyone give an example of when you thought you communicated effectively?
  3. Recall the toothpick activity. Did anyone have difficulty understanding what to build? How was it easier—with the builders silent or with the builders asking questions?
  4. During the Great Communicator and Group Construction, how many different ways did the group use to communicate messages?
  5. Which ways were most effective and why?
  6. In Moving Team Juggle, how many attempts did it take your team to pass the three balls successfully?
  7. Did anyone come up with a plan of action?
  8. Did the team encourage one another after a few dropped balls? Give me an example.

Class 4

A. Discussion: challenge by choice

In their book, *Effective Leadership in Adventure Programming,* Priest and Gass provide the following definition of challenge by choice: "An effort to empower students by proactively informing them that they, not you as the team-building leader, control a major part of determining the degree of challenge, risk and competence with which they will engage during team building." Ask the class to define this paragraph in another way.

We have used challenge by choice for years in our team-building graduate classes with St. Mary's University in Winona, Minnesota. Using this method we have found that Schoel, Prouty, and Radcliffe (1988) were correct when they wrote that the challenge by choice concept offers the following benefits:

- A chance to try a potentially difficult or frightening challenge in an atmosphere of support and caring
- The opportunity to back off when performance pressures or self-doubt become too strong, knowing that an opportunity for a future attempt will always be there

  Note: During our years of conducting team-building classes, we have found that team pressure to conquer a tough challenge can be quite strong. Team members have to buy into the fact that if someone does not feel ready, the team must support that decision.

- A chance to try difficult tasks, recognizing that the attempt is more significant than performance results.
- Respect for individual ideas and choices.

B. Discussion: full-value contract

Discuss the meaning and characteristics of the full-value contract, which is so important in team building and adventure education. Priest and Gass present the full-value contract in depth in *Effective Leadership in Adventure Programming* on page 176. Here are a few highlights of the contract:

- We will work together as a group toward individual and group goals.
- We will adhere to certain safety and group behavior guidelines.
- We will give and receive feedback, both positive and constructive, and work toward changing behavior when it is appropriate.

Discussion of these terms is important because the discussion relates directly to the next activity.

C. Discussion: team building

Explain to the class that how they cooperatively work to solve a challenge is as important as whether or not they solve it. Every member of the team will have to play a part because each will be concerned with the outcome.

During some of the challenges, some teams may fall short of their goals. Teams may even break down if they do not organize and plan. But as the teams continue to try to solve increasingly difficult challenges, team members, we hope, will learn to listen to others, to praise others for ideas and efforts, and to encourage teammates to achieve success.

- Explain to the class that they will start team building with introductory challenges and then move to intermediate and advanced challenges.
- Explain general safety rules.
- Use front-loading questions before team building.

Class 5

Before class the teacher should set up the following five team-building challenges found in chapters 7 and 10:

- Magic Bases
- Rainbow Swamp Trail
- Construction Zone
- River Crossing
- Swamp Machine

Go over safety concerns with the teams. Explain to the teams the function of the challenge card and the organizer card, which can be found in the appendix, as well as the function of the organizer, encourager, and praiser. Tell the teams that these roles must rotate among team members as they move through the challenges.

- By setting up one more challenge than there are teams, one challenge will always be open.
- Teams will not make it to all challenges but should be able to complete at least two or three before the end of class.

Allow enough time for teams to work together and put equipment away. Tell them to remember how far along they were on a particular challenge because they will start at that point in the next class period.

Class 6

Assign each team a challenge or two to set up. Teams must set up their challenges in different locations. This requirement will force all teams to work together to set up safely.

A. Set up the challenges that the teams did not complete during the previous class period.

B. Also set up these challenges:

- Tire Bridge
- Toxic Waste Transfer
- Lifeline

C. Work on solving challenges

D. Allow enough time for teams to work together to put equipment away.

E. Short discussion:

1. How could you change or adapt the challenges that you tried to make them harder or easier?

This discussion will get your students thinking about designing challenges, and they may begin to realize the difficulty of designing a challenge.

Class 7

A. Set up challenges not yet completed during class 6. In addition, set up the Rock and the Whole World in Their Hands. Again, the teams have to communicate as to where these challenges will be placed so they do not interfere with each other. Teammates will also have to discuss who is setting up the various pieces of equipment.

B. Practice challenges

Class 8

A. Each team sits in a circle and fills out a team report card (see chapter 3). Allow discussion within the teams. Allow each team member to fill out one card or assign a secretary to fill out the card after group consensus on the answer.

B. After team report cards, the teams should set up the following challenges:

- Teamwork Walk
- Great Pearl Caper
- Indiana's Challenge
- Building Blocks

C. Teams will get through only two or three challenges. Allow enough time to put equipment away.

Class 9

A. Present more debriefing questions.

1. Communication

a. Can anyone give an example of when you thought you communicated effectively?

b. How do you know that your teammates understood what you communicated?

c. If teammates did not understand your communication, what could you do differently next time to give a clearer message?

d. What could the message receiver do differently the next time to understand the message?

e. How many different ways did the group use to communicate messages?

f. Which ways were the most effective? Why?

g. Did you learn something about communication that will be helpful later? If so, what?

After working through the debriefing questions, set up intermediate challenges that teams did not attempt during the last class period.

B. Allow enough time to put equipment away.

Class 10

A. Allow teams to set up any intermediate challenges that they have not attempted. Also set up these challenges:

- Island Escape
- The Maze
- Stepping-Stones I

B. Practice intermediate challenges and allow enough time to put equipment away.

Class 11

A. Set up any introductory or intermediate challenge that has not been attempted. Also set up these challenges:

- Bridge Over the Raging River
- Human Pegs
- Dynamic Barrier

B. Allow enough practice time and then have teams put equipment away.

Class 12

A. Introduce advanced challenges.

1. Revisit challenge by choice and full-value contract concepts.

2. Assign the groups to set up the following advanced challenges:

- Black Hole
- Stepping-Stones II
- Neutral Zone

- Knights of the Around Table
- Electric Fence

B. Allow teams to attempt advanced challenges. Review safety rules with the class and remind them to be encouragers.

The teams will get to only one or two of these challenges during this class period.

C. Assign the teams the task of setting up the same challenges in the next class period.

D. Have teams work together to put challenges away.

Class 13

A. Start the day with more debriefing questions from the Priest and Gass leadership text.

1. Who assumed leadership roles during the challenges?
2. What were the behaviors that showed leadership?
3. Can everyone agree that these behaviors are traits of leaders?
4. How has the group responded to various leadership behaviors?
5. Did anyone follow an idea even though he or she wasn't sure that the idea would work? Why?
6. Did leadership roles shift to others during the challenges?

B. Set up all the advanced challenges from the last class meeting and continue working. Allow enough time to put equipment away.

Class 14

A. This is the last day of advanced challenges. Allow teams to struggle, but if it looks as if a team may not be able to accomplish a challenge, move them to another challenge so that a different team gets a chance to try. Alternatively, allow some teams to gather around the Electric Fence and offer encouragement.

B. Allow enough time to clean up.

C. Discuss ways to adapt or change challenges to make them easier or more difficult.

Class 15

A. Start class today with a discussion about how the advanced challenges required different solutions than the introductory or intermediate challenges did. You may get responses like these:

1. Challenges were very hard and required specific roles—we had to match individual skills to those roles.
2. We had to assist physically much more than we did before.
3. We had to listen and concentrate much more.

B. Positive adjectives (see chapter 2).

C. Hand out a template (team-building outline) for a class project.

1. Discuss and clarify if necessary.
2. Review: Each team will design a team-building challenge that another team will attempt to solve. Each team must set up and practice its challenge before presenting it. Everyone should get a copy of each team's completed challenge.

D. Have each team sit in a circle and start initial discussion about its project.

Class 16

A. In the classroom, lecture on and discuss canoeing.

1. Parts of a canoe.
2. Parts of a paddle.
3. Demonstrate and practice the proper paddle grip.
4. Explain and demonstrate the following canoe strokes:
   a. Bow stroke
   b. J-stroke
   c. Draw stroke
   d. Sweep stroke
   e. Rudder and bow-stern

B. Practice all strokes in the classroom.

C. Teams meet for further discussion and planning of team-building project.

D. Announce class meeting at pool or pond for next time.

Class 17

A. Practice canoe skills in the water.

1. Equipment needed:
   a. Canoes
   b. Paddles
   c. Life jackets
   d. Pool, pond, lake, or river

A paddle for each person, a life jacket for each person, and a canoe for every two people.

B. Practice the following skills:

1. Embarking and debarking

2. Exchanging positions in a canoe

3. Strokes learned in last class period

Today: Review Bow stroke and J-stroke

C. Discussion questions:

1. What specific skills did you do today that required cooperation?

2. Did you and your partner communicate effectively?

3. What cooperative decisions did you have to make while paddling the canoe?

D. Meet at the same location next class period.

Class 18

A. Embark and paddle to the center of the pond, reviewing the bow stroke and J-stroke.

B. Make a pivot turn using the sweep and reverse sweep strokes.

C. Exchange positions.

D. Paddle to a new location and repeat. Students have to work together and make cooperative decisions to do the activity. They must decide how to do the pivot turn and where to turn on the pond to repeat the sequence. Have students try to do this sequence of skills within a certain time limit.

Class 19

A. Review and practice:

- Bow stroke
- J-stroke
- Sweep strokes (pivot turn)

B. Introduce the two-person canoe lift and portage.

C. Introduce the one-person canoe lift and portage.

D. Decisions and cooperation needed today:

1. Working together to lift and carry

2. Becoming more proficient in propelling the canoe by working together more efficiently

Class 20

A. Review portage techniques.

B. Review and practice canoe strokes.

Class 21

A. Class discussion

1. What do we have to do to have a successful canoe field trip?

2. What food does each team want?

3. Who will buy the food for the team?

4. Who will do the cooking? Who will clean up?

5. What is the plan for setting up camp?

6. Who carries what equipment in canoes?

7. How do we handle camp cleanup?

B. Allow each team to discuss and plan. After discussion, allow teams to work on their team-building projects.

C. In preparation for the canoe field trip the next class period, teams must buy food, pack clothes, and be ready to go.

Class 22

A. Canoe trip

Class 23

A. Evaluation of canoe trip

1. Debriefing questions and decision-making opportunities

Class 24

A. Students use the entire class period to plan their team-building projects.

Class 25

A. Teams must organize equipment, set up their challenges, and practice their projects.

Class 26

A. Team A presents its team-building project. Allow time to set up. Team B attempts the challenge. Other teams observe and take notes.

B. Discussion in class after completing the challenge.

1. How can we change or adapt the challenge to make it better or different?

2. Did the challenge offer participants an opportunity for physical assistance? Be specific.

3. What decisions did the team have to make? Explain.

4. Did the team assign each member a role or task to accomplish the challenge more easily?

5. Did the team complete the challenge the way the originators envisioned it would? Originators explain.

6. Fill out the team report card.

Class 27

A. Team B presents its team-building project. Allow enough time for setup. Other students in class observe the setup so that they will better understand the challenge.

Team C attempts the challenge. Teams A and D observe and take notes.

Put equipment away and report to the classroom.

B. Class discussion.

1. Did the challenge create opportunities for discussion, communication, and planning?

2. Did the challenge offer opportunities for physical support?

3. Give some suggestions for adaptations or additions.

4. In attempting to solve the challenge, did the group assign roles to team members?

5. Did the team attempting the challenge communicate well?

6. Other discussion questions.

Class 28

A. Team C presents its challenge. The other teams observe the setup.

B. Team D attempts the challenge. Teams A and B observe the challenge and take notes.

C. Break down and put equipment away. Report to the classroom for discussion.

Class 29

A. Team D presents its challenge. The other teams observe the setup.

B. Team A attempts the challenge. Teams B and C observe and take notes.

C. Break down and put equipment away. Report to the classroom for debriefing.

Class 30

A. Discuss competition. Set up a competitive volleyball tournament.

1. Trophies will be awarded.

2. Teams will have time to practice.

3. Each team elects a captain.

B. The purpose of the volleyball tournament is to see whether team-building lessons carry over into a competitive game situation. Will you see some carryover in the following areas?

1. Caring and support for teammates

2. Praise and encouragement

3. Effective communication

4. Ability to step out of the comfort zone and compete

   • Go after balls—not stand around

   • Seek success with enthusiasm and communicate that enthusiasm

   • Never give up

C. Allow teams to practice volleyball skills. Use no net. Teams should prepare and organize their own volleyball practices.

Class 31

A. Put three nets up in the gym. Teams must organize and practice volleyball skills.

B. Teams should be ready to play the first round in the next class period.

Class 32

A. Teams set up two nets and start the tournament. The duty of captain should rotate with every game. The captain must make the rotation decisions.

1 versus 2
3 versus 4

Play two out of three or 40 minutes.

Class 33

A. Teams set up nets and continue the tournament. Rotation is the responsibility of the captain.

1 versus 4
2 versus 3

Class 34

A. Teams set up nets and continue the tournament. Rotation is the responsibility of the captain.

1 versus 3
4 versus 2

Class 35

A. Debriefing

    1. How did the aspect of competition affect your ability in the following areas?

        a. Cooperation with teammates.

        b. Did having a captain help or hinder team decisions? Did all captains use the same leadership techniques?

        c. You used a lot of praise and encouragement during team building earlier in the year. Did you find that it carried over into a competitive situation?

        d. How did you decide who played what position? Were all team members happy with the role that the team gave them? If not, what did you do about it?

        e. How badly did you want to win the trophy? Did your competitive feelings cause any stress on the team? If so, how did the team handle that stress?

        f. Without referees, how did you handle disputed calls?

        g. What happened after the game? If you lost, did you congratulate the other team or were you angry?

        h. Did you feel that your team was stronger because of the team building that we did before the tournament? If so, how?

Class 36

A. Hand in portfolios.

B. Have teams talk to the class about their community-building projects.

    1. Whom did it benefit?

    2. What roles did each of you play?

Icebreakers and Communication Activities

cebreakers and communication activities are similar because both activities require students to communicate. These fun and easy activities start students on their way to becoming more relaxed with their new teammates. We usually do three or four icebreakers before we feel that a team is ready to move on to introductory challenges. No set formula tells us how many to do. The teacher must decide when the team is ready to move on. The Great Communicator, Agadoo, Memory Game, and Where Do I Go help participants feel more like a team and reduce the stress that they may feel about talking to their teammates. We do these activities before doing any challenges. Never debrief or prebrief these activities; they are just for fun. These activities have no safety issues, group size restrictions, or age restrictions. Participants of all ages enjoy them.

Agadoo

▷ Description

We use this dance and communication game (see figure 6.1) to break the ice before team building.

▷ Success Criteria

To meet and greet everyone in class.

▷ Equipment

The Agadoo song and dance directions (Children's Party Album, Pop All-Stars).

▷ Setup

Class members can stand anywhere they choose on half of a basketball court. When the music and singing start, the class must perform the dance. When the dance stops and the chorus starts, class members must high-five and say the name of as many classmates as they can before the dance starts again.

When the chorus starts for the second time, participants must double high-five and greet as many classmates as they can before the dance starts again. The instructor can choose different greetings each time the chorus starts.

▷ Rules and Sacrifices

1. Each classmate must attempt to meet and greet as many people in class as possible.
2. Classmates must listen to the music while greeting so that they are ready for the Agadoo dance.

▷ Possible Solutions

For this dance activity, there are no possible solutions that apply.

▷ Conclusion of the Task

When the music is over, the challenge can conclude.

1. Agadoo-do-do
jab index fingers
forward 3 times

2. Push pineapple
pushing movement
forward with hands

3. Shake tree
clasp hands together swing
over left shoulder and right

4. Agadoo-do-do
jab index fingers
forward 3 times

5. Push pineapple
pushing movement
forward with hands

6. Grind coffee
make circles with hands
over each other
roly-poly movement

7. To the left
point left arm in
the air

8. To the right
point right arm in
the air

9. Jump up
both hands in the air

10. And down
bring arms down
to knees

11. Cross over
hands at knees

12. Then bring
hands back

During chorus high-five as many people as you can before verse starts, and when verse starts repeat dance.

Figure 6.1   Doing the Agadoo-do dance.

▷ Additions and Variations

- Use the entire gym. Make the space larger or smaller.
- While greeting classmates, students should learn the names and hometowns of as many people as they can. How many can they remember?

▷ Safety Considerations

If you want the students to run and high–five their greetings, caution them about running into classmates.

Memory Game

▷ Description

This is an enjoyable icebreaker activity to do before team building.

▷ Success Criteria

Students try to meet and greet as many people as they can. Participants greet each person differently, but they must greet each one the same way they did previously.

▷ Equipment

Any type of music the instructor desires.

▷ Setup

The group should be scattered and standing around half of the gym floor. When the music starts, the class should start jogging within the boundaries that the instructor has set. When the instructor stops the music, everyone must find a high-five partner. Students give their high-five partners a high-five and introduce themselves. When the music starts again (the instructor should wait for 5 to 10 seconds), the class resumes jogging. When the instructor pauses the music again, classmates must find a new person to double high-five and then find and single high-five their original single high-five buddy. When the music resumes (after 10 to 15 seconds), the class resumes jogging. The third time the instructor pauses the music, classmates must find a new elbow-to-elbow partner, find and double high-five their double high-five partner, and find and single high-five

their single high-five partner. This sequence can go on and on; each time it will be harder to remember the sequence of greetings.

Possible greetings: Back to back, pinky to pinky, toes to toes, knees to knees, or try exercise partners.

▷ Rules and Sacrifices

There are no rules and schedules for this ice breaker, but you may want to remind the class of the boundaries for this game.

▷ Possible Solutions

The students greet all their greeting buddies in order before the music ends. They must make an effort to remember the order.

▷ Conclusion of the Task

When the students have successfully greeted all their partners in order by music's end.

▷ Additions and Variations

- Classmates must change the way they move every time the music starts playing.
- Shorten or lengthen the amount of time for the sequence of greetings.

▷ Safety Considerations

This game, like Agadoo, is a very safe and fun activity. However, you may want to caution them to be aware of any others in the space.

Group Construction

▷ Description

This activity can be quite difficult for younger students so be sure to read the Additions and Variations section to make modifications.

▷ Success Criteria

To have every team member build the same design with 10 toothpicks.

▷ Equipment

Ten toothpicks for each team member.

▷ Setup

Team members sit in a semicircle with their backs to the center of the circle. They should not be able to see other group members' toothpicks as they build their designs on the floor.

One team member designated as the construction manager sits with his or her back to the rest of the team on the opposite side of the semicircle. The construction manager places his or her toothpicks on the floor one at a time and attempts to build a design of some kind. After placing each toothpick on the floor, the construction manager orally guides the rest of the team to place their toothpicks in the same position. The construction manager tries to get all the builders to construct the same design that he or she is building.

▷ Rules and Sacrifices

1. The construction manager is the only one who can speak.
2. The construction manager must give directions one toothpick at a time.
3. No one may look at the construction manager's design or at any other builder's design before completion.

4. The construction manager may not look at the builders' designs before completion.

After the construction manager gives the direction for the last toothpick, the builders and the construction manager look at each other's designs. How many designs exactly matched the construction manager's design?

▷ Possible Solutions

The builders must concentrate on the construction manager's explanation. The construction manager should speak slowly and give as specific directions as possible.

▷ Conclusion of the Task

All builders will have a completed toothpick design that matches the construction manager's design as closely as possible.

▷ Additions and Variations

- Allow the builders to speak and ask questions of the construction manager.
- Let one student observe and give feedback to the builders based on his or her vision of the design.
- Let the builders work together as one team with 10 toothpicks.
- Add toothpicks.

After one person has had a chance to be the construction manager, allow another student to attempt the challenge.

▷ Safety Considerations

This game presents no safety challenges.

Moving Team Juggle

▷ Description

This activity is a variation of the cooperative team juggle activity from *The Cooperative Sports and Games Book* by Terry Orlick (1978). The adaptation we have made makes this activity much more difficult and interesting.

▷ Success Criteria

To pass the three balls from team member to team member in an exact order while moving around the gym and not allowing a ball to touch the floor.

▷ Equipment

Three foam balls—either footballs or soccer balls.

▷ Setup

The group stands in a circle. One of the team members holds the three foam balls. When everyone is ready, the person starts tossing the three balls, one at a time, to a team member across the circle. Teammates continue to pass the balls around the circle until everyone has had a chance to catch all three balls. The last person to catch should be the person who started the rotation. Each team member must remember to whom he or she tossed the balls and that person's name.

▷ Rules and Sacrifices

1. If a ball hits the ground, the group must start the process over.
2. When the group was standing in a circle tossing and catching, the primary purpose was to learn the rotation. Before starting the balls around a second time, group members must be moving.

3. The team may not move as a unit. Team members must jog in different directions around the gym while attempting to pass and catch in the same rotation as they did in the circle.

▷ Possible Solutions

Students must be very alert as balls will come at them one right after another. Also, students must remember who threw to them and whom they throw to.

▷ Conclusion of the Task

When all three balls have been successfully passed in the correct rotation the task is complete.

▷ Additions and Variations

- Use fewer balls.
- Allow the team to move as a unit.
- At the instructor's signal, team members must change the way they move.

When several teams attempt this challenge at once, the activity becomes quite difficult.

▷ Safety Considerations

The students are not only moving among their classmates in the gym, they are also throwing and catching. Caution them to be aware of others and avoid contact.

Adapted from Terry Orlick 1978

Untying Knots

▷ Description

This is an old activity with a new twist.

▷ Success Criteria

To create a knot or puzzle with the ropes and then untie the knot without letting go of the ropes.

▷ Equipment

Six to eight cloth ropes 8 to 10 feet (2.5 to 3 meters) long

▷ Setup

The team stands in a circle about the width of the basketball center circle. Team members must connect with another person in the circle with a rope. They may not connect with a person next to them. One group member (A) holds one end of a rope in his or her right hand and connects with the right hand of a group member across the circle. Then person A connects his or her left hand with the rope to the left hand of a different group member. This process continues until all group members are connected to one other person's right hand and a different person's left hand. The group may need several attempts to link up properly, but this could be part of the puzzle. See the photo on this page.

▷ Rules and Sacrifices

1. Group members may not let go of their ropes or change hands with the ropes.

2. Group members must communicate and move their bodies and ropes to untie the knot and create a connected circle like the one shown in figure 6.2.

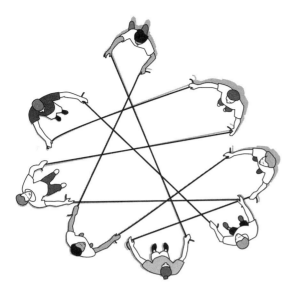

Figure 6.2 Group members that are standing directly next to one another should not be holding the same rope. The right hand of one group member's rope should lead to the right hand of the group member holding the opposite end of the same rope. The same is true for left hands.

Some group members may be facing outward. That configuration is acceptable as long as the rope and bodies form a circle.

▷ Possible Solutions

The students must cooperate and try and figure out who should move in order to untie the knot. Students may have to duck under or step over other ropes to form the finished circle.

▷ Conclusion of the Task

When the ropes and team members form a connected circle the task is completed.

▷ Additions and Variations

- Try different lengths of rope.
- The original way is to reach across the circle and connect hands.

▷ Safety Considerations

This game presents no safety considerations.

Adapted from T. Orlick

Where Do I Go?

▷ Description

This ice breaker is used in groups of two to six. Very specific directions must be given by each group member. We always challenge the participants to see if they can accomplish the challenge in four moves or less.

▷ Success Criteria

To communicate effectively and get a blindfolded team member to cover both objects with his or her feet.

▷ Equipment

Two small objects such as toothpicks, coins, or paper clips.

▷ Setup

The team sits in a circle about the size of the basketball center circle. One team member is blindfolded and stands in the center of the circle. (Caution: Make sure that the person does not move around without direction from the group.) Another group member places the two objects on the ground inside the circle, close enough to one another that the blindfolded person can simultaneously cover one object with each foot. On a signal, each group member can give one direction, such as, "Move your left foot forward 6 inches (15 centimeters)." Team members give directions until the blindfolded person covers the two objects with his or her feet.

▷ Rules and Sacrifices

1. Each group member can give only one direction.
2. The blindfolded person may not speak.
3. Only one group member may speak at a time.

▷ Possible Solutions

The team must give very clear, concise directions to the blindfolded person.

▷ Conclusion of the Task

The task is complete when the blindfolded person's feet are completely covering both objects.

▷ Additions and Variations

- Try this with a partner. Partners change roles after a successful attempt.
- Put down four objects and decide which objects should be covered by a hand and which objects should be covered by a foot.

▷ Safety Considerations

The obvious safety concern here is having one team member's eyes covered by a blindfold. Caution that person to move only when told to by another group member. The entire group must be aware of the insecurity of the blindfolded teammate and look out for his or her welfare.

The Great Communicator

▷ Description

The Great Communicator is an effective challenge for building teamwork. Although it is not a physical challenge like the others, it is helpful in developing listening skills. If group members do not listen to one another, how can they communicate ideas? Group members also need practice in speaking so that they can clearly explain to one another the ideas that they wish to put into action. You can use the Great Communicator with all your groups at one time. Space is not an issue here. This challenge can be done in a classroom or gymnasium.

We suggest that you try this challenge early in your team-building program. As your groups develop (or struggle to develop) you may wish to use this challenge from time to time as a test of communication success.

Group members sit either in a semicircle or in a random pattern in an area assigned only to that group. One member of the group is selected as the Great Communicator.

The Great Communicator attempts to describe a picture in terms that will allow the group members to draw the objects that he or she is describing. But the Great Communicator may not use certain terms that describe shapes, such as *circle, square, rectangle, triangle,* and *arc.* Group members cannot ask the Great Communicator questions or ask for further descriptions. We suggest that you give the task of Great Communicator to a different group member after each picture is completed.

▷ Success Criteria

Unlike our other challenges, this challenge has no defined criteria for success. After the Great Communicator has finished giving the description, each group member shows the rest of the group his or her completed picture. The group will be able to observe whether they as individuals or as an entire group understood the descriptions given.

▷ Equipment

- Each group member needs a pencil and one piece of paper for each drawing.
- You need to give each Great Communicator a picture to describe. See figure 6.3 for examples or make up your own.
- The Great Communicator should use a clipboard so that teammates cannot see through the page.

▷ Setup

The only setup is for group members to have the necessary equipment and for each group to have a working space of a 10-foot (3-meter) circle or square.

▷ Rules and Sacrifices

1. There are no sacrifices in this challenge.
2. The Great Communicator cannot use the designated terms *(square, circle, rectangle, triangle,* and *arc).*

▷ Possible Solutions

The solutions to this challenge will vary according to descriptive skills of the Great Communicator and the listening skills of the group members. The purpose of this challenge is to give group members

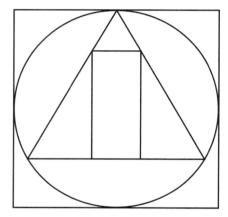

Describe this picture. You may not use the following words: circle, square, triangle, rectangle, arc.

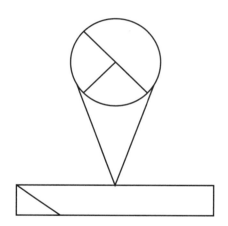

Describe this picture. You may not use the following words: circle, square, triangle, rectangle, arc.

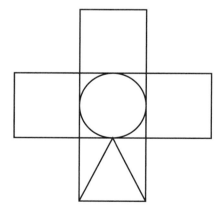

Describe this picture. You may not use the following words: circle, square, triangle, rectangle, arc.

Figure 6.3 Examples of pictures to describe during the Great Communicator challenge.

Reprinted, by permission, from D. Midura and D. Glover, 1995, *More team building challenges* (Champaign, IL: Human Kinetics), Appendix A.

an opportunity to practice communication skills. As they display their drawings and compare them to the Great Communicator's picture, they will get an indication of their success in listening and speaking. Ideally, as the group practices this challenge a few times, group members will see improvement in their communication efforts and skills.

▷ Conclusion of the Task

The task ends when the Great Communicator finishes describing the picture. The group members show their finished drawings to the Great Communicator and to each other.

▷ Additions and Variations

- Feel free to use the picture examples that we have provided.
- As you use this challenge, you or your students can supply your groups with additional or more creative examples to describe.

▷ Safety Considerations

This challenge includes no obvious safety considerations.

Adapted, by permission, from D. Midura and D. Glover, 1995, *More team building challenges* (Champaign, IL: Human Kinetics), 16.

Introductory Challenges

"**S**elf-esteem is most likely to be fostered when children have challenging opportunities to build self-confidence and esteem through effort, persistence and the gradual accrual of skills, knowledge and appropriate behavior. Learning to deal with setbacks and maintaining the persistence and optimism necessary for childhood's long and gradual road to mastery: These are the real foundations of lasting self-esteem."

From "All About Me," by Lillian Katz

In our present-day games and sports, the most aggressive or athletically inclined people dominate decisions and activity. In team building, everyone participates in the decisions, and everyone has to participate in the activity for the group to succeed. We have classified the following activities as introductory ones because they require less sophisticated problem-solving skills. They also tend to be less strenuous both physically and intellectually.

Construction Zone

▷ Description

Like the Great Communicator, Construction Zone is more of a communication challenge than it is a physical challenge. Group members attempt to assemble a large puzzle. One set of group members uses verbal clues and cues to assist construction workers, who will be wearing blindfolds. The challenge is for the sighted group members to communicate in a clear manner so that the construction workers can follow the directions and complete the puzzle.

You can have as many group members blindfolded as you wish. Of course, at least one group member must remain sighted. For our task discussion, let's assume that three or four group members are blindfolded. After blindfolding the designated group members, the sighted group members mix up the parts of the puzzle. Although you or your students could create many types of puzzles, we will assume that the puzzle will become a square when assembled. The sighted group members give verbal directions to the blindfolded members, guiding them to the puzzle pieces and then guiding them to place the pieces in the correct positions. The sighted group members are not allowed to touch the puzzle pieces or the blindfolded group members. We suggest that you clear the working area of obstructions or other physical structures.

▷ Success Criteria

Teams master this challenge by correctly assembling the puzzle.

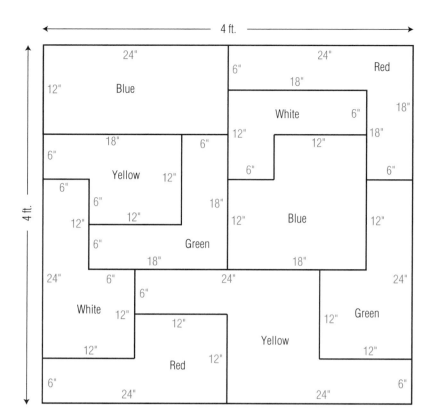

Figure 7.1 The Construction Zone puzzle pieces can be painted on one side to make the challenge easier for younger participants (not using blindfolds).

Adapted, by permission, from D. Midura and D. Glover, 1995, *More team building challenges* (Champaign, IL: Human Kinetics), 19.

▷ Equipment

You need one to four blindfolds and a construction puzzle (see figure 7.1). The puzzles could be made from quarter-inch (60-millimeter) plywood 4 feet (120 centimeters) square or even tag board.

▷ Setup

This challenge does not require a great deal of space. The task could be done in a classroom, hallway, or gymnasium space. A 10-by-10-foot (3-meter-by-3-meter) area with no obstructions is adequate.

▷ Rules and Sacrifices

1. Only blindfolded team members may touch the puzzle pieces. If sighted members touch puzzle pieces, the group must mix up the puzzle again and start from the beginning.

2. The sighted group members may not touch the blindfolded group members. The same sacrifice as in rule #1 applies.

3. No one may use put-downs or last names.

▷ Possible Solutions

The solution to the task is simply to assemble the puzzle. The level of difficulty depends on the verbal skills of the sighted group members and the manipulative skills of the blindfolded construction workers. Of course, you can increase the level of difficulty by providing puzzles that are more difficult.

▷ Conclusion of the Task

When the group has assembled the puzzle, the blindfolded group members remove their blindfolds.

▷ Additions and Variations

• You may wish to put a time limit on each construction group.

- You could tape an outline of the puzzle onto the floor to help the group in the construction process.
- To give all group members a turn as blindfolded construction workers, have the group rebuild the puzzle with new blindfolded members or provide the group with a new puzzle.

One additional note is that using large puzzles seems to be more motivating for both the people involved in the task and those observing the challenge.

▷ Safety Considerations

Blindfolded team members should not be allowed to wander from the working area or walk around unattended. In addition, blindfolded team members must be careful when handling and passing the puzzle pieces. If someone were to jerk or jab a puzzle piece carelessly toward a blindfolded teammate, he or she could be hit hard or could be hit by a sharp corner of a puzzle piece.

Reprinted, by permission, from D. Midura and D. Glover, 1995, *More team building challenges* (Champaign, IL: Human Kinetics), 18-19.

Geography Masters

 DVD

▷ Description

This challenge was created after buying a large rubber (poly) map of the United States from a sporting-goods catalog. The procedure for this challenge can be similar to that of Construction Zone or changed by either adding or omitting different forms of communication.

The team attempting this challenge starts with the 50-piece puzzle of the United States either in a box or with the puzzle pieces stacked in a large pile. For the purpose of this description, the challenge will be for the group to assemble the puzzle without using any form of oral communication. This is one of the few challenges in which having team members compete against a stopwatch might add value to the challenge.

▷ Success Criteria

The team masters the challenge when it has assembled the puzzle without using any form of oral communication (speaking, coughing, throat noises, and so on).

▷ Equipment

- A large United States puzzle is required. We recommend a puzzle like the USA Poly Puzzle sold by Gopher Sport. This puzzle includes the Great Lakes as well as the states. You may decide to supply the group with a picture map of the United States.

- One of the variations calls for blindfolds for at least half of the group.

- If timing the group becomes part of the challenge, a stopwatch is necessary.

▷ Setup

A space about 8 feet (2.5 meters) square should provide enough room for a group to perform the challenge. Place the puzzle pieces in a box or stack the pieces in a pile in the middle of the work space. After the group has read the challenge and organizer cards, they can turn over the box or simply start sifting through the stack of puzzle pieces.

▷ Rules and Sacrifices

1. No one may use any form of oral communication (speaking, throat noises, coughing, or any other sound coming from the mouth or throat).

2. If the group breaks rule #1, it must restack the puzzle pieces and start from the beginning.

▷ Possible Solutions

The solution is that the puzzle will be assembled to look like a map of the United States.

▷ Conclusion of the Task

Group members throw their hands in the air when they complete the puzzle. This signal should get the attention of the instructor, who then can stop the stopwatch.

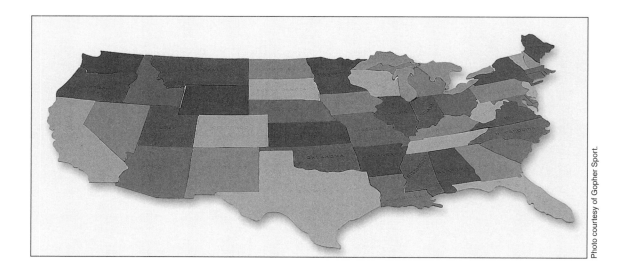

Photo courtesy of Gopher Sport.

▷ Additions and Variations

We have found that fourth grade students can handle this challenge using an outline map of the United States without the names of the states appearing on the map. You might consider providing younger children a map of the states with names. You might decide against using a map at all with older participants. Another possibility is to provide the map but keep the map 15 or 20 feet (4.5 to 6 meters) away from the group, thereby creating a situation in which group members must run to another place to get clues for putting the puzzle together. Additionally, you could create a relay-running adaptation in which group members must run to an area where the puzzle pieces are located, run back with a puzzle piece, give it to an installer, and then send another runner to get an additional piece. This task can also use rules similar to those of Construction Zone, in which half of the group is blindfolded. The sighted people may use oral communication, but they may not touch the puzzle pieces or their blindfolded teammates. Note that if you use an adaptation of this challenge, you should provide the necessary changes in the rules and sacrifices, the directions on the challenge card, and the questions on the organizer card.

▷ Safety Considerations

If groups do this task with all members sighted, it includes no obvious safety concerns. If some team members are blindfolded, they should not wander or walk around unattended by sighted teammates.

General Hospital, Emergency Room

▷ Description

This challenge is another group task that can serve as a regular team-building challenge or as a communication activity. The challenge was created after buying a 7-foot (2-meter), 21-one piece vinyl skeleton puzzle from a sporting-goods catalog. General Hospital, Emergency Room closely follows the Construction Zone challenge.

Half of the group members are blindfolded, and the other half remain sighted. Group members receive the skeleton puzzle, either in a container or stacked up in a single pile of puzzle pieces. They then construct the skeleton.

▷ Success Criteria

The task is to assemble the skeleton with the puzzle pieces connecting in the correct manner. The sighted group members cannot touch the blindfolded team members nor may they touch the puzzle pieces during construction of the skeleton.

▷ Equipment

- The group receives the skeleton puzzle either in a container or piled in a single stack of puzzle pieces.
- Blindfolds for at least half of the group are required.

- You may include a drawing of the skeleton, depending on the age of the group.
- A working area of approximately 8 feet (2.5 meters) square should be sufficient for this task.

▷ Setup

Place the puzzle pieces in the working area. Provide enough blindfolds and the skeleton diagram if necessary.

▷ Rules and Sacrifices

1. Sighted group members may not touch the puzzle pieces.
2. Sighted group members may not touch the blindfolded group members.
3. If group members break either rule, they must mix up the puzzle pieces and start the task from the beginning.

▷ Possible Solutions

The solution is that the puzzle will be assembled with all the pieces in the correct places.

▷ Conclusion of the Task

The sighted group members call the instructor to the working area to approve the skeleton construc-

Photo courtesy of Gopher Sport.

tion before the blindfolded group members may remove their blindfolds. The blindfolded members may then remove their blindfolds to view their wonderful creation.

▷ Additions and Variations

- Groups can do this challenge without blindfolds. For this variation we recommend that you prohibit oral communication.

- You can also add competition by timing the construction of the skeleton.

- You can add to the difficulty by placing the skeleton drawing a distance away from the group so that group members have to run a short distance to consult with the picture of the skeleton.

▷ Safety Considerations

As in the two previous challenges, safety concerns are absent if all group members participate as sighted teammates. If some team members are blindfolded, they should not be allowed to wander or walk around unattended by sighted teammates.

Atom Transfer

▷ Description

In this challenge, group members attempt to transfer a ball resting on one post to another post using ropes that are attached to a metal ring. Team members may only hold onto the handles attached to the ropes. The other ends of the ropes are attached to the metal ring. Gopher Sport created this challenge. Sporting-goods companies that market team-building activities sell the equipment as a set. Although you could probably make the equipment, it is reasonably priced. In its initial form, this challenge is good for young children (ages 5 to 8). For older participants, we recommend using some of the adaptations.

Group members must transfer the atom (ball) from post A to post B. They may manipulate the ball only by holding onto the rope handles. The ball may not touch the floor or any group member.

▷ Success Criteria

The group completes the challenge by successfully moving the ball from post A until it rests on post B, with the metal ring lowered to the floor and the ropes lying on the floor as well.

▷ Equipment

- The Atom Transfer set includes a metal ring with 8 to 10 ropes attached to the ring. Each rope also has a handle.
- A rubber ball about the size of a softball or baseball serves as the atom.
- Two stationary posts are needed. These posts, approximately 3 feet (90 centimeters) high, must be able to support the ball.
- If groups are to attempt adaptations to this challenge, you may need some extra equipment as described in Additions and Variations.

▷ Setup

You need a space approximately 20 feet (6 meters) long and 15 feet (4.5 meters) wide to accommodate this challenge. Set a post at each end of this rectangular space. The ring slips over post A and at its base. The ropes extend away from the post, and the ball rests on top of it.

Photo courtesy of Gopher Sport.

▷ Rules and Sacrifices

1. Group members may hold only the handles of the ropes.

2. The ball cannot touch the floor.

3. The ball may not touch a group member.

4. No one may call others by their last names or use put-downs.

5. If the group breaks a rule, it must place the ball back on post A after slipping the ring back over the post and placing it on the floor.

▷ Possible Solutions

The ball will be carried to the second stand. All group members should be holding at least one rope handle. The ball will be placed on the stand so the ring slips over the stand.

▷ Conclusion of the Task

After placing the ball on post B, the team must lower the ring and ropes to the floor without dislodging the ball from the post. The team is done when all the rope handles are lying on the floor.

▷ Additions and Variations

• For students older than third grade, you might try having half of the group wear blindfolds.

• Another variation requires group members to weave their way through obstacles that they cannot touch.

▷ Safety Considerations

This challenge presents no apparent safety concerns. If blindfolds or obstacles are used, care must be taken so that teammates do not trip over obstacles on the floor.

Riverboat

▷ Description

Riverboat is an introductory challenge that requires a group to transport itself across a large open space. This task generally has one basic solution, but groups usually use the better part of a class period to complete the challenge.

Group members transfer themselves from one end of a basketball-court-sized area to the other end without touching the floor with their bodies.

The group uses two tumbling mats (folded) to create a riverboat. The group must move the mats so that they do not come unfolded. The group must also prevent the mats from crashing onto the floor and making a loud noise.

▷ Success Criteria

The group masters the Riverboat challenge when all members have successfully crossed the gym space (river) without touching the floor with their bodies. The group must take all assigned equipment to the opposite side of the river as well.

▷ Equipment

- Two standard-size tumbling mats
- Two small tires (preferably boat trailer tires)
- Two long jump ropes (or sash cord)

▷ Setup

You need a long open space the length of a standard basketball court. A wide hallway would also provide adequate work space.

▷ Rules and Sacrifices

1. If a group member touches the floor with any part of his or her body, the entire group must go back to the starting position.
2. The group must take all the equipment across the river.
3. The mats must remain folded. If the mats (the riverboat) fall apart, the entire group returns to the starting position.
4. If a mat crashes to the floor (explodes) and makes a loud noise, the group must start again.
5. No one may call teammates by their last names or use put-downs.

▷ Possible Solutions

Generally, the group places one mat on the floor and then passes the other mat to the front. Group members move to the front mat and then lift, pass, or slide the other mat to the front and transfer themselves to the new front mat in a leapfrog manner.

Often, they use the tires as tugboats to assist in the passing of the tumbling mats. As lifeboats, the tires also offer a less crowded situation on the riverboat. Groups usually tie the jump ropes to the tires to move them more efficiently.

▷ **Conclusion of the Task**

The group completes the challenge when it has successfully crossed the river with all the equipment.

▷ **Additions and Variations**

- You may wish to make this task more difficult by creating obstacles in the river or requiring the group to perform a portage.

- You might want to create a storm story whereby the group must reach certain points within time limits or risk taking on more baggage (such as additional equipment).

▷ **Safety Considerations**

Students should be aware that lifting a heavy tumbling mat awkwardly or incorrectly could result in back muscle pain. Sometimes students put their feet in the tires to hop while moving the equipment. In doing so, they could fall forward and injure themselves if they are not prepared to catch themselves.

Reprinted, by permission, from D. Midura and D. Glover, 1995, *More team building challenges* (Champaign, IL: Human Kinetics), 21.

Swamp Machine

▷ Description

The Swamp Machine challenge requires group members to transport themselves across a defined space using a tumbling mat. The mat must have its Velcro ends attached so that group members can get inside the unit to operate the machine as they would the tracks of a military tank. We will describe this task using a 6-foot-by-12-foot (180-centimeter-by-360-centimeter) UCS mat with 1-foot (30-centimeter) segments (see Additions and Variations for using other mats).

Group members begin on one side of the gym at a designated island or land space (two unfolded tumbling mats, side by side). Two, three, or four group members get into the swamp machine and maneuver it across the swamp to the other island or land space. Some of the group members then get out of the swamp machine. At least two group members must remain in the swamp machine as it travels back across the swamp to pick up more group members. Group members have to trade places often because two, three, or four members must always be in the machine as it travels back and forth across the swamp. No group member may take more than two consecutive trips across the swamp. The group continues the challenge until all members have successfully crossed the swamp to the second land space.

▷ Success Criteria

The group masters the Swamp Machine challenge when all group members are standing on the second land space with the swamp machine.

▷ Equipment

You need four standard tumbling mats to create two land spaces (two mats, side by side, for each land space). We recommend a 6-foot-by-12-foot (1.8-meter-by-3.6-meter) UCS tumbling mat with 1-foot (30-centimeter) segments (most standard mats are made in 2-foot [60-centimeter] segments) with Velcro ends to attach the ends together for the swamp machine.

▷ Setup

Place two standard tumbling mats, unfolded, side by side, to create a land space. Place the other two mats in a similar fashion 30 to 40 feet (9 to 12 meters) away to create a second land space (about half the length of a basketball court or the entire width of your court). Alternatively, any long, open space such as a hallway or cafeteria would be sufficient for this challenge. Place the swamp machine on the first land space with the Velcro ends attached.

▷ Rules and Sacrifices

1. If a group member touches the floor (swamp), that person and one successful person must go back to the first land space.

2. If the swamp machine falls apart, no sacrifice is required if the group members in the swamp machine repair it while it is in the swamp. If the group members in the swamp machine cannot repair it while it is in the swamp, the entire group must return to the first land space.

3. No group member may take more than two consecutive trips across the swamp. If a group member does so, that person and one person from the second land space must go back to the first land space.

4. Two, three, or four group members must always be in the swamp machine as it crosses the swamp. If one or more than four members occupy the swamp machine, the entire group must start the challenge from the beginning.

5. Group members may not use last names or put-downs.

▷ Possible Solutions

Generally, group members get inside the swamp machine and roll it forward to the other land space. One or two group members get out of the machine, stand on the second land space, and send the machine back to the starting area. The swamp machine may veer off to the side if group members try to go too fast or do not work together carefully. As the swamp machine goes back and forth, group members must make sure that the Velcro ends stay together. They should check the ends after each trip.

Group members need to determine some of their sequences mathematically so that they do not leave teammates stranded near the completion of the challenge. Group members may reach the second land space thinking that they have completed the task only to find that they need to get back into the machine to retrieve additional teammates.

▷ Conclusion of the Task

To conclude the task, all group members will be standing on the second land space with the swamp machine safely parked on shore.

▷ Additions and Variations

- You may wish to create a story sequence by saying, "A storm is approaching. You have 10 minutes to get your group to safety on the other shore."

- You may wish to challenge the group to get their teammates across the swamp in less than four moves.

- If you do not have a mat as we described (a 1-foot segmented mat such as those manufactured by UCS), you may wish to attach standard tumbling mats together. Make sure that the Velcro ends hold together well.

▷ Safety Considerations

If any group members are claustrophobic, suggest that they work near the outside edge in the swamp machine. They will have access to the outside air and will not feel quite as enclosed. Caution group members that their shirts might creep up on them when they are moving inside the machine. Suggest that they tuck their shirts into their pants so that no embarrassing moments occur.

When moving the swamp machine, participants may incur injury if they choose to do fast or uncontrolled forward rolls while inside it. While doing forward rolls, team members could fall into one another or could injure their heads or necks by rolling improperly. In addition, suggest that team members remove items from their pockets when participating in this challenge.

Reprinted, by permission, from D. Midura and D. Glover, 1995, *More team building challenges* (Champaign, IL: Human Kinetics), 24.

The Whole World in Their Hands

 DVD

▷ Description

This challenge offers several solutions. A group can solve this challenge quickly if teammates work well together (and have some good luck); the challenge can also be difficult to master. This task requires group members to move or use body parts in ways quite different from those that they use to solve other challenges. This is a good introductory challenge.

The group tries to transfer a large cage ball, 48 inches (120 centimeters) in diameter or larger, from one end of a gymnasium to the other, a distance of 45 to 60 feet (14 to 18 meters). The larger the ball, the more interesting the challenge. The cage ball starts out resting on an automobile tire. The goal is to move the ball to a second tire at the other end of the gym. The group has to move the ball without letting it touch the floor and without any group member touching it with the hands or arms. The group moves the ball from tire to tire four times. Each trip involves moving the ball in a new manner.

▷ Success Criteria

Group members master the challenge when they move the cage ball from tire #1, transfer it across the gymnasium space, and balance it on tire #2. The group then moves the ball back to tire #1 on the second trip. They make four trips altogether, with each trip or method of transfer differing from the others. The cage ball may not touch the floor.

▷ Equipment

- Two automobile tires
- One large cage ball, 48 inches (120 centimeters) in diameter or larger, or a large earth ball (commercially sold), inflated to its maximum size
- A long, open gymnasium space

▷ Setup

Choose an open working space. In addition, the large ball will be easier to control away from walls.

Group members start by standing around the cage ball. During the challenge, they may move to other positions.

▷ Rules and Sacrifices

1. The cage ball cannot touch the floor.
2. Group members cannot touch the cage ball with their hands or arms.
3. If the group breaks a rule, it must return the ball to tire #1 and begin the task again.
4. Group members may not use last names or put-downs.
5. The group must successfully move the ball four times.

Photo courtesy of Gopher Sport.

▷ Possible Solutions

We've found multiple solutions to this challenge, and undoubtedly you and your students will find others. We offer four solutions.

1. Group members lift the cage ball off tire #1 with their feet and crab walk or slide across the gymnasium floor; they use feet, legs, and upper bodies to keep the ball from rolling over group members and onto the floor. When team members get the cage ball to tire #2, they lift the ball onto the tire, again using all body parts except hands and arms.

2. Group members lie in two lines similar to railroad tracks. Two group members roll the ball down the lines of bodies, using their bodies to keep the ball from rolling onto the floor. As the cage ball moves, the people on the floor change their positions to lengthen the lines. When the cage ball approaches tire #2, at least four group members should be in position to help get the ball onto the tire.

3. Group members also lie on the floor in this solution, but this time they lie side by side like railroad ties. Again, at least two group members guide the ball across the bodies of their teammates, and group members adjust their positions after the ball crosses them to extend the line.

4. Team members stand with their backs to the ball while one or two group members try to raise the ball high enough with their legs so that their teammates can press against the ball with their backs. The group then tries to walk the ball to tire #2. The teammates who raised the ball with their legs quickly join the group to help control the ball.

▷ Conclusion of the Task

The group achieves success when it rests the cage ball on tire #2.

▷ Additions and Variations

- Consider allowing younger students limited use of the hands or arms.
- To encourage students to think for themselves, you may want to require a group to find a solution different from another group's solution.
- Asking students to move the ball from the end back to the starting tire, using either the first solution or a different method, is a task that requires participation by everyone in the group.

▷ Safety Considerations

Do not allow students to jump on the ball because they could roll over the top of it and land precariously on the floor. We have seen participants attempt to lift the ball by using their teeth to hold the laces of the ball. No way! This method is neither wise nor safe. If a team loses control of the ball, team members may, to regain control, run into or chase the ball through the working area of another group. Discourage the occurrence of this type of event. Caution group members not to try to keep the ball up by heading it (as they might in soccer). The weight of the large ball could hurt the neck or cause a head injury.

Reprinted, by permission, from D. Glover and D. Midura, 1992, *Team building through physical challenges* (Champaign, IL: Human Kinetics), 39.

The Snake

 DVD

▷ Description

The Snake is a shape-building challenge in which groups use a tug-of-war rope as the material to create the desired shapes. After group members create a shape with the rope, they cover the rope with their bodies. This challenge is an easy one to solve, but groups will need time to create the number of shapes assigned.

Group members begin this challenge using either a large open space or a floor space covered by tumbling mats or carpeting. The tug-or-war rope is placed in the middle of the working space, coiled. The teacher gives the group a list of shapes, or the group may negotiate with the teacher to build other shapes. We suggest that the groups each make eight different shapes such as numbers, letters, names, words, or designs.

▷ Success Criteria

The group masters the challenge when it completes the number of shapes that the teacher has assigned. All group members must be part of each shape created. Group members must completely cover the tug-of-war rope each time they create a shape. Each shape will be considered completed when the teacher approves it.

▷ Equipment

The challenge requires one tug-of-war rope.

▷ Setup

All you need is a large open space, although you may wish to cover the floor with tumbling mats. Place the tug-of-war rope in the center of the working space. Curl the rope into a coil.

▷ Rules and Sacrifices

1. Make the shape using a tug-of-war rope.
2. All group members must lie on or cover the rope.
3. Group members must completely cover the tug-of-war rope.
4. The teacher must approve each shape before the group begins to form another.
5. Group members cannot use last names or put-downs.

This challenge includes no sacrifices, but you should require group members to form clearly identifiable shapes to gain approval.

▷ Possible Solutions

Group members find certain shapes, letters, or numbers easy to build. You may wish to include some easy, moderate, and difficult shapes in the assignment. Group members may find that the rope is longer than the combined lengths of their bodies. They may need some time to discern that they can double the rope over if necessary.

▷ Conclusion of the Task

The group solves the challenge when it forms the designated number of assigned shapes. The group should leave the rope in a neat coil at the center of the working area for the next group.

▷ Additions and Variations

- If you do not have a tug-of-war rope, you can substitute jump ropes tied together or clothesline rope 40 to 50 feet (12 to 15 meters) long. You could also use electrical cords 50 to 100 feet (15 to 30 meters) long. (Please don't plug them in!)

- If you use simple or familiar shapes, you may wish to add time limits to each task and award points for reaching certain goals, or you could have groups compete in a timed activity.

- You could combine groups and create extra large projects. Displaying pictures of a successful group making its shapes would motivate students.

▷ Safety Considerations

This challenge presents virtually no safety problems, but remind the group not to step on one another when finding their places.

Tire Bridge

▷ Description

Tire Bridge is another challenge in which a group moves from one end of a large space, such as a gymnasium, to the other. The group uses automobile tires to construct a moving bridge to cross a river. This task is time consuming but not difficult.

▷ Success Criteria

The group masters the task when all group members have crossed the river and stand together with the tires stacked vertically.

▷ Equipment

You'll need one tire per group member and one additional tire. Large tires are harder to move and therefore create work that is more physical. Small tires, such as boat trailer tires, are easier to move, but they may be harder to balance on. Clean the tires before use. Bias-ply tires, difficult to find these days, are less likely to have problems such as exposed belts or threads. Beginning and ending lines are also necessary (usually the boundary lines of a basketball court).

▷ Setup

Place the tires near the starting position. If you are using a basketball court or similar space, provide a clear path. The ending position should have enough space so that students can stand "on land" and stack the tires in a column there as well. This challenge does not present safety concerns if the group stays away from equipment and walls.

Because this task is not physically difficult, group members need to encourage one another to concentrate. Groups who do not concentrate may break rules #3 and #4, which follow.

▷ Rules and Sacrifices

1. The students must begin standing on land.
2. Only one person may be on a tire at a time.
3. If any group member touches the river (the floor) with any part of his or her body, the group must move the bridge back to the starting position.
4. If two people step on one tire at the same time, the group must move the bridge back to the start.
5. If any group member uses last names or put-downs, the group must start over.

▷ Possible Solutions

As they step on the tires and form a line with the tires, group members pass the last tire to the front of the line, and, one by one, they step forward. Some groups carefully place the tires on the floor ahead; daring groups may toss the tires forward. If group members do not coordinate their moves, someone may step on an occupied tire, requiring the group to start over.

A group may lose control of a tire. A student can place both feet inside the tire and jump toward the runaway tire, but it would be difficult and tiring for the entire group to travel across the river this way.

▷ Conclusion of the Task

The group achieves success when group members have crossed the river and have stacked the tires vertically. Group members cannot step into the

river. After you approve the group's accomplishment, have members carry the tires back to the starting position.

▷ Additions and Variations

Here are some ways to vary this task:
- Give the group more tires to pass. This variation requires a greater amount of physical labor.
- Place a time limit (such as 20 minutes) on completing the task.
- Create a zigzag path rather than a straight line.
- Provide islands for resting or regrouping.

▷ Safety Considerations

As with any challenge that uses tires, make certain that the tires have no exposed steel belts that can cause cuts, scratches, or puncture wounds. If you are using large tires, instruct participants to lift properly so that they do not strain their back muscles. Prepare participants to look out for one another so that they can help balance teammates if they should lose their balance. An injury could occur if someone falls awkwardly off a tire onto the floor.

Reprinted, by permission, from D. Glover and D. Midura, 1992, *Team building through physical challenges* (Champaign, IL: Human Kinetics), 43.

Toxic Waste Transfer DVD

▷ Description

The Toxic Waste Transfer challenge requires the group to transport an object across an open space without directly touching the object. The group manipulates a bucket filled with small objects using ropes attached to the bucket.

Group members form a circle around a 5-gallon (20-liter) bucket. The bucket has numerous ropes attached to it, and group members hold onto the end of the ropes. Working together, group members transport the bucket from one terminal to the other terminal by manipulating the ropes. By manipulating the ropes, the group transfers the contents of the first bucket into the second bucket. If a toxic waste spill occurs, the group must select a toxic waste expert (from the group) to dress into the protective clothing, put the spilled toxic material back into the first bucket, remove the clothing, and then continue the transfer process. Each time a new spill occurs, a new group member must dress into the protective clothing.

▷ Success Criteria

The group masters the challenge by successfully transferring all the contents of the first bucket into the second container without leaving any material on the floor.

▷ Equipment

- You need to make a toxic waste transferring bucket. Attach 10 to 12 ropes to a 5-gallon (20-liter) pail. The ropes should be at least 10 feet (3.05 meters) long. You can simply drill holes into the bucket, slip the rope through, and tie a tight knot in the end of the rope (see figure 7.2).
- You need a second bucket or box to act as the disposal container.
- You may wish to create a costume for the toxic waste expert. A snowmobile suit or coveralls, boots, hat or helmet, and oversized gloves make a good costume (optional).
- You may want to set out two distinctive boundaries for the two containers, such as two tumbling mats, hoops, or bicycle tires.
- You may also want a box or backpack in which the group can carry the protective clothing.
- Use colored tape to mark the area of the rope that students can handle. For example, mark the end of the rope with green tape. Place a piece of red tape 12 inches from the end. Students may hold the rope only between the tape lines.
- For the toxic waste material, fill the container (not to the very top) with packing peanuts, golf balls, or plastic golf balls.

▷ Setup

Place the container with ropes and toxic waste material on the floor approximately 40 to 50 feet (12 to 15 meters) from the second container. A distance of three-fourths of a gym space would be adequate.

Figure 7.2 Toxic waste transfer bucket.

Adapted, by permission, from D. Midura and D. Glover, 1995, *More team building challenges* (Champaign, IL: Human Kinetics), 36.

Set out the container of protective clothing for the group to carry as well.

▷ Rules and Sacrifices

1. If the toxic waste bucket touches the floor, the entire group must start the task from the beginning.
2. If a group member touches any toxic waste from the first container without wearing the protective clothing, the group must start the task again.
3. If a rope touches the floor, the group starts again.
4. If the toxic waste expert places the spilled contents into the wrong container, the group must go back to the starting spot.
5. The group cannot continue the process after a toxic spill until the expert has taken off all the protective clothing. The sacrifice is to start from the beginning.
6. No one may touch the rope between the red tape mark and the container.
7. Group members cannot use last names or put-downs.

▷ Possible Solutions

One basic solution meets this challenge, but groups will have to struggle to meet the success criteria. Group members carefully transport the contents of the toxic waste container by moving together and manipulating the ropes. As they transfer the contents of the first container into the second, they must work slowly and carefully. If a toxic waste spill occurs, the group must be careful not to let the first container touch the floor. One group member must quickly dress into the protective clothing (another group member may assist in this process), clean up the spill, and place the spilled material into the first container. The toxic waste expert must remove the protective clothing and join the group in its effort to complete the exchange.

If another spill occurs, a different group member must dress into the protective clothing.

▷ Conclusion of the Task

The group completes the task when it has transferred all the contents of the first container into the second container without leaving any of the material on the floor.

▷ Additions and Variations

You may allow groups to rest the first container on the floor in designated areas (such as inside hula hoops or bicycle tires) if the group needs to reorganize itself or wait for the toxic waste expert to clean up.

Allow younger children to hold the rope much closer to the bucket. For example, put colored tape 3 feet away from the bucket for second graders.

▷ Safety Considerations

This challenge presents one possible safety concern that we can see. Participants could fall if they walk backward and trip over an object lying on the floor. This challenge is extremely safe.

The Rock

Although it appears simple, the Rock challenge requires the group to balance for a specified amount of time on an object (the rock). The object that you use as the rock determines the difficulty of this challenge.

▷ Description

All group members must balance on the rock (or be off the floor) for a slow count of "one-and-two-and-three-and-four-and-five." Group members need to find a way to help each other maintain balance, which means that they may experience close encounters with one another.

▷ Success Criteria

The group masters the challenge when the entire group is on the rock (or off the floor) for a slow count of five. The instructor must see the task completed and count to five.

▷ Equipment

You'll need a rock—a 13-inch (33-centimeter) automobile tire or a heavy-duty box—and several tumbling mats to place under the rock. The size of the tire used in this challenge can make a significant difference in difficulty, so issue smaller tires for smaller-sized groups. A large group (such as 10 group members) may need a 14- or 15-inch (36- or 38-centimeter) tire.

▷ Setup

This task does not require much setup, but you should place the tumbling mat far enough away from walls or other objects so that should a student fall, chance of injury is lessened. The mat should be unfolded. We suggest three 5-foot-by-10-foot (150-centimeter-by-300-centimeter) mats. Place the rock in the center of the mats.

At first, most groups believe that this task is too easy. However, success does not always come quickly. Because this task requires students to hold on to one another closely, some students will debate whether death is more desirable than touching someone of the opposite sex. Others will love the close encounter.

▷ Rules and Sacrifices

1. All group members must be off the floor (tumbling mat) and on the rock.
2. All group members do not have to be touching the rock as long as they are off the floor.
3. Once a group member has been on the rock, touching the floor (or mat) for even an instant means that the group must start over with no one on the rock.
4. No one can use last names or put-downs.

Note that the mats are considered part of the floor space. If a group member gets off the floor or mat and then steps back down onto the floor or mat, a sacrifice occurs.

The group needs to practice until group members are confident that they will succeed when they call the instructor to witness the solution.

▷ Possible Solutions

Most groups fail at first. Group members step onto the rock, hold on to one another tightly, start counting to five, and fall off. After a few such failures, group members learn that they must plan to step onto the rock and hold on to others while maintaining balance. One method is for each group member to hold on to someone directly across from him or her on the rock. As more group members get onto the rock, balancing becomes more difficult. Some groups try to have everyone put one foot on the rock and then all add the second foot on the count of three. Some group members may try to stand in the middle of the rock and have others surround them. Alternatively, a group may try to have its members lie horizontally on the rock and on top of one another. Another group might try having some members sit on teammates' shoulders as they step onto the rock. Discourage this last solution because it is unsafe.

As groups practice, remind them that rule #3 is very specific. A student may start to fall, barely touch the mat, and pop back onto the rock. If anyone touches the mat even for an instant, all group members must get off the rock and start over.

As we said, some students, especially those in upper-elementary grades, may find touching one another difficult. Tell them that they cannot complete the task without physically helping one another. By reinforcing positive group behavior, you will help students find satisfaction when they work well together.

▷ Conclusion of the Task

When group members have practiced their solution and are confident that they can succeed, they should call the teacher to the working area. The teacher begins the slow count of five when all group members' feet are off the floor. Although the actual conclusion takes only five seconds, the cheering lasts far longer.

▷ Additions and Variations

- To vary this challenge, you may choose to lengthen the time limit.
- You may wish to use a smaller tire, such as an 11- to 12-inch (28- to 30-centimeter) boat trailer tire.

A 13-inch (33-centimeter) tire works well as a rock. A variation that adds difficulty is to consider the hole in the tire part of the floor. To compensate, let students place their feet inside the tire without touching the floor. To ease the challenge for a large group or a group having considerable difficulty, count the center of the tire as part of the rock.

▷ Safety Considerations

Choosing a good solution usually means that no one will be put into a risky situation. Group members sometimes fall as a group when trying to balance on the tire. This event usually occurs because the group is laughing and being silly. Caution group members that they could be hurt if they fall onto one another carelessly. Make certain that enough mats cover the working area. Occasionally a group has one group member lie on the tire and then builds a tower of teammates by stacking themselves one on top of another. Although there will be some laughter at first, the people on the bottom will eventually feel the pain of the group. At times like this, a teacher must step in and insist on better behavior. The teacher could do this privately or with a specific group if its members are not working safely.

Reprinted, by permission, from D. Glover and D. Midura, 1992, *Team building through physical challenges* (Champaign, IL: Human Kinetics), 28.

River Crossing

▷ Description

River Crossing is a physical challenge that requires a group to cross a designated space. In this task the group travels across a river that is half the length of a gymnasium or basketball court using two scooters, two deck tennis rings, and a long jump rope.

All group members must get from the clearly marked beginning shore or land area across the river to the opposite shore. They must use the designated equipment when crossing the river, and they cannot touch the river with any part of their bodies. All floor space between the shores is considered part of the river.

▷ Success Criteria

The group masters the task when all group members have crossed the river without touching it. All designated equipment must cross the river as well.

▷ Equipment

You'll need two sitting scooters, two deck tennis rings, and one long jump rope. A 14- to 16-foot (4.3- to 4.9-meter) sash cord jump rope works best. Starting and finishing lines are also necessary; they can be tape lines or the end boundary and midcourt lines of a basketball court. The space should be free from obstacles or structural hazards.

▷ Setup

The starting and finishing lines should be clearly marked, and the equipment should be lying at the starting line. Set one deck tennis ring on each scooter. Fold the jump rope and lay it across the two scooters. Although this challenge can be done in half a gymnasium space, a wide working area is helpful, such as half the width and half the length of a basketball court.

Team members travel across the river using the scooters. They can use the rope to pull a team member on a scooter. They can use the deck tennis rings to help propel the scooters or tie the rings to the rope to create a pulling device. Usually students try to give their teammates a push start on the scooters to get them partway across the river, but they must avoid pushing so hard that teammates fall forward.

▷ Rules and Sacrifices

1. The river is the entire area between the designated lines.
2. If any part of a person's body touches the river (floor), that person and another who has successfully crossed the river must be sacrificed and those two must start over.
3. The first person across the river cannot be sacrificed. The group can keep one person across the river for the remainder of the challenge.
4. If a person touches the river while trying to rescue equipment, a sacrifice is required.
5. Although the group cannot sacrifice the first teammate who successfully crosses the river, that person cannot touch the river. If that happens, the team must sacrifice a teammate who later crosses successfully in place of the first person.
6. No one may use last names or put-downs.

▷ Possible Solutions

A common solution to this challenge is for one person to go partway across the river on a scooter and then use one or two deck tennis rings to push the rest of the way across. The first person tries to push the scooter back across the river and rolls the deck tennis ring back to the waiting group. If the first person did not take the jump rope across, group members will throw the rope to the first teammate safely over the river. Those who successfully cross the river can then throw out the jump rope as a lifeline to pull other group members across.

▷ Conclusion of the Task

To solve the task, all group members and all designated equipment must be across the river at the ending line.

▷ Additions and Variations

- If the width of the river is greater than 35 or 40 feet (11 or 12 meters), you may wish to use two long ropes or one long rope and one short rope. If the width is less than 35 feet (11 meters), two long ropes make the task too easy. Make sure that the combined length of the ropes is shorter than the width of the river.

- To make the challenge more difficult, add obstacles in the river. These obstacles could create path diversions, or they could require sacrifices if touched.
- You could also require group members to carry an object such as a stuffed animal with them, or you could require the group to return safely across the river to the starting line.

A group may want to use the deck tennis rings as skates. If you do not want them to use the rings in this manner, specify that in the list of rules.

▷ Safety Considerations

As suggested before, whenever group members transfer scooters across a space, they must take care so that an errant scooter doesn't strike anyone. In addition, if a team decides to push someone on a scooter, team members must take care so that the person does not fall face first onto the floor.

When returning equipment to the starting area, group members must take care not to hit others with it. For example, a teammate should not throw an empty scooter across the river. The rope is intended to be used as a transferring device, not as a tightrope. When group members attempt to walk across the rope, they cannot help but touch the floor with their shoes.

Reprinted, by permission, from D. Glover and D. Midura, 1992, *Team building through physical challenges* (Champaign, IL: Human Kinetics), 25.

Lifeline

▷ Description

Lifeline has become one of our standards when presenting challenges. The basic solution to this challenge includes several variations. The task requires the group to travel about three-fourths the length of a basketball court using two scooters and a tug-of-war rope as the means to transport the group.

Group members begin at one side of the swamp with only one scooter. Another scooter rests on a tire halfway across the swamp. A tug-of-war rope lies just beyond the end line, on the other side of the swamp. The tire in the middle is an island; therefore, it is not movable. Group members must cross the swamp to retrieve the second scooter and the tug-of-war rope so that they will have enough equipment to get all group members across to the other side. Although this challenge has a basic solution, you will see groups use the equipment in different ways.

▷ Success Criteria

The group is successful when all group members have crossed from the starting line to the ending line, about three-fourths the length of a basketball court. Not all equipment has to be across the swamp with the team.

▷ Equipment

- Two 12-inch (30-centimeter) scooters, or two 16-inch (40-centimeter) scooters for older students, adults, or participants with special needs
- One automobile tire
- A tug-of-war rope 50 to 75 feet (15 to 23 meters) long that will reach across the swamp

▷ Setup

Set one scooter upside down (so that no one steps on it) just behind the starting line. Set an automobile tire halfway across the swamp. Set a second scooter upside down on the tire. Place the tug-of-war rope across the end line. Have the rope coiled so that the group does not have to spend a lot of time untangling it. Make sure that the rope stretches all the way across the swamp area.

▷ Rules and Sacrifices

1. No one may touch the floor with any part of his or her body or clothing.
2. No one may stand on a scooter.

3. If a person breaks a rule, that person and a successful teammate (or the teammate who has advanced the farthest) must go back to the starting line. They may not take a scooter back with them unless it was the first scooter that the group used.

4. No one may call others by their last names or use put-downs.

▷ Possible Solutions

A common solution to this task is to send one team member to the tire on one scooter. This person usually gets onto the island and sends the two scooters back to the team. Another team member then goes to the island and, with the help of the person on the island, goes across to the side with the tug-of-war rope. Usually these methods of travel include pushing the person on the scooter and that person doing some wiggling or air swimming to propel himself or herself forward. Once a team member reaches the tug-of-war rope, the easiest way to succeed is to string the rope across the swamp so that succeeding team members can pull themselves to the other side. Often the team member on the tire helps stabilize the rope for safe and fast travel. If groups use two scooters for each person, the process often goes faster. Rarely, however, do teams use the scooters in this fashion. Teams will more likely send one scooter for each person.

Elementary-aged students often use a solution in which they get the rope across to the tire and then pull each group member across to the ending side. This method tends to take longer, and the groups usually work extremely hard to transfer the rope back to the tire repeatedly.

▷ Conclusion of the Task

The group completes the task when the entire group has successfully crossed the swamp without touching the floor. If anyone touches the floor, he or she as well as a successful teammate must start the task from the beginning. If a mistake occurs before a group member has been successful, that person and the person advancing the farthest must be sacrificed. Group members need not have all the equipment with them, although they usually do.

▷ Additions and Variations

We have had to develop few variations to this task.

- One common variation is to use a 16-inch (40-centimeter) scooter rather than a 12-inch (30-centimeter) scooter for students with special needs.

- Another variation is to tape two scooters together for a student who could not fit on one scooter because of an ambulatory problem.

We recommend that you not allow participants to stand on scooters even if they are accomplished skateboarders.

▷ Safety Considerations

Team members need to take care if they choose to push a teammate on the scooter. Remind participants that they need to keep their fingers away from the wheels as well. When transferring the scooters from one side of the swamp to the island or to the starting area, students need to push the scooters carefully, not throw them carelessly across the working area. In addition, team members need to show care when trying to get the tug-of-war rope across an open area. A team member who throws the rope in an unsafe manner could hit a teammate with it.

The Wall I

▷ Description

Maybe it is just the nature of children to love climbing, but the Wall I challenge creates a lot of fun and excitement every time we use it. This challenge requires a group to climb over a wall of mats or crash pads. To accomplish this, group members must work together and develop positive team-building skills.

Choosing the correct height for the wall is important; it should be high enough to make the task challenging yet reasonable enough to keep the task safe. Getting tall or heavy group members over the wall challenges the whole group, and getting the last person over the wall is usually the most difficult aspect. If you create a wall of sufficient height, group members must help one another.

▷ Success Criteria

The group masters the task when all group members have crossed the wall.

▷ Equipment

You'll need a large folding crash pad standing on end, at least 5 by 10 feet (150 centimeters by 300 centimeters) and 12 inches (30 centimeters) thick when unfolded, and two tumbling mats (unfolded) to place under the wall. If no crash pad is available, use a stack of folded tumbling mats 5 to 6 feet (150 to 180 centimeters) tall. To keep the wall from falling over, tie jump ropes or strapping material around the mats or crash pads.

▷ Setup

A space 15 feet (4.5 meters) square away from walls and equipment is sufficient for this challenge. First, lay two unfolded mats on the floor side by side (not end to end). Stand the crash pad on end with the sides folded inward. Center the crash pad on the two mats. Tie jump ropes or strapping material around the crash pad so that it does not come apart. Mark a

dividing line on the floor, dividing the mats. Students cannot cross the line unless they go over the wall.

▷ Rules and Sacrifices

1. The wall (crash pad) may not fall over.
2. Students climbing may not grasp crash pad handles or ropes holding the crash pad together (group members who are not climbing may hold these objects to support the wall).
3. Students may not step over the line dividing the mats into two sections.
4. If the group violates rule #1, the entire group must start over.
5. If a group member violates either rule #2 or rule #3, the person making the error and one person already across the wall must start over.
6. If a group member uses last names or put-downs, the entire group must start over.

▷ Possible Solutions

Group members must help each other over the wall. Because getting the last person over the wall can present the most difficulty, the group may need to keep at least one person on top of the wall to help lift the last person. If top heavy with group members, the wall could fall over. Group members on the floor can support the wall and hold up those on top of the wall. This challenge is enjoyable, especially for elementary-age students. Make safety a top priority. You could eliminate jumping down from the wall. Group members should not pull on teammates' clothing when assisting them. Besides damaging clothing, some embarrassing moments could occur.

▷ Conclusion of the Task

The group completes the challenge when all group members have crossed the wall.

▷ Additions and Variations

- To make the task more difficult, require group members to remain on the mats when they are not touching the wall. This rule restricts movement and prevents group members from running and jumping up to the wall.
- To promote planning, prevent group members from climbing on top of the wall to help others more than once. This restriction requires group members to plan how to help teammates up to the wall, how to help them climb over, and how to support those on top of the wall.

▷ Safety Considerations

This challenge presents few safety problems, although you should make sure that the wall does not fall over because of careless or reckless behavior. Students should not jump off the wall or slide off the wall headfirst.

Group members must be committed to the safety of their teammates. They must not drop a teammate whom they are lifting. Make certain that your floor mats cover the entire working space. Care must be taken so that the wall does not fall or get knocked over. A teacher should be present to monitor and possibly spot this activity.

You may see people trying to boost others over the wall or see group members on their hands and knees allowing others to step on their backs. Some group members may try to jump up on the wall, which could knock the wall over. Monitor this type of attempt and consider eliminating it if it appears unsafe or unmanageable.

Reprinted, by permission, from D. Glover and D. Midura, 1992, *Team building through physical challenges* (Champaign, IL: Human Kinetics), 46.

Magic Bases

▷ Description

A physical educator in Missouri gave us this challenge. Although we have placed this task in the introductory challenge section, a few minor adjustments to the spacing of the equipment can make it much more difficult. One of the unique elements of this challenge is that group members must maintain a hand-holding arrangement throughout the entire challenge.

During this challenge, teammates must hold hands as they travel through a figure-eight pattern of 12-inch-diameter (30-centimeter-diameter) poly spots. Team members may step on the poly spots only after they enter the path. They may not touch the floor or speak to one another during the journey. Group members may touch the floor when they step off the exit base, but they may not release their hands from their teammates.

▷ Success Criteria

The group completes Magic Bases when all members have successfully passed through the figure-eight pattern of bases and exited from the last base.

▷ Equipment

You need at least one 12-inch (30-centimeter) poly spot for each group member. If you do not have this piece of equipment, you can use 12-inch (30-centimeter) square vinyl bases or make bases from carpet squares as long as you can secure them to the floor.

▷ Setup

Set up the bases in a figure-eight pattern, with one loop open. Designate one base as the starting base and select another as the exit base. Set the bases about a big step apart. The age of your participants will play a role in your choice of distance. The distance between bases should not exceed 2 feet (30 centimeters).

▷ Rules and Sacrifices

1. The team must travel the figure-eight pattern with members holding hands. Hands may not come apart.

2. Team members may not touch the floor between the entry base and the exit base.

3. No more than four feet may be on one poly spot at a time.

4. No one may call others by their last names or use put-downs.

5. If a rule is broken, the entire group must start the task from the beginning.

▷ Possible Solutions

The team must proceed slowly, and team members must help one another balance on the bases. A student who hops or jumps to a new base could pull a teammate with whom he or she is holding hands off balance. When team members meet at the crossroad or intersection of the figure eight, they have to communicate nonverbally about how they will pass by their teammates. Teammates may have to hold their arms low so that the lead person can step over them, or they may have to raise their arms so that others may cross beneath their connected arms. Team members have to take turns passing under or over their teammates at the intersection of the path.

▷ Conclusion of the Task

The group masters the challenge when all team members have successfully traveled the figure-eight pattern of bases without touching the floor or become disconnected.

▷ Additions and Variations

- Once a teammate steps on a base, he or she may speak. Group members may not speak until they reach the first base. This variation allows group members to offer suggestions during the challenge.

- Give the team a time limit or time the challenge so that the team can compare its time with that of other groups.

- No more than two feet may touch a base. This makes the challenge more difficult.

- Spacing the bases closer together or farther apart can significantly alter the difficulty of this challenge.

- Here is a tough but fun variation. After the first person in line reaches the fifth base, the team must figure out how to have that person become the last one off the path.

- Alternate the direction that each person faces as group members line up to hold hands.

▷ Safety Considerations

Put tape on the bottom of the poly spots or bases to prevent them from slipping. Caution group members to let go of a teammate's hand if they lose their balance and cannot regain it. Starting the challenge over is better than causing team members to fall on top of one another.

Reprinted, by permission, from D. Glover and L. Anderson, 2003, *Character education* (Champaign, IL: Human Kinetics), 128.

Geo Sphere

▷ Description

Tom Heck (www.teachmeteamwork.com) created and gave us this challenge. Geo sphere can be found in sporting-goods catalogs such as Gopher Sport. This challenge is unique in both the equipment used and in the fact that the challenge is more difficult for older and larger participants.

The team must set up the geo sphere so that it is balanced and stands upright in the container provided. The team then plans travel routes through the geo sphere that will not cause it to collapse. The instructor determines the level of difficulty for the group by establishing the path or by requiring the group to create a unique path for each participant. All group members must travel through the geo sphere. A person may touch the geo sphere, but group members may not hold the geo sphere or support it with their bodies.

▷ Success Criteria

The group masters the challenge when all team members have passed through the geo sphere without causing the equipment to collapse.

▷ Equipment

- One geo sphere
- One multipurpose bucket or container
- Possibly a picture or drawing of the geo sphere in the setup position

Photo courtesy of Gopher Sport.

▷ Setup

Place the collapsed geo sphere and holding container on the floor. Team members gather around the geo sphere and discuss how to set up the equipment. After completing the setup, team members must decide the order of travel and how they will get through the equipment.

▷ Rules and Sacrifices

1. Team members must travel through the geo sphere one at a time.
2. If the geo sphere falls down, the group starts over from the beginning.
3. Teammates may help one another verbally and physically.
4. No one may hold onto the geo sphere.
5. No one may jump or dive through the geo sphere.
6. Once a group member goes through a pathway, another group member cannot use that sequence again. Each path must be different.
7. No one may call others by their last names or use put-downs.

▷ Possible Solutions

The team should discuss its plans before beginning the challenge. Team members need to understand that they must create different routes. Generally, group members talk teammates through the openings and assist them by holding their hands or guiding their feet. Most attempts have group members working slowly and deliberately as they try to squeeze through the different openings.

▷ Additions and Variations

- Challenge the group to have its members hold hands as they travel through only one path. If a hand break occurs, the group must start again.
- Suspend a string with a ball or bell from the top of the geo sphere. This item is a barrier or additional obstacle to avoid.
- Have group members work in pairs. Sighted group members coach their blindfolded partners through the geo sphere.
- Require group members to pass a large object through the upper half of the geo sphere as they travel through the lower half.

Younger participants may find it easier to get through the geo sphere simply because they are smaller. You might consider allowing primary-aged students to follow the same path through the obstacle.

▷ Safety Considerations

We have not seen any safety problems with this challenge. But it is possible that a group member could trip and fall while attempting to travel through the geo sphere. Having group members spot or be in position to help team members as they enter and exit the geo sphere should reduce any possibility of a fall.

Reprinted, by permission, from D. Glover and L. Anderson, 2003, *Character education* (Champaign, IL: Human Kinetics), 135.

CHAPTER 8

Intermediate Challenges

Intermediate challenges are a little more difficult than introductory challenges. They usually involve the use of more equipment, and groups need more time and more teamwork to achieve success.

Island Escape
 DVD

▷ Description

Island Escape is a favorite challenge of many age groups. This task requires a group to transfer its members across a large open space using a series of islands. Each island has specific equipment that the group may use (options for equipment substitutions are listed below). Students must transfer from island to island without skipping islands. As part of the uniqueness of this challenge, the group must leave the designated equipment at each island when the last person leaves that island. In this environmentally sound challenge, groups may use the resources, but they are not to abuse them.

All group members must transfer across the gym, stopping at each of the designated islands. When the group completes the challenge, the equipment originally assigned to each island must remain there, except one scooter. That scooter may be with the group members as they stand on their side of the lake. Group members may not skip islands, nor may they send teammates so far ahead that islands between team members are empty.

▷ Success Criteria

The group masters the task when all group members have crossed the designated lake. They may have only one scooter with them. All other equipment must be on the islands (in the hula hoops, in or on the tires).

▷ Equipment

- Five hula hoops or tires for the islands
- Six scooters
- Five long jump ropes

- Five balloons or cones, preferably 18-inch (45-centimeter) cones
- A space approximately the length of a standard basketball court and 10 to 15 feet (3.0 to 4.5 meters) wide

▷ Setup

Place the hula hoops (or tires) in a zigzag fashion about 15 feet (4.5 meters) apart. Place one jump rope, one balloon (or cone), and one scooter in each hula hoop. Place one scooter at the beginning line (the edge of the lake). The hula hoops (islands) should be slightly farther apart then the length of the jump ropes. You can use one more or one fewer island if your working space dictates a change.

▷ Rules and Sacrifices

1. If a group member touches the floor, that person and the person who has advanced the farthest must return to the beginning.

2. If a sacrifice occurs after people are across the lake, the group may take one scooter back to the starting area.

3. The group may not skip an island. If a group member advances so far ahead that an island between that person and a teammate is unoccupied, the person ahead must go back one island before another group member attempts to advance.

4. Group members cannot move the hula hoops (or tires).

5. No group member may use last names or put-downs.

Photo courtesy of Gopher Sport.

▷ Possible Solutions

The common solution to this task has the group sending one team member to the first island. The first member uses the scooter provided. The team carefully pushes the first person to (or at least toward) the first hula hoop (or tire). That person sends the scooter back to the group members on shore. As the team sends a second person, the first person uses the jump rope on the island to help pull the second person to that island.

At this point, the group may begin to do two things at once. One person can begin going toward the second island, while a teammate sends a scooter back to the starting line. The group can send a third person toward the first island, while the first two people work on getting one of them to the second island. Group members do not have to advance in any specific order, but they must not skip islands or leave unoccupied islands between group members.

An advantage to using cones for this challenge, is that team members can use them to help balance themselves or use them as oars to help propel a scooter to the next island. We have had students put the cones between their feet and hop to the next island.

Groups can tie scooters together to make travel easier. Although the procession from one island to the next is somewhat slow, there is a significant amount of group interaction and group members must provide a great deal of help to one another.

▷ Conclusion of the Task

The group masters the challenge when all group members have traversed all the islands and have safely reached the opposite shore. They must leave one scooter, one balloon (or cone), and one jump rope at each island when they leave.

▷ Additions and Variations

Other than the aforementioned equipment variations, we have not found a need for many additions and variations. This challenge incorporates so much interaction that the only necessary variation has been for students with special physical needs. Usually, we have solved this situation by tying scooters together for those students.

- Possible additions would be to have groups carry objects across the lake (wounded group members) or to add additional obstacles in the lake, but we have not used these additions yet.
- You may decide to eliminate the use of hopping on the cones because this tactic allows group members to work independently without helping one another.

▷ Safety Considerations

Because participants use scooters in this challenge, you would be wise to go over the safety issues related their use. Remind students to be careful if they decide to push teammates using the scooters. Group members often get off the scooters, climb onto the tires, and then later get back on the scooters. Although participants are only a few inches (centimeters) off the ground, they can fall or slip getting on a scooter if they are not careful. Groups often pass scooters from island to island without anyone on them. Participants must not throw scooters or push them so hard that someone is hit or a scooter interferes with another group.

Reprinted, by permission, from D. Midura and D. Glover, 1995, *More team building challenges* (Champaign, IL: Human Kinetics), 32.

Plunger Ball

▷ Description

Plunger Ball is a unique challenge that requires a group to build a conveyor system to transfer basketballs from a designated area into a basketball hoop. In addition, the balls must drop through the hoop into another container. Group members must devise a plan to move the balls without touching them with their hands. They use certain pieces of equipment to manipulate the basketballs.

Group members must work together to form a conveyor using the five sets of tinikling poles. The basketballs must travel down the sets of poles toward the designated basketball hoop. In addition, as the group is transferring the basketballs, the balls must be over the heads of those holding the poles. As a ball comes across the last set of poles, some of the group members must help lift the ball onto the tall plunger. To accomplish this part of the challenge, group members use the small plungers to guide or lift the ball. They then need to lift the ball carefully up to the designated basket, drop it into the hoop, and then catch it in a large container resting on the floor. After group members get a ball into the receiving cart, they repeat the procedure with the next ball.

▷ Success Criteria

The group completes the task when its members have dropped all the basketballs through the hoop and into the large container.

▷ Equipment

- Five sets of poles 8 to 10 feet (250 to 300 centimeters) long
- Three basketballs
- Three deck tennis rings on which to place the basketballs
- Four small bathroom plungers
- One plunger mounted onto a 5- to 6-foot (150- to 180-centimeter) mop handle and a large container such as a custodial cart

▷ Setup

You need a space about three-fourths the size of a basketball court (see figure 8.1). Set the three basketballs onto the deck tennis rings. Place the rings on one free-throw line (three-quarters of the distance from the basket to which the group will travel). Set the poles in pairs lying end to end down the center of the basketball court. Set two small plungers at each end of the line of poles. Place the tall plunger near the designated hoop into which the basketballs must fall. Set the large container under the basket.

▷ Rules and Sacrifices

1. If a ball touches the floor, the group must start at the beginning.

2. If a ball touches any part of a group member's body, the ball must go back to the starting position. The one exception is that the ball

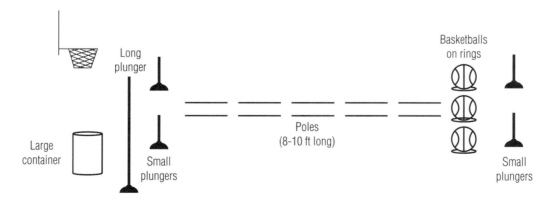

Figure 8.1   Plunger Ball setup

Adapted, by permission, from D. Midura and D. Glover, 1995, *More team building challenges* (Champaign, IL: Human Kinetics), 44.

may roll over the hands of those holding the poles.

3. A group member may hold onto only one plunger at a time. If a group member holds onto two or more plungers, the group must return the ball to the beginning position.

4. When the ball goes through the basketball hoop, it must fall into the large container. If it misses, the group must return the ball to the beginning position.

5. No one may use put-downs or last names.

▷ Possible Solutions

The most common solution is to have two group members, each holding a small plunger, lift a basketball onto the first set of poles. Two other group members hold the poles. Those holding the poles may be standing, kneeling, or lying on the floor. They try to roll the ball across the set of poles and transfer it to the next set of poles. The two group members with the plungers may help steady or guide the ball as it rolls along the poles. The ball makes its way across all five sets of poles. As the ball reaches the end of the line, one group member holds the tall plunger (a plunger head placed on a mop handle or broom handle, five to six feet [150 to 180 centimeters] long). Other group members may use the other available plungers to lift or guide the ball onto the tall plunger. The group then slowly lifts the ball toward the basketball hoop. As the ball drops through the hoop, it must land into the large designated receiving container (a large garbage can or custodial cart works well). One or more group members may try to manipulate the cart so that the basketball falls into it.

Groups may choose slightly different ways to hold the poles. Group members might work in pairs so that two people work with a set of two poles. These people may have to set their poles down and go to another set after they transfer the ball to the adjacent set of poles. Some groups may use a method of having some group members at the ends of two different sets of poles to create a railroad track effect.

Groups may stand, kneel, or lie on the floor as long as the ball moves above group members' heads from one set of poles to the next.

▷ Conclusion of the Task

The group completes the task when all the balls go through the basketball hoop and successfully land in the receiving cart or large container.

▷ Additions and Variations

- You may choose the number of balls that you have the groups use. We recommend three basketballs.
- The challenge is more difficult if group members are required to stand when transferring the balls from one set of poles to another.

- If you do not have tinikling poles, use plastic PVC plumbing pipe. Pipe that is 1.5 inches in diameter is fine. Use 8- to 10-foot (2.5- to 3-meter) lengths. You can find plungers at discount stores, outlet stores, hardware stores, or full-service lumber and remodeling businesses.

You may find additions or variations that meet your needs. Because this challenge is time consuming and requires a lot of group participation and interaction, other variations may not be necessary.

▷ Safety Considerations

Group members need to use caution when manipulating the poles. Someone can easily lose concentration or forget where teammates are positioned. If this happens, a person may drop the poles on a teammate. Rarely would the ball dropping on someone cause injury. Group members must handle the plungers carefully to avoid hitting teammates.

Reprinted, by permission, from D. Midura and D. Glover, 1995, *More team building challenges* (Champaign, IL: Human Kinetics), 43.

The Maze

 DVD

▷ Description

Two students in a team-building class for Saint Mary's University (Minnesota) presented us with the Maze. We consider this challenge one of the standards for any group participating in a team-building program. Although the Maze certainly fits into the communication section of activities, we include it among the intermediate challenges because you can change the level of difficulty and do it in a limited space with little equipment. The Maze can be done in a classroom setting as well.

The Maze could also be called the memory game. Most participants are familiar with memory game activities and usually feel comfortable or confident the first time they see this task. Group members need to discover a path through the maze by trial and error. During the challenge, the group receives a signal if a group member makes an error going through the maze. Correct moves are noted by no signal. The group must memorize correct moves so that each person going through the maze can respond to the correct pathway. We recommend using the 16-base maze before trying a maze with more bases.

▷ Success Criteria

The group completes the task when all members successfully go through the maze without stepping on the incorrect bases. Each person must eventually pass through the maze, not just one.

▷ Equipment

You create the basic maze by using 16 poly spots or vinyl bases (carpet squares will also work). If you choose to make a larger maze, you will need to add the corresponding bases to your equipment list.

▷ Setup

Set the bases or spots in four rows of four bases, spaced 12 to 24 inches (30 to 60 centimeters) apart. If you have options for color, we recommend that the starting base be one color and the other bases be a different color. If you are setting up a few different challenges at one time, you can place this challenge in a small space.

The instructor creates a maze ahead of time (see figure 8.2). The instructor can monitor the challenge or put one group member in charge of beeping his or her teammates off the path when an error occurs. We

Puzzle 1   Puzzle 2

Puzzle 3

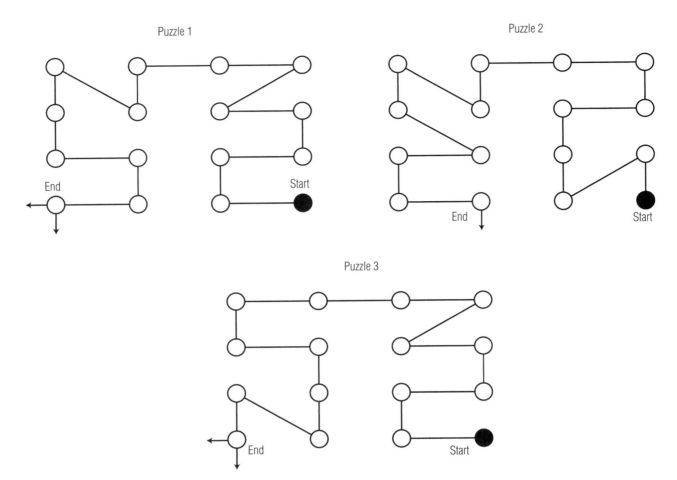

Figure 8.2   Teachers can make up their own mazes once these examples become familiar to students.

Adapted, by permission, from D. Glover and L. Anderson, 2003, *Character education (Champaign*, IL: Human Kinetics), 124.

recommend an oral "beep" or "buzz" to designate an incorrect move. We also suggest that the group be told where the entry spot is located. The group must then discover the path and the exit base.

▷ Rules and Sacrifices

1. If a group member steps on a wrong base, his or her turn ends and the next person begins.

2. Once a person steps off a base or spot, it is considered a move. A person may not step back to a previous base.

3. When attempting the second maze, no one may speak or use any type of oral communication. If this happens, the person moving through the maze must step out of the maze and let the next person begin.

4. No one may use last names or put-downs. If this happens, the person traveling through

the maze must step off the path and let the next person begin.

▷ Possible Solutions

The solutions follow the designated paths created ahead of time (refer to figure 8.2). Groups will need varying amounts of time to solve the problem. Groups discover solutions only through trial and error.

▷ Conclusion of the Task

A group completes the challenge when every group member successfully follows the correct path through the maze. As an example, if Audrey makes it through the maze, she is done. If Jordan follows and makes an error, he must wait until the other group members try to make it through the maze before he takes another turn. Once through, group members may help their teammates figure out the correct path. For the group to be successful, everyone must make it through the maze.

▷ Additions and Variations

We have had no need to make variations based on special needs. Variations can add difficulty.

- An example would be adding rows of bases. Instead of four rows of four, you could have five rows of five.

- Another variation is to reduce the forms of communication that team members can use. An example of would be disallowing any oral forms of communication, prohibiting any type of hand or foot signals, or not allowing group members to touch one another physically while moving through the maze.

- We recommend giving each group two different mazes to conquer. The second maze should have at least one variation or change. For example, students may not use verbal communication.

▷ Safety Considerations

Unless you choose a variation of this challenge that requires participants to be blindfolded, no perceived safety considerations apply to this challenge. If you use blindfolds, refer to the section in chapter 4 about how to use them.

Adapted, by permission, from D. Glover and L. Anderson, 2003, *Character education* (Champaign, IL: Human Kinetics), 123.

Stepping-Stones I

▷ Description

Stepping-Stones I can be a difficult challenge to master, but groups can solve it using many different solutions. The difficulty of the task lies in the reluctance of most students to touch someone physically. Verbal communication is exceptionally important in solving this challenge.

In this task, students stand in specific order, using bases placed in a straight line, and then reverse their order by moving from base to base.

Lay out a straight line of bases on the floor, 12 to 15 inches (30 to 38 centimeters) apart. The students begin on a base and then move from base to base until they are in reverse order from their starting positions. Use one more base than you have group members (for example, with eight students, use nine bases) so that students can shift positions. Group members need to help one another move and maintain their balance, which is vital to this task.

▷ Success Criteria

A group masters the challenge when its members are standing in reverse order from their starting position, as in the following example.

Starting position:

Sally –Luke –Tasha –Megan –Matt –Ericka –Ann –Seth

Ending position:

Seth –Ann –Ericka –Matt –Megan –Tasha –Luke –Sally

▷ Equipment

You'll need one base for each group member and one extra base. Have extra bases available to handle large groups. Flat, indoor bases are best. If you have no bases, tape 12- to 15-inch (30- to 38-centimeter) squares on the floor or use carpet squares cut to that size.

▷ Setup

Outline the bases with tape so that students know where the bases belong and so that the bases are more likely to remain stationary. This procedure also helps you set up the task for the next class or the next day.

You may want to have students take a number (1 through 8) to help them remember their positions at the end of the challenge.

▷ Rules and Sacrifices

This task has many rules, so the group needs extra time for reading.

1. Only one person may touch a base at a time.
2. When moving from base to base, a person may move in either direction to a neighboring base.
3. Group members may touch a new base only if it is empty.
4. Group members cannot move the bases except to make minor adjustments; no pen-

alty is necessary if the group member does not get off the base to adjust it.

5. Shoes are considered part of the person, which means that participants may not remove their shoes, put them on the floor, and use them as extra stepping-stones.

6. No one may touch the floor with any part of the body.

7. If a group member breaks any rule, the entire group must start the task again.

The rule prohibiting more than one group member from touching the same base at the same time does not mean that a group member cannot lift or hold a teammate off an occupied base or step on the feet of a teammate to move along.

▷ Possible Solutions

In the most common solution to this challenge, a person on one end works toward the other end by jumping or stepping over neighbors, who squat as low as possible. The student on the move, of course, needs an empty base on which to step. Look back at the example under Success Criteria for this challenge. The group needs to leave an empty base between Ann and Ericka so that a base is available for Seth. Ann gets as low as possible so that Seth can step or leap over her. Ericka prepares to help Seth keep his balance. (Another approach is for Ann and Seth to exchange positions.) After Seth goes by, Ann moves to the end base, where Seth began. Seth moves over next to Ann, and Ericka moves next to Seth, leaving an empty base between Ericka and Matt. Seth tries to get past Ericka to the next position, and Matt prepares to assist Seth. The group continues this procedure until Seth makes it to the opposite end of the line. Then it's Ann's turn. She moves down the line until she is next to Seth. Then it's Ericka's turn, then Matt's, then Megan's, and so on until the group has fully reversed its order.

Rather than jump or step over each other, teammates could step on their neighbor's shoes (without touching the base) and move to the next base. Group members could lift one another over to a new base. Leapfrogging over one another is another option.

Regardless of the method used, teammates need to help each other maintain their balance so that no one touches the floor or touches a base already occupied. The size of the bases allows little margin of error for maintaining balance. Group members who work well together will have nonmoving members reaching toward their teammates to support them physically.

A difficulty observed in this challenge is that when a group member makes an error, the group abandons its first plan and attempts a different solution. Another problem arises when a group attempts an improbable method (such as having group members crawl over the backs of squatting teammates) but does not quickly see the futility of its efforts.

▷ Conclusion of the Task

The group solves the task when its members are standing on the bases in reverse order of their starting positions (cheering joyfully, of course).

▷ Additions and Variations

The section on possible solutions covered some variations. Groups whose members do not work well together find this a difficult challenge, but groups whose members are willing to help each other can do this task quickly. Seeing teammates help each other is fun!

▷ Safety Considerations

Tape the bases to the floor so that they do not move or slide when group members move from base to base (see the earlier discussion in chapter 4 about bases). Tell participants that if a solution causes pain, it probably is not a good solution. We have listened to groups discuss the solution of having members crawl over the backs of teammates who place themselves in squatting positions. Occasionally group members will lose their balance and fall to the floor. Remind participants that they must always be prepared to help their teammates. We often see participants watch their teammates lose their balance and fall to the floor but forget to reach out to help them.

Reprinted, by permission, from D. Glover and D. Midura, 1992, *Team building through physical challenges* (Champaign, IL: Human Kinetics), 33.

Bridge Over the Raging River

▷ Description

Bridge Over the Raging River is a terrific challenge that requires all group members to be integral parts of the solution as they cross a river using four automobile tires, two 8-foot-long (2.5-meter-long) boards, and two ropes. This challenge is not intellectually difficult, but most groups find it physically difficult. This challenge is one of the first we ever did.

Group members travel from one end of a space (land) to the other end without touching the floor (river). The length of a basketball court works well. The group must carry all equipment to the other side.

▷ Success Criteria

The group masters the task when all group members cross the river without breaking the rules and with their equipment.

▷ Equipment

- Four automobile tires (large tires are harder to use).
- Two 8-foot (2.5-meter) two-by-fours (boards about 3.8 centimeters thick and 9.0 centimeters wide).
- Two jump ropes as shown in figure 8.3. Eight- to 14-foot (2.5- to 4.3-meter) lengths of sash cord work best.

▷ Setup

Label distinct starting and ending lines and use a straight-line open area (the length of a gymnasium) free from any objects or walls.

The group creates a series of movable bridges using the two-by-fours to close the gaps between tires. Groups often use one tire as an island to stand on as group members transfer equipment forward. They tie the jump ropes to a tire or two-by-four to pull the equipment forward.

Remind participants that they must move the two-by-fours safely. They must be careful not to hit teammates accidentally with a board or to step on one end of a board so that it flips up.

▷ Rules and Sacrifices

1. Group members may not touch the river (floor).
2. A group member may not step on a two-by-four if it has one end in the river (the two-by-four may sag into and touch the river without penalty).
3. If a group member breaks a rule, the group must take the bridge back to the starting position and start over.
4. No one can use last names or put-downs.

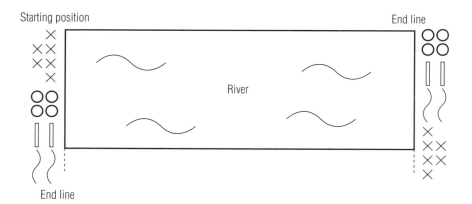

Figure 8.3   Starting and ending positions for Bridge Over the Raging River.

Reprinted, by permission, from D. Glover and D. Midura, 1992, *Team building through physical challenges* (Champaign, IL: Human Kinetics), Appendix.

▷ Possible Solutions

Most groups follow one basic pattern to solve this task. Groups make a movable bridge. As the group advances, it passes the tires and two-by-fours forward. Group members must share space on a tire.

Participants need good balance and must hold on to or physically assist teammates throughout the challenge. They have no choice but to help one another constantly! The group also needs to communicate how it intends to pass the equipment along. If someone tries to roll a tire to a teammate who is unaware of the plan, the tire may roll off course, causing an unwanted detour. Participants may attempt to move tires by getting their feet inside a tire and jumping along with it (hard to do but possible). Most groups attempting the challenge find it difficult to have several teammates balance on a tire at once. Multiple mistakes often occur, which generally means that the group must start the task over.

▷ Conclusion of the Task

The group is successful when it crosses the river (the length of the gymnasium or basketball court) with all assigned equipment in its possession. You may institute a time limit, basing success on criteria other than crossing the river. When group members complete the challenge, have them take the equipment back to the starting position for the next group to use.

▷ Additions and Variations

- Smaller tires, such as boat trailer tires of 11 to 12 inches (28 to 30 centimeters), create a crowded area and make it more difficult for several people to maintain good balance.
- You might place obstacles (cones, balance beams, parallel bars) in the river that the group must travel around, over, or under.
- Another variation is to have the group carry some object, such as a football blocking dummy, that represents an injured group member who must be rescued.

▷ Safety Considerations

Participants need to move the two-by-fours carefully. They must not drop them, leave them standing on end, throw them, jerk them, or otherwise handle them recklessly. We have already mentioned that participants must avoid stepping on one end of a board if the other end is not supported. If a board were to flip up, if could hit someone, an especially painful event if a teammate is straddling the board with his or her feet. Teammates should not grab onto one another and cause one or both to fall off the bridge in a careless manner. This challenge includes a lot of lifting and moving of tires. Participants need to lift properly and safely.

Reprinted, by permission, from D. Glover and D. Midura, 1992, *Team building through physical challenges* (Champaign, IL: Human Kinetics), 52.

Human Billboard, Skywriters

▷ Description

Human Billboard and Skywriters are essentially the same challenge. In Human Billboard, participants create a series of letters while climbing on a cargo net. In the Skywriters challenge, group members create a series of shapes. In describing this challenge, we will use Skywriters as the primary illustration. The appendix includes a challenge card and an organizer card for each challenge.

Skywriters is a challenge that uses a hanging cargo net. Groups attempt to build a series of shapes or patterns on the cargo net using all group members to form each figure. If you do not have a cargo net, you can modify a few directions so that the students can create the same patterns on the floor or on mats covering the floor. Accomplishing Skywriters on a cargo net is physically demanding. Performing Skywriters on the floor or on tumbling mats is more appropriate for young students.

Group members build a series of shapes or patterns. They begin by standing on the mats under the cargo net. All members must be on the cargo net to form the shape. After you approve each shape, all group members must get off the cargo net before they construct the next shape. By using paper and pencils, the group can prepare a plan whereby each person has a specific assignment as part of the designated shape. You can give the group a specific checklist of shapes from which to choose their skywriting, or you can have them create their own assignment. See figure 8.4 for sample checklist of Skywriters.

▷ Success Criteria

Using all members of the group, the team constructs a designated number of shapes from the checklist provided to them. The group masters the challenge when it has constructed all the shapes. We suggest that groups construct a minimum of six shapes. If you are using the cargo net, the group must create all shapes on the net. For Human Billboard, we recommend a checklist of 10 to 12 letters. Group members can then choose a predetermined number of letters to create (such as 6 or 8). The following is a sample checklist for Human Billboard:

Human Billboard checklist

Choose 6 of the following letters:

_____	A	_____	L
_____	E	_____	M
_____	F	_____	N
_____	H	_____	T
_____	I	_____	V
_____	K	_____	Y

▷ Equipment

- A cargo net
- Mats or crash pads under the net for safety
- A checklist of shapes to be built
- Paper and pencils for drawing and preparing plans

▷ Setup

As you prepare for this challenge, set out enough mats or crash pads under the cargo net to provide safety. Give a copy of the checklist to the group. Provide paper and pencils so that the group can make plans before climbing onto the cargo net.

▷ Rules and Sacrifices

1. All group members must be on the cargo net and off the floor when they construct the shape.
2. All group members must be on the same side of the cargo net (you may wish to modify this rule if your group is large and the cargo net is small).

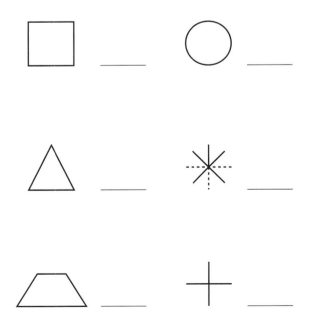

Figure 8.4 Skywriters checklist

3. All group members must get off the cargo net before they create the next shape.

4. This task has no sacrifices, but you must approve the construction of each shape before the group can start the next one. If you do not approve a shape, the group must work out whatever is necessary to correct the difficulty.

5. No one can use last names or put-downs.

▷ Possible Solutions

Groups usually follow a similar pattern to reach the solution to this challenge. Group members position themselves on the cargo net so that each of their bodies becomes a part of the shape that they are building. Some group members may have to assume a diagonal, horizontal, or vertical position. Groups may find it helpful to have one member remain on the floor until the shape is just about completed. This person can offer suggestions about the placement of teammates and whether they need to be straighter or more curved in a particular pattern. After the group completes a shape, it must get the attention of the teacher so that he or she can approve the shape.

All group members must then come off the cargo net, being careful not to step on one another when descending from their positions.

▷ Conclusion of the Task

The group completes the challenge by building the designated number of shapes. Group members should be sitting on the tumbling mats ready to give each other words of praise or encouragement.

▷ Additions and Variations

- The size of your cargo net or the number of group members may cause you to develop variations. If your cargo net does not accommodate a large number of students, you may wish to have group members on both sides of the net or have only a specific number of students construct each shape.

- Some schools have stall bars on the walls. Groups could possibly do the challenge on stall bars.

- As mentioned before, you can modify this challenge for younger children by having them construct shapes on the floor or on floor mats.

This challenge looks easy on paper, but groups will have to work to succeed on the cargo net. Do require groups to meet some quality standards. Straight lines should look straight, and curved lines should bend properly. Do not require students afraid of heights to climb high. Remind students who frequently climb high that they need to rest or stop if they become tired.

▷ Safety Considerations

Because of the nature of this challenge, group members run the risk of stepping on the hands of their teammates while climbing up and down the cargo net. To ensure safety, group members must offer constant communication and encouragement when moving or changing positions on the net.

Remind participants not to position themselves higher on the net than a level at which they feel safe. Encourage them to get on and off the cargo net in an orderly manner so that they do not step on one another's hands or heads. Do not allow participants to jump off the net from their positions on the net.

Adapted, by permission, from D. Midura and D. Glover, 1995, *More team building challenges* (Champaign, IL: Human Kinetics), 55.
Adapted, by permission, from D. Midura and D. Glover, 1992, *Team building through physical challenges* (Champaign, IL: Human Kinetics), 27.

Jumping Machine

▷ Description

Jumping Machine challenges a group to complete 10 consecutive jumps over a turning long rope.

The group selects two members to turn the long rope as they would a jump rope. Other group members try to jump the rope 10 consecutive times. The entire group (minus the turners) must jump the rope at the same time. The rope turners may change places with a jumper who needs to rest.

▷ Success Criteria

The group masters the challenge when all members complete 10 consecutive jumps without a miss or without stopping the rope between jumps.

▷ Equipment

You'll need one long rope and a space large enough to turn the rope safely as a jump rope. Because the rope is long, you may need the space of up to half a basketball court. If you do not have a long enough rope, tie two long jump ropes together. (Ropes made of sash cord are better than speed ropes.) If you have enough rope, you might try tying ropes parallel to one another to make a strand two or three ropes thick and 25 to 30 feet (7.5 to 9.0 meters) long.

▷ Setup

Many groups assume that this is an easy challenge, and for some it may be. But to be successful, the group needs a plan for entering the turning rope and may need to have several group members practice turning the long rope. The jumpers can't jump well if the rope turners don't turn the rope well. Because of the weight and length of the rope, it must travel through a high arc. To accomplish this, the rope turners will need to use their upper-body strength. The rope turners need not hold the long rope at the ends, so they should try different ways of turning the rope to find the best hand placement. The weight of the rope, rather than the length, is what adds difficulty to this challenge.

▷ Rules and Sacrifices

1. Only one group member may be at each end of the rope. All other group members are jumpers.

2. To be counted, the jumps must be consecutive.

3. The rope must pass over the jumpers' heads and below their feet.

4. If they miss, the jumpers begin the task again.
5. The turners do not have to hold the very end of the long rope.
6. Team members may call teammates by first names only and may not use put-downs.

▷ Possible Solutions

We generally find that a group will use either of two approaches to this challenge. One solution has the jumpers standing in a straight line, close together, 1 to 2 feet (30 to 60 centimeters) apart. On a signal, all jumpers start jumping at the same time. The second solution has the jumpers start jumping the rope one or two at a time. In the second solution the group does not start counting jumps until all team members have entered the turning rope.

If the rope turners get tired or have trouble doing their job, teammates could take their place. If new turners take over, they should have a chance to practice.

Rarely will a group be immediately successful with this challenge. Because of repeated failures, groups often try to circumvent the rules, often by slowing the speed of the turning rope so that group members can step over the rope in slow motion. The group must turn the rope at a challenging pace.

▷ Conclusion of the Task

The group masters the challenge by completing 10 consecutive jumps. Group members should count their successful jumps aloud so that they always know the status of their effort. When the group counts aloud, the teacher won't have to watch the group all the time because the nature of the counting usually causes students to be dependable and honest.

▷ Additions and Variations

Challenge the group to devise a plan to exit the turning rope successfully.

▷ Safety Considerations

Jumpers should not fall deliberately or act silly while jumping. We have gone away from using a tug-of war rope in this activity. Some tug-of-war ropes are extremely heavy and could hurt a jumper, especially if the rope hits the jumper in the head. A heavy rope could also knock the feet out from under a jumper, causing a fall.

Reprinted, by permission, from D. Glover and D. Midura, 1992, *Team building through physical challenges* (Champaign, IL: Human Kinetics), 58.

Human Pegs

▷ Description

Human Pegs is a challenge that resulted from a class assignment in one of our summer classes. Bill Butterman and Ryan Johnson helped create this challenge along with Dan Midura. This challenge is an adaptation of a children's game that uses golf tees or marbles that are placed on a wooden board. The object of the game is to jump the pegs, remove the jumped pegs from the game, and wind up with only one peg. In this adaptation, the pegs are group members who try to jump each other, one at a time, until only one person remains on the playing area.

Create a triangular play area with 10 bases, equally spaced from one another (see figure 8.5). Each group member stands on one base. If you do not have nine team members in the group, you can place a tall cone on a base in place of a person.

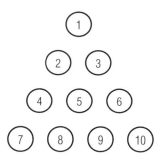

Figure 8.5   Human Pegs setup

▷ Success Criteria

The group achieves success when its members can jump teammates and eliminate them one by one until only one team member is left on the bases. The group may make multiple attempts to find the correct solution.

▷ Equipment

You can use 10 vinyl bases, poly spots, or carpet squares to create the game board. If a group does not have nine members, have enough tall cones available to serve as substitutes for real bodies. You need an area only about 8 feet (2.5 meters) square to accommodate this challenge.

▷ Setup

Set the bases an equal distance from one another, approximately 12 inches (30 centimeters) apart. The setup will form a triangle. Group members can choose where each person will stand, and they place cones on bases where needed. If a group leaves base #5, #1, #7, or #10 open, it will be unable to reach a solution. We suggest that you let group members struggle to find these things out for themselves.

▷ Rules and Sacrifices

1. Group members may not touch the floor before they are eliminated.

2. Team members may go over one another to a new base. They may not walk around one another.

3. Only one person may touch a base at a time.

4. Group members can make moves only by jumping over one base at a time. Teammates may not simply step from one base to an open base.

5. No one may use last names or put-downs.

6. If a group member breaks a rule, all group members get back on a base, but they must leave a new base open as the empty base.

▷ Possible Solutions

We have provided six different solutions. With 10 bases and team members occupying 9 of them, a group cannot do the task if it leaves base #5 open. A group will be unable to get down to one person left if it leaves base #1, #7, or #10 open to start the activity. Groups must leave base #2, #3, #4, #6, #8, or #9 as the open base (see Human Pegs Possible Solutions on the following page).

▷ Conclusion of the Task

The group should be able to complete the task within a few attempts. If the challenge seems too easy, have group members show you the solution after they have completed the challenge. Require them to prove their solution to you. Their turn ends when no member can make a jump. If they do not get down to one player, have them try again.

Human Pegs Possible Solutions

Open space #2	Open space #3	Open space #4	Open space #6	Open space #8	Open space #9
7 to 2	10 to 3	1 to 4	1 to 6	10 to 8	7 to 9
9 to 7	8 to 10	7 to 2	10 to 3	3 to 10	10 to 8
1 to 4	1 to 6	9 to 7	8 to 10	7 to 9	3 to 10
6 to 1	4 to 1	2 to 9	3 to 8	2 to 7	8 to 3
7 to 2	10 to 3	10 to 8	7 to 9	10 to 8	1 to 6
1 to 4	1 to 6	3 to 10	2 to 7	7 to 9	4 to 1
4 to 6	6 to 4	7 to 9	10 to 8	9 to 2	10 to 3
10 to 3	7 to 2	10 to 8	7 to 9	1 to 4	1 to 6
End on 3	End on 2	End on 8	End on 9	End on 4	End on 6

▷ Additions and Variations

- This task can be done by adding another row of 5 bases to make a pattern of 15 bases, meaning that people or cones must occupy 14 bases.

- To simplify the challenge, allow group members simply to walk around to another base as their move rather than jump a teammate.

- To make the challenge more difficult, space the bases farther apart.

- Additionally, you could eliminate oral communication during the challenge.

- You could also modify this activity for a team as small as one or two by just using cones and not having any people on bases.

▷ Safety Considerations

This challenge does not present obvious safety considerations. But if jumping over teammates becomes a requirement for this challenge, make certain that the bases or poly spots do not slide on the floor.

The Wall II

▷ Description

The Wall II is like a sequel to a good movie or theater performance. The Wall II incorporates the additions and variations of the Wall I (chapter 7) to create a more difficult challenge for older students. This task is only moderately difficult for students older than sixth grade. As with the Wall I, the Wall II allows students to climb, an activity that elicits lots of excitement and enjoyment.

The group must plan how to get everyone over the wall, especially large teammates and the last person. This wall should be higher and wider than the wall used in the Wall I, yet it needs to be constructed safely. Safety also requires complete cooperation from all teammates.

▷ Success Criteria

A group masters the challenge by crossing the wall. Group members must remain on mats during the challenge except when climbing the wall.

▷ Equipment

- Three large crash pads or a double stack of tumbling mats 6 to 7 feet (180 to 210 centimeters) high
- Two more tumbling mats (unfolded) to place under the crash pads
- A tape line that divides the working area into two equal spaces

▷ Setup

A space 15 feet (4.5 meters) square should be adequate for this challenge. First, place two unfolded tumbling mats on the floor side by side (not end to end). Then center the crash pads on the floor mats and stack the pads on top of each other. If crash pads are not available, stack folded tumbling mats in a double-wide, horizontal column. Stack the mats as stably as possible by alternating the direction of each layer. Secure the stack with strapping material

or jump ropes. Don't set up this challenge close to a wall or other structure.

▷ Rules and Sacrifices

Because the Wall II is not the same as the Wall I, make sure that group members study the rules, understand the differences, and follow them carefully.

1. Students may not grasp crash pad handles or strapping material that holds the wall together. (They should treat the face of the wall as if it were solid.)

2. Students may not step over the line that divides the working area.

3. After group members get down from the wall, they may not climb back up to help their teammates.

4. All group members must remain on the floor mats when not on the wall and must not touch the floor next to the mats.

5. If a group member breaks any rule, the person who made the mistake and one person who has crossed the wall must start over.

6. No one may use last names or put-downs.

▷ Possible Solutions

Students often jump and try to grasp the top of the wall by themselves. Instead, group members need to plan how to get each other to the top of the wall, one by one. Because group members must remain on the mats during this task, they cannot take a running start. Teams may use several methods to boost the first person up to reach the top of the wall, but without proper communication, the first person often continues over the wall to the floor below. Remember that in the Wall II, group members cannot climb back up to help their teammates after they get off the wall.

Monitor students as they help each other climb to the top of the wall. If too many are on top of the wall, it could become top-heavy and perhaps tilt or even tip over. You may want to stipulate how many group members can be on top of the wall at one time (a maximum of three is recommended).

The group also needs a plan to help one another get off the wall safely. Because getting the last person over the wall can be the most difficult task, someone needs to stay on top of the wall to help lift this person. Group members on top of the wall also need support from teammates. To reemphasize safety, consider adding a rule that requires all group members to have a teammate's help when getting down from the wall.

Remind group members that they should not pull on teammates' clothing while assisting them. Doing so could damage clothing and embarrass a group member.

▷ Conclusion of the Task

All group members will be off the wall and standing on the opposite side of the wall from where they started.

▷ Additions and Variations

You could require each team member to carry something over the wall. Group members cannot throw the item or hand it over. We have used a cone, a basketball, and a football dummy.

▷ Safety Considerations

Because most group members must be lifted up in this challenge, teammates must make certain that they do not drop one another. Take precautions so that the wall does not tip or fall over. Require that group members accept help getting off the wall. Do not allow anyone to come off the wall headfirst. Limit the number of participants who can be on top of the wall at any given time. You do not want the wall to become overloaded on top.

Reprinted, by permission, from D. Glover and D. Midura, 1992, *Team building through physical challenges* (Champaign, IL: Human Kinetics), 68.

Indiana's Challenge

▷ Description

Indiana's Challenge, created in one of our summer classes, has become one of our core challenges not only because of its clever design but also because it doesn't require much space and uses very little equipment. In addition, the challenge has multiple solutions.

Group members gather around a 10-foot (3-meter) diameter circle, such as the jump-ball circle of a basketball court. The challenge is to remove a basketball that is balanced on an 18-inch (45-centimeter) cone from the middle of the circle. Group members have jump ropes that they use to get the ball out of the circle. One element of the challenge is that the group must find three different ways to remove the ball. One of the three methods must include flinging the ball so that a group member can catch it in the air. Another element of the challenge is that the ball may not touch the floor either inside or outside the circle. In addition, no group member may step over the line or touch the inside of the circle with any body part. Whenever the ball falls to the floor, one group member may cross the line to place the ball onto the cone. While in the circle, this group member may not help manipulate any of the ropes.

▷ Success Criteria

The group completes the task when it invents three methods of removing the ball from the cone and getting it into the hands of a group member outside the circle. As stated previously, at least one method must include flinging the ball so that a group member catches it in the air. The group must use some combination of the ropes.

▷ Equipment

Provide a basketball and four jump ropes, approximately 10 to 12 feet (3.0 to 3.6 meters) long. We recommend sash cord rope.

▷ Setup

Place the 18-inch (45-centimeter) cone on the center of the 10-foot (3-meter) circle. Make sure that the cone has an opening that will allow a basketball to rest on the top of it. Place the ropes outside the circle. If you do not have an existing circle in your

facility, create one with chalk or vinyl tape. You could use another shape, but a circle adds an interesting dimension when the group tries to move around.

▷ Rules and Sacrifices

1. If the ball touches the floor, one group member may cross the circle line to replace the ball on the cone.
2. Participants may not cross the line at any time while trying to remove the ball.
3. The teammate replacing the ball on the cone may not manipulate the ropes while in the circle.
4. The ball may never touch the ground inside or outside of the circle.
5. No one may call others by their last names or use put-downs.
6. If a group member breaks a rule, the group must stop, replace the ball, and begin again.

▷ Possible Solutions

Almost every time we use this challenge, we see groups come up with new twists to solving it. One method is to cross the ropes so that two ropes are perpendicular to two other ropes. The group then creates a small cradle in which to rest the ball. Group members lift the ball and carry it out of the circle.

They also use this method to lift the ball and fling it into the air so that a group member can catch it. In both cases, group members must hold the rope tight so that the ball does not slip through. Another method is to create a channel with the ropes. One side lifts its end of the ropes and rolls the ball to the other side of the circle, where a group member catches it. We have also seen a group place two ropes parallel to one another about 8 inches (20 centimeters) apart and then weave the other ropes back and forth to create a long, skinny net. The group uses this net to carry the ball out of the circle, roll the ball out of the circle, and fling the ball out of the circle.

▷ Conclusion of the Task

The group completes the task when it creates three different methods of removing the ball from the cone. Group members should then replace the ball on the cone, untie any knots that they may have made, and place the equipment neatly outside the circle.

▷ Additions and Variations

We have seen so many solutions to this task that we have not felt the need to create any variations.

▷ Safety Considerations

This challenge presents no obvious safety issues.

Teamwork Walk

▷ Description

The Teamwork Walk challenge is easy to figure out but hard to do. Groups enjoy solving it, but it requires practice and teamwork. Every group member plays an equal role in solving the task.

The group tries to follow a designated path, usually the length or perimeter of a basketball court. The group uses team skis, made of long two-by-six boards (boards about 3.8 centimeters thick and 14.0 centimeters wide) or four-by-four beams (about 9.0 centimeters square) with rope-type handles so that group members can hold on to the skis while trying to move the skis. You may need to construct the team skis because it is hard to find commercially made skis that allow more than six people to participate at one time.

▷ Success Criteria

A group masters the challenge when it completes the designated path without any member touching the floor or wall. The path can vary in length or difficulty depending on the space you have available and the ages of the participants.

▷ Equipment

The group uses team skis or long walking boards. You will need two 12-foot (3.6-meter) two-by-six or four-by-four pine or fir boards. (Length can vary to meet your needs.) You also need sash cord, clothesline rope, or strapping material to make the handholds.

Drill holes through the two-by-sixes so that the rope or strapping material can pass through the boards. If you drill the holes about 18 inches (45 centimeters) apart, you will be able to fit eight or nine sets of handholds on a 12-foot (3.6-meter) board. Group members should be able to remove their feet from the skis easily if they fall.

▷ Setup

Provide the group with a set of team skis and a designated walking path. The path should be long enough to make the challenge interesting. Remember that the skis will be 8 to 12 feet (2.5 to 3.5 meters) long, so choose a space that allows a sufficient challenge and adequate turning space.

▷ Rules and Sacrifices

1. Group members may not touch the floor with any part of their bodies.
2. Group members may not use walls or stationary structures to help them maintain their balance.
3. If a group member breaks a rule, the group starts over.
4. No one can use last names or put-downs.

▷ Possible Solutions

Teamwork is the solution for this challenge. Using a group leader or organizer helps because someone must coordinate the team's movements. For instance, team members must move their feet simultaneously. Having someone count cadence helps. Group members may need to assist one another physically by holding on to the hips, waist, or shoulders of the group member directly in front of them. When making turns, clear verbal communication is essential. Be aware that if one person falls during the task, others may too. Deliberate carelessness could put teammates into precarious positions.

▷ Conclusion of the Task

The group is successful when it crosses the finish line. (You should decide whether a team finishes when the first person reaches the finish line or when the entire team crosses the finish line.)

▷ Additions and Variations

This challenge is open to a variety of additions or variations. As you observe your groups perform this challenge, we are sure that you will see variations that we have not tried.

- Groups must complete the challenge within a time limit.
- Use both a time limit and distance goal. How far can the group travel in a given time? A large gymnasium or long hall lends itself well to this variation.
- Devise an obstacle course or zigzag path, or require specific turns as variations. A 360-degree turn might be a tough challenge.
- Don't let students hold on to one another.
- Place a number of objects along the path for the group to pick up, such as a ball, jump rope, base, or hoop. The team stops to let team members pick up one object each.
- Send the group under a lowered parallel bar or volleyball net.

This challenge generates a lot of laughter and fun.

▷ Safety Considerations

Because participants are working in a line, one person ahead of another, the group must avoid falling like dominoes if someone should lose his or her balance. Many commercially made buddy boards or team walkers allow only two, four, or six teammates to work at one time, but they do incorporate handheld ropes. We too have moved away from footholds to handheld ropes, which allow participants to remove themselves from the skis more quickly if the group loses its balance.

Reprinted, by permission, from D. Glover and D. Midura, 1992, *Team building through physical challenges* (Champaign, IL: Human Kinetics), 37.

Great Pearl Caper

▷ Description

This challenge requires special equipment. It is quite difficult for students at the primary level but is ideal for those at the intermediate and middle school levels. The team must successfully transport the giant pearl back to its rightful place. With some clever variations this challenge could be much more difficult. We will offer those variations at the end of the description.

The team has two pearl track transports. Team members must work together to transport the pearl across the gym and then must figure out how to place it in its pearl stand, which is a crate (or tire). They must remember that they cannot move forward when the ball is in their pearl track transport.

▷ Success Criteria

The group completes the challenge by placing the pearl on the second pearl stand (crate or tire).

▷ Equipment

- Two pearl track transports (handmade or purchased from a sporting-goods supplier such as Gopher Sport)

- One 22-inch (56-centimeter) or larger ball
- Two 15-inch (38-centimeter) tires or two crates

▷ Setup

The pearl (cage ball) should be sitting on the tire at the starting line. The finish line is located at the midcourt line of the gym (this distance can vary depending on the space available or the age of the participants). The pearl tripod stand, a crate (or tire), is located at the finish line. When the group deposits the pearl in this stand, the challenge is complete. Team members, the pearl, and the pearl track transports are all located at the starting line.

▷ Rules and Sacrifices

1. Team members may not touch the pearl with any part of their bodies.
2. The team can transport the pearl only with the pearl track transports.
3. After part of the team has the pearl in a track transport, those teammates cannot move toward the pearl stand. They can move anywhere if they are not in possession of the pearl.

Photo courtesy of Gopher Sport.

4. The pearl may never touch the ground.

5. No one may call others by their last names or use put-downs.

6. If the team breaks any rule, it must return to the starting line, replace the pearl on the first crate (or tire), and attempt the challenge from the beginning.

▷ Possible Solutions

The group uses one pearl track transport to push the pearl off the first crate and onto the other pearl track transport. The receiving pearl track transport must receive the ball off the ground, and the team must balance it until the other part of the team moves into place to receive the ball. Team members continue to pass the ball to one another as they make progress toward the second crate. If they move too fast, the ball may drop to the floor. They must carefully roll it down their track and onto the waiting track of the other teammates. After the pearl arrives at the second crate, the team must carefully attempt to roll the ball onto the crate. The other part of the team can attempt to steady it with its transport track. This

method works best if the students pull the ropes tight to widen the track.

▷ Conclusion of the Challenge

When the group places the ball on the second crate (or tire), it has mastered the challenge.

▷ Additions and Variations

- Do not allow students to balance the ball on the transport using the rope handles. Make them pull the ropes tight.
- Make team members step over mats or under a high-jump bar as they move toward the pearl stand.
- Use a story line to create a dilemma whereby the group must transport the pearl quickly (under a time limit or time them to set a standard for other groups).

▷ Safety Considerations

This challenge presents no obvious safety issues.

Reprinted, by permission, from D. Glover and L. Anderson, 2003, *Character education* (Champaign, IL: Human Kinetics), 143.

Stomp It

▷ Description

Stomp It is now a commercially manufactured challenge, but it is possible to build your own launching device. Groups do this challenge in two or more stages. One group member stomps on the ball launcher, while the rest of the group members catch the balls hurled into the air before they touch the ground.

The team must decide which group member will stomp on the ball launcher to launch the balls. The remaining group members must stand or kneel on poly spots or bases surrounding the launcher and catch the flung balls before they touch the ground. During the first stage, any group member may catch the balls. In the second stage, group members will be assigned to catch a specific colored ball. If any launch attempt fails, the group rotates so that a new group member becomes the launcher on every attempt.

▷ Success Criteria

The group accomplishes the challenge when it has completed both stages of the task. During the first stage, group members must catch all the balls before they touch the ground. In the second stage, group members identify which specific colored ball they will catch.

▷ Equipment

Give the group a ball launcher or stomp-it board with five different colored balls. In addition, give the group poly spots or bases on which to stand or kneel.

▷ Setup

Place the stomp-it board on the floor or on a firm tumbling mat. Place the balls in the launcher holes. Set poly spots or bases around the ball launcher a few feet (a meter or so) from the launching device.

Group members must stand or kneel on the poly spots or bases until the stomper hits the launcher with his or her foot.

▷ Rules and Sacrifices

1. If teammates do not catch all the balls, the balls are replaced on the ball launcher and the group rotates so that a new group member becomes the stomper.

2. In the first stage, group members must catch all the balls.

3. A group member may catch only one ball.

4. Anytime a ball touches the floor, a new stomper rotates to the ball launcher and takes a turn stomping.

5. In the second stage, each group member declares which colored ball he or she will catch before the stomper launches the five balls.

6. If a ball touches the floor in the second stage or a group member catches the wrong ball, the group members rotate and they try again.

7. No one may call others by their last names or use put-downs.

▷ Possible Solutions

Group members should study the flight pattern of the balls and communicate that pattern to other members of the team. In addition, the stompers should try to stomp with similar force each time.

This will ensure that the flight path of the balls will be consistent.

▷ Conclusion of the Task

The groups having success are usually quite vocal when group members all catch the correct colored balls. Most groups engage in a lot of discussion about stomping force, direction of flight, and who needs to stand where to catch the flying balls. When all five balls are caught at one time—one ball by each team member—(not counting the stomper) the task is complete.

▷ Additions and Variations

Generally, groups take quite a while to achieve success in the two stages. We have seen two variations.

- One is a math variation in which each ball has a point value. Team members continue to catch the stomped balls until they reach a point requirement.

- The second variation is for a batter to hit a stomped ball (the stomper launches one ball at a time) with team members then catching the batted ball. The team must make a specific number of catches (such as 6 to 10).

▷ Safety Considerations

Teammates could possibly collide when attempting to catch balls if one teammate's ball crosses paths with another's ball.

Adapted, by permission, from D. Glover and L. Anderson, 2003, *Character education* (Champaign, IL: Human Kinetics), 145.

Missing Bucket

▷ Description

This challenge, developed in one of our summer classes by David Moran and Brent Lakas, is definitely an outdoor activity. In this task, sighted team members direct blindfolded teammates through a maze of obstacles. In addition, the blindfolded team members carry water with the intention of filling an empty container.

Sighted teammates give oral directions to blindfolded team members as they fill cups to carry through an obstacle-laden course. The blindfolded team members take numerous trips as they attempt to fill a water container placed approximately 30 feet (9 meters) from the starting bucket of water (the main source). The sighted team members stand outside the travel area (out of bounds) as the blindfolded members navigate through the maze. Sighted teammates direct blindfolded team members back to the starting line on a route on either side of the maze area.

▷ Success Criteria

A group completes the challenge when the blindfolded members have filled the empty receiving container to the top or to a designated line.

▷ Equipment

- Use long jump ropes to mark the starting line, the finish line, and side boundary lines. As an alternative, use athletic spray, marking paint, or field chalk to mark the lines and boundaries.
- A 5-gallon (20-liter) bucket can serve as the main water source.
- Use a 1-gallon (4-liter) container such as a milk jug or ice cream container to receive the water transported in the challenge.
- Have enough plastic or paper drinking cups to supply half the team's members.
- Use 8 to 12 poly spots or vinyl bases for obstacles. Do not use obstacles that would cause the blindfolded team members to trip.

▷ Setup

Place the boundary markers so that they create an area 10 to 12 feet (3.0 to 3.6 meters) wide and 20 to 25 feet (6.0 to 7.5 meters) long. Set the obstacles in a random pattern to eliminate the assistance that a logical pattern offers blindfolded team members. Place the water source at the starting line and the receiving container at the finish line.

▷ Rules and Sacrifices

1. Blindfolded group members may not step on a mine (flat obstacle).
2. Blindfolded members may not cross the side boundary lines.
3. Sighted group members may not touch a blindfolded teammate.
4. Sighted team members may not touch the bucket, the receiving container, or a water-carrying cup.
5. No one may use last names or put-downs.
6. If the group breaks a rule, a blindfolded team member loses the water in his or her cup and returns to the starting line.

▷ Possible Solutions

The most common solution is for a sighted team member to direct one blindfolded teammate from the water source to the receiving container. Team members work in pairs until they fill the receiving container. Another solution is for the blindfolded team members to form a human chain and travel together through the maze to fill the empty container. The blindfolded team members could carry the bucket through the maze to the finish line and then fill the receiving container.

▷ Conclusion of the Task

The blindfolded teammates can remove their blindfolds when they have completely filled the receiving container or have filled it to the designated mark.

You may wish to require that all blindfolded team members be at the finish line before they remove their blindfolds.

▷ Additions and Variations

- You can declare that the water-source bucket must remain stationary.
- The blindfolded team members could change places with their sighted teammates after each completed turn.

- You can create different levels of difficulty with the receiving container by having a large opening, allowing a funnel, or requiring the blindfolded team members to pour the water into the narrow neck of a milk jug.

▷ Safety Considerations

Refer to the section on using blindfolds in chapter 4.

Great Balls of Color

▷ Description

This challenge was presented to us in one of our summer graduate classes. Currently, Gopher Sport markets a similar challenge called Cooperative Maze Game. Great Balls of Color uses a homemade sheet with cutout holes, and Cooperative Maze Game uses a manufactured tarp with holes cut out for balls to drop through.

The colored balls must pass through the corresponding colored holes in the sheet into a container beneath the sheet, without touching the floor or any body parts of group members trying to solve the task. Group members hold either the edges of the sheet or a scoop. They manipulate the colored balls by moving the sheet so that the balls fall through the correct holes and land in the catching container. The scoopers attempt to catch any balls that fall off the sheet or fall through the holes in the sheet and do not land in the catching container. Balls that fall off the sheet, pass through the wrong hole, or miss the container must be placed back onto the sheet.

▷ Success Criteria

The group completes the task when all the balls pass through the correct holes in the sheet and land in the container.

▷ Equipment

- A sheet (twin-size top sheet) with five holes cut out and marked with different colors
- Five colored softball-sized Wiffle balls, with colors corresponding to the holes in the sheet
- A container to catch the balls, such as a 5-gallon (20-liter) bucket, a recycling container, or an 18- to 20-gallon-sized (68- to 75-liter) plastic storage bin
- Two scoops (manufactured scoops or milk jugs with the ends cut out)

The Cooperative Maze Game set, from Gopher Sport, has all the equipment except the scoops and container.

▷ Setup

You need an area only slightly larger than the size of the sheet. A space the size of a basketball free-throw lane will work. Team members may hold the corners and sides of the sheet or tarp. Place the container under the middle of the sheet. Scoopers may move around and under the sheet. Group members then place the balls on the sheet.

▷ Rules and Sacrifices

1. The hands of group members must remain on the edges of the sheet or tarp.

2. No hands or other body part may touch a ball.

3. Group members may not move the container.

4. If a ball goes through the wrong hole, the group must start the task again (unless a scooper catches the ball).

5. If a ball touches the ground, the group must start the task over.

6. Scoopers may catch a ball that falls off the sheet or through the wrong hole. If they make the catch, they place the ball back on the sheet.

7. Scoopers may not touch the sheet with their bodies or the scoop.

8. Group members may not call teammates by their last names or use put-downs.

▷ Possible Solutions

This challenge has one basic solution. Group members lift and lower the sheet to maneuver the balls from side to side. They must direct the balls through the correct holes and have them land in the container. Teammates holding the sheet often want to use their feet to kick the ball from beneath the sheet. This tactic breaks rule #2. To achieve success, group members should remain calm. Frequently, a group member makes a rapid movement or jerks the sheet to redirect the path of a ball.

This action often causes the ball to fly up or off the sheet. If you buy the Cooperative Maze Game, be aware that the rules sent with the challenge differ from those presented here. You can do the challenge with either method. The balls with the manufactured challenge are foam and therefore a little lighter.

▷ Conclusion of the Task

A group completes the challenge when all the colored balls pass through the corresponding holes in the sheet and land in the catching container beneath the sheet.

▷ Additions and Variations

- Do not allow talking.

- Designate one communicator to speak.

- Allow the scoopers to direct the ball into the container from beneath the sheet.

- Allow group members holding the sheet to block the ball with their bodies to keep it from falling off the sheet.

- Allow balls that have passed through the correct holes and fallen in the container to remain there if another ball touches the floor or a group member.

- Try one ball at a time for younger children.

In the initial version of this challenge, the middle hole in the sheet was colored black. No ball could pass through that hole. Only four other colored balls were used. These balls passed through the holes closest to the corners. If a ball passed through the black hole, the group started the challenge from the beginning.

▷ Safety Considerations

This challenge presents no conspicuous safety concerns. If group members do not know the location of the container, however, they could trip over it if the group holding the sheet moves significantly from its starting position.

Juggler's Carry

▷ Description

This challenge, created as a project in one of our classes by Jeff Lagoo, Kim Poppin, and Tammy Bernard, has some similarities to the Whole World in Their Hands. The challenge uses four large balls.

The team must transfer four large balls halfway across a gym space (such as a basketball court). The group makes four trips, and on each trip the group adds one ball. On the first trip, the group transports one ball. On the second trip, the group adds another ball and transports two. This process continues until the team completes the fourth trip by transporting four balls.

▷ Success Criteria

The group masters this challenge by picking up all four balls, one at a time, and crossing the designated finish line (which also is the starting line).

▷ Equipment

You need four large inflatable or rubber balls. We suggest using either a 48-inch (120-centimeter) ball and three smaller balls, a 32-inch (80-centimeter) ball, a 24-inch (60-centimeter) ball, and a 22-inch (56-centimeter) ball, or four 32- to 36-inch (80- to 92-centimeter) balls. The balls could be the light rubber roto-molded balls, beach balls, or cage balls. They can be inflatable or another type of ball approximately these sizes. The size of the balls depends largely on the age and size of your students. As an example, four 22-inch (56-centimeter) balls will work with primary-aged children. You will also need a rope 20 to 30 feet (6 to 9 meters) long and two chairs or large cones to create a barrier.

▷ Setup

Place two balls behind the start–finish line, which could be the end line of the basketball court. Place

two more balls in the center of the gym behind the half-court line. If no basketball court is available, mark two lines with tape 30 to 50 feet (9 to 15 meters) apart. In the middle of the area place two chairs with a rope tied between them. The rope should be about the height of the participants' knees.

▷ Rules and Sacrifices

1. No ball may touch the floor between the starting and ending line.
2. Team members may not touch the balls with their hands.
3. A different person or different group of people must pick up a ball on each trip.
4. When traveling across the gym, all team members must be connected to one another and must be touching a ball.
5. No one may use last names or put-downs.
6. If a team member breaks a rule, the team must start over from the line where it completed the last successful trip.

▷ Possible Solutions

Students need to communicate about who is picking up the ball and how they will transport it with everyone touching the ball. During each trip, students add a ball to the group support system and move with the whole group supporting the balls. Alternatively, team members may decide to break into smaller groups but still maintain connection to one another as they transport the balls.

▷ Conclusion of the Task

The group completes the task when all four balls pass across the original starting line, now serving as the finish line.

▷ Additions and Variations

- If the team touches the rope, it must restart the task from the previous ball.
- Require the team to find a different way to pick up the ball and add it to the group trip.
- Make the trips longer or shorter.
- Depending on the age of the team, use two or three smaller balls.

▷ Safety Considerations

This challenge presents few safety considerations. If participants walk backward, teammates should coach them to prevent anyone from tripping. Stepping over the rope obstacle should also elicit help from teammates if the obstacle is hard to see because of the method that the group uses to move the balls. The rope should be strung in a manner that would cause the rope to fall if touched rather than trip a participant.

Reprinted, by permission, from D. Glover and L. Anderson, 2003, *Character education* (Champaign, IL: Human Kinetics), 114.

Frankenstein

▷ Description

This beat-the-clock challenge reinforces the structure of the human anatomy. It uses the same skeleton equipment as General Hospital, Emergency Room does. Normally we do not make the challenges competitive in nature, but part of the fun of this challenge is trying to do it as fast as possible.

Participants attempt to put together the skeleton puzzle in the shortest time possible. The team has to earn the right to put parts of Frankenstein together by successfully tossing and catching a deck tennis ring. Each time team members have successfully passed the ring, the team gets to add three more bones to Frankenstein. A minimum of seven trips of tossing the ring will be required to build Frankenstein. The group creates a system of tossing, catching, running, and building the puzzle.

▷ Success Criteria

The group masters the Frankenstein challenge when all bones are correctly arranged.

▷ Equipment

- One skeleton puzzle
- One deck tennis ring
- One storage crate or container
- Five indoor bases

▷ Setup

Place the bases 10 to 15 feet (3.0 to 4.5 meters) apart in a straight line. Modify the distance depending on the age and ability of your students.

Five team members each stand on a different base. The remaining team members must be in the building area close to base #1. The storage crate holding the skeleton puzzle should be at the opposite end of the working area, or about 15 feet (4.5 meters) from base #5. See figure 8.6.

▷ Rules and Sacrifices

1. Team members must toss the deck tennis ring from base #1 to base #2. The person on base #2 must catch the ring and successfully turn and toss it to the person on base #3. This process continues until the ring has traveled all the way to base #5 and back to base #1. If a team member drops the ring, it must be sent back to the team member who last tossed it.

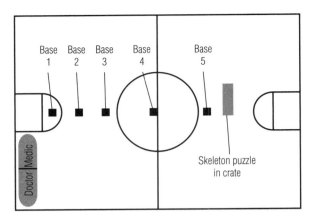

Figure 8.6   Frankenstein setup

2. Once the ring gets back to base #1, the medic runs to the storage crate at the opposite end of the gym and brings back three bones. The medic cannot leave the building area (the lab) until the ring gets back to base #1.

3. When the medic returns, he or she must give the bones to the doctors, who begin assembling the puzzle. When the doctors receive the bones, all players rotate positions. The medic goes to base #1, the person on base #1 goes to base #2, the person on base #2 goes to base #3, the person on base #3 moves to base #4, and the person on base #4 moves to base #5. The person on base #5 becomes a new doctor, and one of the doctors becomes the new medic. Team members cannot rotate positions until the medic returns to the building area with three bones.

4. The ring must make seven successful round trips to get all the puzzle pieces to the building area. After the last medic has delivered the last three puzzle pieces, team members can hustle to the lab and confer about any changes they need to make to Frankenstein to make him complete. When they think that they have put Frankenstein together correctly, the last medic yells, "Lightning." This is the signal to stop the clock. The instructor then checks the puzzle for accuracy. If the puzzle is correct, the time stands. If it is incorrect, the clock starts again as the team rearranges the bones.

This process continues until the team assembles Frankenstein correctly.

▷ Possible Solutions

The team should communicate before the challenge starts about where teammates should position themselves to start the challenge. Certainly, a team would want the best catchers on the bases, and a teammate who is a good doctor should plan to rotate to the lab when most of the bones are there. The team runs through the challenge in a relay manner.

▷ Conclusion of the Task

The group completes the task when the team assembles Frankenstein correctly and the clock stops.

▷ Additions and Variations

- Allow team members to assign permanent roles so that they can match the team members' skills with the challenge.
- Lengthen or shorten the distance of the toss.
- Allow participants to bring back more or fewer bones to shorten or lengthen the time of the challenge.

▷ Safety Considerations

This challenge presents no specific safety issues other than the possibility that the deck tennis ring may hit someone who is not looking when a teammate tosses it.

Reprinted, by permission, from D. Glover and L. Anderson, 2003, *Character education* (Champaign, IL: Human Kinetics), 121.

Dynamic Barrier

▷ Description

This challenge does not require a lot of equipment and can be adapted to students of all ages. Dynamic Barrier is one of the two challenges that uses a turning jump rope.

The team must pass through the twirling barrier (rope) from one side to the other without touching the rope. In addition, all equipment must pass through the barrier. Because the twirlers or rope turners must also pass through the barrier, the group must decide when to change twirlers.

▷ Success Criteria

A group masters this challenge when all group members and all equipment have passed from one side of the barrier to the other side of the barrier without touching it.

▷ Equipment

- One long jump rope
- One large 22- to 34-inch (56- to 86-centimeter) ball
- Three deck tennis rings
- One hula hoop
- One gym scooter

▷ Setup

You need a working area large enough to accommodate a turning jump rope. Make sure that participants have sufficient room to run through the rope or scoot through on a scooter. An area too close to a barrier, such as a wall, may impede a group's chance for success and compromise safety. The twirlers must practice turning the rope because their proficiency will be crucial to the group's success.

▷ Rules and Sacrifices

1. All group members and all equipment must pass through the barrier without touching it.
2. Group members must roll the large ball through the barrier, and a group member must accompany it. In other words, a team member and the ball must pass through the barrier together, but the ball must be rolling.
3. Team members must toss the deck tennis rings through the barrier, and a team member on the opposite side must catch them. If a

team member drops a ring, the team must start the challenge over from the beginning.

4. The scooter must carry a team member through. The team must decide who will sit on the scooter and then push that person through the barrier. Caution: Teammates may assist and push the scooter and their teammate through, but they must be aware of their proximity to the walls. As soon as the scooter gets through the barrier, the rider should stop it and not coast into teammates or equipment.
5. Two teammates must pass through at the same time while holding the hula hoop.
6. All remaining students on the team must pass through the barrier together. Although they do not have to be connected, they must pass through at the same time.
7. If any teammate or any equipment touches the barrier, then that person or that piece of equipment and all team members who have already successfully passed through the barrier must go back to the start.
8. No one may call others by their last names or use put-downs.

▷ Possible Solutions

The rules indicate how groups must solve this challenge. Groups use one basic solution to this challenge, although the order of travel will differ from group to group. The team must decide which team members will pass through the barrier with equipment and which team members will pass through the barrier with other teammates. The team must also decide who will throw and catch the deck tennis rings, who will start as the twirlers, and who will replace the original twirlers when it is their turn to pass through the barrier.

▷ Additions and Variations

You can use an infinite number of variations in this challenge. Here are a few:

- Don't use equipment, but time the team. See how long it takes a team to pass through the barrier one at a time, including the switching of twirlers. The clock stops only when all team members have passed through.

- Have teams try passing through the barrier and back to the starting point all connected together. The team should select its best twirlers because they do not have to pass through in this variation.
- Add equipment from activities used in other curriculum units, such as basketballs, footballs, volleyballs, tennis equipment, and so on.
- Have teams choose an order of travel based on an unusual criterion. Examples include chronological birth date order; numerical order using only the day of the birthday month (August 1 would start before February 3); alphabetical order based on first names, middle names, mothers' first names, or other scheme; or order by height (tallest or shortest starting first).

- Give the group a maximum number of rope turns to get everyone through the barrier, or count the number of turns as a competitive feature between teams.

▷ Safety Considerations

Because this challenge uses a scooter, refer to the section in chapter 4 on safe use of scooters. Group members should not deliberately slide through the turning rope. Teammates who throw objects through the barrier should be certain that the receivers are looking and ready to catch the thrown items. Do not place group members too close to a wall on the ending side of the barrier.

Reprinted, by permission, from D. Glover and L. Anderson, 2003, *Character education* (Champaign, IL: Human Kinetics), 116.

Tower of Tires

▷ Description

The Tower of Tires challenge is a takeoff on a children's game commonly called the Tower of Hanoi, among other names. This challenge is a math game that requires participants to restack a set of items while observing a few simple rules. The result finds the original stack in a different place, but the original order of the items remains the same. This challenge requires little room or equipment.

The challenge uses five tires, each a different size. The tires are numbered 1 through 5, from smallest to largest. Stack the five tires on one large cone in order so that the largest tire (#5) is on the bottom and the smallest tire (#1) is on the top. Place two additional large cones about three feet (one meter) to either side of the cone holding the five tires (see figure 8.7). The group moves the tires one at a time, from cone to cone, until the stack of tires rests on a different cone.

▷ Success Criteria

The team completes the challenge when it has successfully moved all the tires from one cone to another cone while following the specific rules for moving the tires. The tires must be in the same order as they were at the start, from #1 to #5, with tire #1 on top.

▷ Equipment

- Five different sized tires
- Three large cones, preferably 36-inch (90-cemtimeter) cones
- Tape for making numbers on the tires
- A clipboard with paper and pencil for recording the moves

▷ Setup

Set the five tires on one large cone with the largest on the bottom and the smallest on the top. Set the

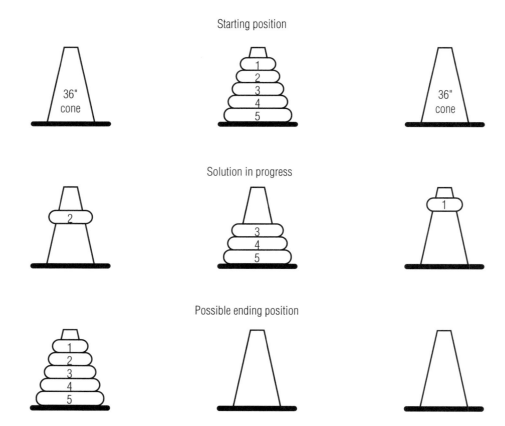

Figure 8.7   The progression of Tower of Tires from start to finish and somewhere in between.

other two cones in line with the middle cone approximately three feet (one meter) to either side.

▷ Rules and Sacrifices

1. The team can move only one tire at a time.

2. A tire may not be stacked on top of a smaller tire.

3. Two teammates must move each tire, with each person using two hands.

4. Each time the team moves a tire, a different combination of teammates must move it.

5. When team members move a tire, they must move it onto a cone (the cone may be empty or have another tire on it). A move is considered complete when one or both teammates let go of the tire.

6. No tire may touch the floor unless it is on a cone.

7. If a team breaks a rule, team members must restack all tires in the original position.

8. No one can use put-downs or last names.

▷ Possible Solutions

The fewest number of moves required to reach the solution is 31. Teams can complete the challenge using more than the minimum number of moves.

An example of how a team might perform the challenge follows. Two teammates move tire #1 onto the empty cone on the right. Two other teammates move tire #2 onto the empty cone on the left. Another combination of two teammates moves tire #1 over to tire #2, allowing yet another combination of teammates to move tire #3 onto the empty cone. This process continues until the team is able to move the bottom tire (#5) to a different cone. The team members then try to reverse the process so that they can move tire #4 onto tire #5 and so on, until they restack all the tires.

We suggest that students write down all their moves. The time will likely come when the team has used every possible combination of team members to make a move. When this occurs, the team may repeat combinations on the list.

▷ Conclusion of the Task

As noted previously, the team completes the task when it has moved the entire stack of tires to a different cone with the tires stacked in their original order. Have the group members move the stack of tires back to the center cone before going on to the next challenge.

▷ Additions and Variations

Groups can do this challenge using a different number of tires. We have found that using five tires takes a reasonable amount of time and presents a good challenge.

- Three tires can be moved in 7 moves (minimum moves).
- Four tires can be moved in 15 moves (minimum moves).
- Five tires can be moved in 31 moves (minimum moves).
- Six tires can be moved in 63 moves (minimum moves).
- Seven tires can be moved in 127 moves (minimum moves).

▷ Safety Concerns

This challenge does not present any inherent safety concerns. As with any task using tires, make sure that no steel belts are exposed. Group members should lift tires safely so that no back muscle problems occur.

Factor In

▷ Description

This is another challenge created by teachers in the team building program offered through Saint Mary's University. This challenge was created by Marc Bachman and Jay Ehlers. The unique thing about this challenge is that it incorporates math and puzzle skills into a great team building challenge.

The team must remain connected and move through a maze of numbered bases. The team members must stand on various bases in the maze, but the bases they are using must have a total number that can be factored by three.

▷ Success Criteria

The task is mastered when all group members move from one side of the maze to the other while connected, keeping the sum total of the bases being used a factor of three.

▷ Equipment

Twelve round bases with numbers written or taped on top

▷ Setup

The bases should be set on the floor in the following pattern:

12	11	10
7	8	9
6	5	4
1	2	3

▷ Rules and Sacrifices

1. Team members must stay connected during travel.
2. Team members may only move one base at a time.
3. Team members may move in a straight or diagonal path.
4. Teammates must remain one base away from the immediate person they are connected to.
5. Only one team member may enter the maze at a time. When a teammate gets to the last row of the maze, that teammate may step out of the maze but must stay connected with the others.
6. After each team member enters or exits the maze, the total-sum number (of the bases team members are standing on) must be a factor of three. Otherwise, the team must start again.
7. Only one person on a base at a time.
8. No one should call others by last names or use put-downs.

▷ Possible Solutions

As each team member enters or exits the maze, the team needs to add up the numbers they are standing on. If the numbers add up to a factor of three, the team can continue.

▷ Conclusion of the Task

When the whole team has successfully moved through the maze and is standing together at the finish, the challenge is complete.

▷ Additions and Variations

- To make the challenge easier, eliminate the row with bases 12, 11, and 10.
- To make the challenge more difficult, randomly place the bases. One factor of three should be in each row.
- Time the challenge.
- Add more rows.

▷ Safety Considerations

This challenge presents no safety issues.

Created by Marc Bachman and Jay Ehlers.

Advanced Challenges

The challenges found in this chapter are physically or intellectually more difficult than the introductory and intermediate challenges. Instructors rarely give advanced challenges to students below sixth grade. We always start every age group with introductory challenges. The younger the age group, the longer we stay with the introductory challenges. We move to intermediate and advanced challenges after teams show that they can accomplish the introductory challenges. Age is not as important in determining whether to give a group an advanced challenge as is the readiness of the group, the instructor's trust in the group, or the demonstrated maturity level of the group.

Nevertheless, the older the group, the sooner we move to the advanced challenges because the introductory challenges are easier for older students.

The advanced challenges require more planning, physical assistance, and encouragement from all team members than the introductory and intermediate challenges do. The advanced challenges teach students to persevere after failure. All advanced challenges can be modified to allow even young children to attempt them. Youngsters in the primary grades probably could not do the Black Hole, but they could do any of the others if modified appropriately.

Black Hole

▷ Description

The Black Hole is both physically and intellectually challenging. In addition, it requires team members to cooperate and trust each other. Group members try to pass through a hula hoop suspended from a basketball hoop. Students cannot touch the hoop (known as the black hole), nor can they dive through it. The challenge is designed so that group members must help each other and offer lots of physical support. If group members have not worked together before, they may not have developed sufficient team-building skills to master this challenge.

Group members begin on one side of the hula hoop and must remain on the tumbling mats during the challenge. To pass through the hoop to the other side, group members need help from teammates.

▷ Success Criteria

A group masters the challenge when all group members have moved through the black hole, from the outer-space side of the hoop to the Earth side.

▷ Equipment

- Two tires
- One hula hoop
- A rope and masking tape to suspend the hoop between the tires and the basket
- At least four tumbling mats (see figure 9.1)
- Mats or crash pads at least 4 inches thick

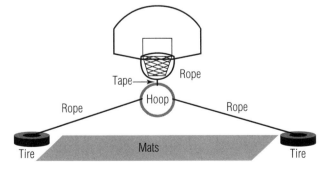

Figure 9.1 Black Hole equipment and setup.

Reprinted, by permission, from D. Glover and D. Midura, 1992, *Team building through physical challenges* (Champaign, IL: Human Kinetics), Appendix.

▷ Setup

Suspend the hula hoop between the tires so that the bottom of the hoop is approximately 3 feet (1 meter) off the floor. You may need to modify the height of the hoop to accommodate shorter students; setting the hoop height so that the bottom is about waist high on most of your students should be sufficient.

Next, place at least four tumbling mats in the working space, at least two on each side of the hoop. Place the crash pad on the exit side of the hula hoop. You can use a tape line to divide the working area into two distinct spaces, much like the centerline of a volleyball court. Provide enough cushion in the working space so that a group member who falls will be well protected.

▷ Rules and Sacrifices

1. All group members must go through the black hole.
2. No person may touch the black hole (hoop) or the ropes connected to the hoop.
3. No one may step over the dividing line.
4. No one may dive through the hoop.
5. Group members may not reach under, around, or over the hula hoop to help. They may reach through the hoop to help.
6. Group members must remain on tumbling mats during the challenge.
7. No one may use last names or put-downs.
8. If a group member breaks a rule, that person and a teammate who has passed through the hoop must start again.

▷ Possible Solutions

Most groups start by lifting and sliding one group member through the hoop while keeping his or her body straight. After the first person passes through the hoop, group members will be on both sides of the black hole to help their teammates through the hoop. Getting the last person through the hoop presents the greatest difficulty. Teammates on the Earth side of the black hole may reach across to the

outer-space side as long as they do not touch the hoop or the floor on the outer-space side.

▷ Conclusion of the Task

At the conclusion of the task, all group members stand on the Earth side of the black hole and remain on the mats until the teacher gives them approval.

▷ Additions and Variations

Here are a few additions and variations to this challenge:

- You can lower the height of the hoop for younger children and raise it for more mature groups.

- Assigning group members to bring back moon souvenirs may add difficulty and interest to the task. Group members would carry various objects (a football, basketball, beach ball, floor hockey stick, or other item) with them to Earth. The object must remain in contact with the person carrying it. Students cannot simply pass the items to one another through the hoop.

- You could establish a time limit (15 or 20 minutes) for the challenge. Develop descriptive story lines to enhance the task for younger groups ("Darth Vader will be here in 15 minutes . . .").

As we said before, this challenge involves trust and cooperation. Because no one can succeed without the help of teammates, this task is an excellent progression from intermediate challenges.

▷ Safety Considerations

Use enough mats so that the working space is well cushioned and safe. Group members must lift and move each other carefully. If group members fall on the hoop, the hoop could break (but better to lose a hoop than have a student be injured). Under no circumstances should you allow participants to dive through the hoop or throw a teammate through the black hole. Before the task begins, discuss the fact that teammates are putting their trust in the group. Group members must do everything they can to keep teammates supported (physically) when helping them move. Make certain that the floor area is well covered with mats and crash pads. When attaching the hoop to an overhead rope, attach the hoop to the rope with a piece of masking tape. That way, if someone falls onto the hoop, the tape will immediately snap, and the person passing through the hoop will not be caught on the hanging hoop. Reattaching the hoop with another piece of tape is easy.

Stepping-Stones II DVD

▷ Description

Stepping-Stones II is a real brain buster that requires much thinking and communication. This challenge, the most difficult thinking task in the book, does not require the group to work hard physically; it is more a human chess game. Cooperation and planning are essential to solving the task.

You may want to use this challenge after students have completed several other challenges or assign it to groups that demonstrate exceptional team-building skills. Refer to Additions and Variations for ideas on simplifying this challenge for younger students and others.

The group tries to rearrange itself from a specific starting order to a specific ending order. Group members stand in a straight line on bases, which they cannot move. The team divides itself into two equal groups, and the groups face each other. Having an even number of participants is helpful but not necessary.

▷ Success Criteria

The group masters the challenge when it has moved from its beginning order to its assigned final positions.

Example: Eight students using nine bases
Starting order:

| A | B | C | D | empty base | 1 | 2 | 3 | 4 |

Ending order:

| 1 | 2 | 3 | 4 | empty base | A | B | C | D |

▷ Equipment

You need one base per group member and one extra base. We use eight group members in our example, so we need nine bases.

▷ Setup

A space 5 to 8 feet (1.5 to 2.5 meters) wide and about 20 feet (6 meters) long will be adequate. Place the bases in a straight line, about 18 inches (45 centimeters) apart. One group member stands on each base, and the empty base is in the middle of the line.

The team divides into two groups. Each teammate gets a letter or number to designate starting position. Alternatively, provide colored jerseys so that group members can identify their sections.

▷ Rules and Sacrifices

1. Each group member must remain on a base except when moving to another base.

2. A person may only move forward to another base.

3. Only one person at a time may occupy a base.

4. When moving to a new base, a group member may move forward one base or around one teammate to another base. But team members may not move around two teammates in one move.

5. Only one group member at a time may move.

6. If a group member breaks a rule or if a group cannot make another move, the group must go back to its starting order.

7. No one may use last names or put-downs.

▷ Possible Solutions

The solution to this challenge is so specific that you might want to practice it by making your own board game. Draw nine squares on construction paper, place numbers and letters on eight checkers or domino pieces (see figure 9.2), and practice these moves:

Step 1—D moves forward to empty base.

Step 2—1 moves around D to empty base.

Step 3—2 moves forward to empty base.

Step 4—D moves around 2 to open base.

Step 5—C moves around 1.

Step 6—B moves forward to open base.

Step 7—1 moves around B.

Step 8—2 moves around C.

Step 9—3 moves around D.

Step 10—4 moves forward to open base.

Step 11—D moves around 4 (D completes switch).

Step 12—C moves around 3.

Step 13—B moves around 2.

Step 14—A moves around 1.

Step 15—1 moves forward (1 finishes).

Step 16—2 moves around A (2 finishes).

Step 17—3 moves around B.

Step 18—4 moves around C.

Step 19—C moves forward (C finishes).

Step 20—B moves around 4 (B finishes).

Step 21—A moves around 3.

Step 22—3 moves forward (3 finishes).

Step 23—4 moves around A (4 finishes).

Step 24—A moves forward (the task is complete).

Whew! Got that? See why we called it a human chess game? Group members need to communicate constantly with one another.

▷ Conclusion of the Task

The group masters the challenge when group members have moved from their beginning order to the designated ending order. As mentioned before, to prevent frustration, group members may need to practice the challenge as a board game before trying it as a physical challenge.

▷ Additions and Variations

- Have group members start by practicing in a four-person group (this task takes eight moves) or in a six-person group (this task takes 15 moves).

- To give your group visual help, tape a letter or number to each member's jersey. One group could wear red jerseys with letters A, B, C, and D. The other group could wear blue jerseys with numbers 1, 2, 3, and 4.

This difficult challenge is not suitable for groups that had trouble with easier tasks. Make modifications that we have overlooked. Keep in mind that this challenge requires more mental gymnastics and communication skill than it does physical skill. Groups that master this challenge should be considered proficient, cooperative problem solvers.

▷ Safety Considerations

This challenge presents no safety concerns.

Reprinted, by permission, from D. Glover and D. Midura, 1992, *Team building through physical challenges* (Champaign, IL: Human Kinetics), 90, 92.

| A | | B | | C | | D | | | | 1 | | 2 | | 3 | | 4 |

Figure 9.2 Solving the Stepping-Stones II challenge.

Alphabet Balance Beam

▷ Description

Alphabet Balance Beam, one of our first tasks, requires group members to help each other as they alphabetize themselves while remaining on top of a high balance beam.

Students cannot touch the floor or the supporting legs of the balance beam during this challenge.

Group members try to rearrange themselves alphabetically. They begin by sitting in random order on the beam. Give numbers to group members to help them remember the starting order. Before students read their instructions (the challenge card), you first specify

1. the name that the group will use for the alphabetical order, such as proper name, middle name, last name, mother's first name, father's first name, or other name, and

2. whether students will alphabetize themselves from right to left or left to right.

▷ Success Criteria

The group masters the challenge when all group members are standing on top of the balance beam in assigned alphabetical order.

▷ Equipment

You will need a high balance beam, 8 to 10 tumbling mats, and at least two crash pads. Cover the entire working area with tumbling mats.

▷ Setup

Choose a space away from walls or other equipment. Place two unfolded mats on the floor, end to end, and set the balance beam on the mats. Place one or two tumbling mats between the support legs of the beam to cover any leg extensions that touch the floor. Use more mats to cover the outside of the legs. Place mats or crash pads behind where the group will stand on the beam. Make sure that the working area is safe.

As students begin, they need to discuss which names (first, middle, last, or other) they will use in the task. You may need to help some students spell certain names. Students need to communicate how they need help and how they can help others.

▷ Rules and Sacrifices

1. All group members must remain on the beam during the task.

2. If anyone touches a mat, the floor, or the legs of the beam, the entire group must get off the beam and start over.

3. If anyone calls another by last name or uses a put-down, the entire group starts over.

▷ Possible Solutions

In solving this challenge, group members often hold tightly to the balance beam while a teammate steps carefully over them. Some students try to change

positions while everyone is standing, and you may even see some students maneuver under the beam. Some group members will probably lose their balance, so group members must guard against a fall. No one should be deliberately careless.

If group members help one another, this task is easier. Some will need additional support just to maintain their balance while sitting.

▷ Conclusion of the Task

The group completes the task when its members are standing on the beam in the correct order. Standing up on the beam may be harder than alphabetizing. Students need to plan how to stand and how to support each other. Don't be surprised to see a group make errors at this stage.

When the entire group is standing, have the group recite the names it used to achieve alphabetical order. Have group members recheck their alphabetized names before they stand.

▷ Additions and Variations

- You may need to experiment to find the height at which to set the beam so that students cannot touch the mats with their feet while sitting on the balance beam. Also, when assigning order, see that the group members are not already seated alphabetically.
- Vary the direction of order often so that students can't anticipate the upcoming task. If a group has to change only a few places to achieve success, the task becomes less challenging and less fun.

▷ Safety Considerations

As with many challenges, you must make sure that mats cover all floor area. Additionally, cover any metal base parts of the beam with mats. Check the beam for any possibility of splintered wood. Have crash pads behind and in front of the beam to protect participants from dangerous falls.

Find out whether any participants have a fear of heights. Standing on the beam may be a fearful prospect for some people. Be sure to use a beam that can support the weight of the participants.

Reprinted, by permission, from D. Glover and D. Midura, 1992, *Team building through physical challenges* (Champaign, IL: Human Kinetics), 22.

Knights of the Around Table

▷ Description

Team building has given us the opportunity to meet with many teachers. These meetings often evolve into a lively exchange of team-building ideas. Knights of the Around Table, a difficult and unique challenge, was created during one of these workshops. This challenge is a good lead up to Electric Fence on page 148.

The group stands behind the starting line, which runs the length of a sturdy table and is positioned 3 feet (1 meter) from the side of the table. The group must transfer all members over, under, and then over the table again, without touching the floor. All group members must exit the top of the table beyond the finish line, which runs the length of the table opposite the starting line. The finish line should also be 3 feet (1 meter) from the table (see figure 9.3).

▷ Success Criteria

The group masters the challenge when all group members successfully cross over, under, and then over the table again and stand behind the finishing line.

▷ Equipment

The only equipment needed for this challenge is a sturdy table and a roll of tape. We do not recommend using a folding table because of the possibility that

it will collapse. In addition, use two large folding mats.

▷ Setup

Place the mats side by side. Set the table on top of the mats. Make sure that the table is not wobbly and that all table legs are secure. Place a tape starting line that runs the length of the table and is 3 feet (1 meter) from the side of the table.

▷ Rules and Sacrifices

1. Group members may not touch the floor between the starting line and finish line.

2. Group members standing behind either tape line may assist a team member get on or around the table but may not touch the table. Or, allow three people to touch the table (instructor's discretion).

3. After a group members gets off the table and crosses the finish line, he or she may not get back on top of the table.

4. No one may call others by their last names or use put-downs.

5. If a group member breaks a rule, that person and one successful person (or the person who has advanced the farthest) must start the task again.

▷ Possible Solutions

A team will succeed in this challenge only if it has a strategy to provide physical assistance to all team members. Team members should select the most athletic person to go first, and the team should assist that person as best they can from behind the starting line. After the first person travels under the table and successfully reaches the top, he or she should stay on top of the table to assist others. Another strategy is to send two people to the top of the table before anyone attempts to crawl under and over.

Getting someone to the finish line and allowing him or her to help from that position is helpful. Remember, providing physical assistance from behind the starting and finish lines is permitted as long as those providing assistance do not touch the table.

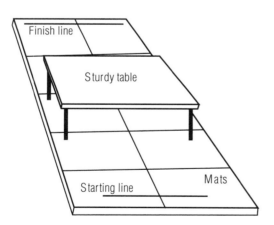

Figure 9.3 Setup for Knights of the Around Table.

Adapted, by permission, from D. Midura and D. Glover, 1995, *More team building challenges* (Champaign, IL: Human Kinetics), 48.

▷ Conclusion of the Task

The group masters the task when all group members have traveled over, under, and then over the table again and are standing behind the finish line.

▷ Additions and Variations

- Use a wider table for older students and a narrower table for younger students.
- Adjust the distance of the starting and finish lines.
- Have the team attempt to transport a football dummy (injury victim) over, under, and then over the table.
- Put a time limit on the journey.
- Allow a certain number of students that are behind the starting or finish line to touch the table while assisting.

▷ Safety Considerations

Because teammates will be leaning and hanging over, under, and around a table, the likelihood of getting bruises is significant. Participants can lose their grip and fall, especially while hanging under the table. Teammates need to be careful when helping a group member. If they hang on to a teammate too tightly or carelessly, they could cause a fall or stretch muscles. Group members attempting to go under the table should not go feetfirst because they could slip or lose their grip and land on their backs or hit their heads on the tumbling mats. Make sure that the table does not have any sharp edges or splintered surfaces that could cause a cut or splinter.

Reprinted, by permission, from D. Midura and D. Glover, 1995, *More team building challenges* (Champaign, IL: Human Kinetics), 48.

Electric Fence

▷ Description

Students of all ages enjoy Electric Fence, and you can easily modify it for your students. This task requires a group to progress from one end of a high balance beam to the other end. The catch is that group members must go under a net (electric fence) hanging perpendicularly above and touching the beam. But the students can't touch the net. Even in modified form, this challenge is one of the more physically demanding tasks in the book.

All group members must crawl, slide, or hang like monkeys as they move from an entry mat (at one end of the beam) to an exit mat (at the other end). The group also must cross under the electric fence (a net hanging above the beam).

▷ Success Criteria

The group masters the task when all group members successfully cross under the fence and stand on the exit mat.

▷ Equipment

- A high balance beam
- At least seven tumbling mats
- A badminton or volleyball net
- Two badminton or volleyball net standards

▷ Setup

Place two mats end to end on the floor and set the balance beam on them. The beam should be high enough so that the tallest student cannot touch the floor when hanging under the beam. Put additional mats under the beam to cover its legs and their extensions. Next, set a folded tumbling mat at each end of the beam and perpendicular to the beam. These mats, which may also be called the ledges, serve as entry and exit mats. Place the net so that it bisects the beam. The net should hang from the standards so that it brushes the top of the beam. Cover all floor space beneath the working area with tumbling mats.

To complete this challenge, students hang under the beam and move like monkeys. Group members on the entry mat (ledge #1) support a guider on the beam. Group members on the exit mat (ledge #2) help a guider on the other side of the beam. This challenge is difficult, and the group may need several attempts to succeed.

▷ Rules and Sacrifices

1. The students must begin the task by getting on top of the balance beam.
2. The students may not touch the floor or tumbling mats between the entry and exit mats (ledges #1 and #2).

3. Group members must go under the net without touching it.

4. The students must get back on the top of the beam before getting off the beam.

5. After a student gets off the beam and onto the exit mat, he or she may not get back onto the beam.

6. Only group members on the beam may help those hanging under the beam.

7. Group members must be on the ledge in order to help a teammate on top of the beam. Students on the ledge may not assist a student hanging under the beam.

8. If a group member breaks a rule, that person and a teammate who has crossed the beam must start over.

9. If a group member calls a person in the group by last name or uses a put-down, that person and a teammate who has crossed the beam must start over.

▷ Possible Solutions

Students climb onto the beam one at a time, turn upside down, monkey style, and try to move along the beam and under the net. While a group member tries to go under the beam and under the net, group members on both sides of the net should offer help. Most students need help getting their feet under the electric fence and getting back on top of the beam. Group members need to decide when to get off the beam (refer to rule #5) because if they get off the beam too soon, they may not be available to help their teammates. Constant encouragement and physical assistance are necessary during this challenge. Making a good choice of the first and last group members to travel the beam is also vital to solving the challenge.

▷ Conclusion of the Task

To reach their goal, all group members must cross under the electric fence and stand on the exit mat (ledge #2). After you approve their success, have the group sit down at the exit mat so that the recorder and the summarizer can state the group's accomplishments. Group members should spend time using positive reinforcers to recognize the encouragement and praise that took place.

▷ Additions and Variations

We have found that the following variations work well:

- Place a tire on the floor (under the beam) for students to use as a support.
- Reduce the travel distance for younger students and then let them drop off carefully.
- Use a lightweight football dummy as an additional group member. The students can pretend that that they are rescuing an injured group member.
- Assign a time limit. (Example: "A storm is coming. You have 20 minutes to complete the task.")

▷ Safety Considerations

Make certain that tumbling mats cover the floor space. Cover any metal feet of the beam with mats. Suggest to participants that they wear long-sleeved shirts and long-legged pants (such as sweat pants or running pants). This task can cause some bruises when participants attempt to get on top of the beam after hanging beneath it.

Grand Canyon I

▷ Description

This challenge requires group members to work together to swing by rope across an imaginary canyon. Most groups find this a favorite task; something about swinging on a rope is exceptionally attractive to students. As with all team-building tasks or challenges, for individuals to succeed, the entire group must master the task.

All group members move from a ground-level starting point (one canyon rim) to the top of a vaulting box (the other canyon rim). The distance between canyon rims is the Grand Canyon. Group members cross the canyon swinging on a rope.

▷ Success Criteria

The group masters the task when all group members have crossed the Grand Canyon and are standing on the opposite canyon rim.

▷ Equipment

- A climbing rope
- A vaulting box (or four folded tumbling mats stacked on one another)
- Four to six tumbling mats placed on the floor for safety

▷ Setup

The distance between the starting line, climbing rope, and vaulting box depends on group members' ages and abilities. You may need to experiment by swinging across the canyon yourself or by letting students experiment. Place the canyon rims far enough apart so that group members must work together.

For example, place a 15-foot-long (4.5-meter-long) tape line about 8 feet (2.5 meters) from the climbing rope to represent the beginning canyon rim.

Place tumbling mats over the entire floor area where students might swing while using the rope. Place a vaulting box (or stack of mats) 6 to 8 feet (1.8 to 2.5 meters) on the other side of the climbing rope 14 to 16 feet (4.3 to 4.9 meters) from the starting line. If you use a vaulting box, put an unfolded tumbling mat over the box so that it covers the top, front, and back of the box. Remember that the distance between the canyon rims must be far enough to make the task somewhat difficult yet safe. If the rope is close to a wall, place a crash pad against the wall to prevent injury.

The students swing over the Grand Canyon and onto the vaulting box. Group members need to help one another get onto both the rope and the vaulting box. To be safe, students should not crash into the vaulting box.

▷ Rules and Sacrifices

1. The Grand Canyon is the area between the starting line and the vaulting box.

2. If any member of the group touches the floor anywhere in the Grand Canyon, a student who has successfully crossed the canyon and the person who touched the floor must start over.

3. If a group member falls or jumps off the vaulting box, that person and one other person must start over.

4. Group members must call teammates by first names only or face a sacrifice. Stepping over the starting line violates rule #2; strictly enforce this rule.

▷ Possible Solutions

Group members swing over the canyon one at a time. The group should recognize that its best swingers should go first and last. The group also should recognize that if it has trouble getting a particular person across, the next person should be one who can easily cross the canyon. In the event of a sacrifice, the group will become discouraged if it has to bring back members who had trouble crossing the canyon. Therefore, the group should send back its best swingers in the event of a sacrifice.

As we suggested before, the distance between canyon rims should be enough to require the group to plan how to help each other. The swinger, grasping the rope about shoulder height, needs a push from teammates to swing across the canyon. If the swinger does not make it across, he or she either swings back to the start or slides down the rope to

the floor. A swinger who successfully crosses the canyon assists other swingers onto the vaulting box. As more group members successfully cross the canyon, the helpers should support one another so that no one falls off that canyon rim. Do not allow careless swinging or other unsafe behavior.

The excitement of the challenge can cause group members to forget important strategy. Group members may jump off the vaulting box in anticipation of a required sacrifice. If group members step off the vaulting box, a sacrifice is required; they cannot just step back onto the vaulting box.

▷ Conclusion of the Task

The group completes the task when all group members are standing on the vaulting box, cheering and happy, of course. After you approve their success, have them listen as the recorder and the summarizer recognize the encouragement and praise that took place during the task.

▷ Additions and Variations

You may find that a student absolutely cannot swing across on the rope. Designate a student to swing in place of the nonswinger, who nonetheless becomes a helper on the vaulting box.

- Use a football blocking dummy to represent an injured group member who needs to be rescued.

- Eliminate the vaulting box for very young children and use a folded tumbling mat.

- Set a time limit for completing the task.

- Have group members begin the challenge by standing on a folded tumbling mat and grasping the rope higher than they would if standing on the floor.

▷ Safety Considerations

Cover floor area with mats. Use a vaulting box that cannot tip over. You might need to place a mat over the vaulting box to absorb the shock of team members swinging into the box if they do swing high enough to get on top of it. Participants can fall off the box if they do not help one another balance. Therefore, make sure that mats surround the box on all sides. Make sure that the swinging rope is in an area where team members will not swing into a wall.

Adapted, by permission, from D. Glover and D. Midura, 1992, *Team building through physical challenges* (Champaign, IL: Human Kinetics), 82.

Grand Canyon II

▷ Description

Grand Canyon II is an advanced challenge. It differs from Grand Canyon I both in its setup and in the complexity of teamwork required. Group members travel across an open space from one cliff to another using a climbing rope as the means to swing across the Grand Canyon.

The group transfers its members from one cliff to another. They attempt to swing across the open space between the cliffs and land safely on the second cliff. Group members need to assist one another in both the swinging process and the landing process. The placement of the rope in relationship to the first cliff determines the difficulty of this challenge.

▷ Success Criteria

The group masters the challenge when all group members have safely crossed the Grand Canyon and are standing on the second cliff.

▷ Equipment

You need one climbing rope for swinging and two large crash pads for the two cliffs (if you do not have crash pads, you may safely stack tumbling mats to create the two cliffs). You also need additional mats between the cliffs and over any floor space where the group may be working. When in doubt, mat the area.

▷ Setup

Set the first cliff almost directly under the climbing rope, perhaps 1 to 2 feet (30 to 60 centimeters) away. The closer the rope is to the cliff, the more difficult the challenge is. Locate the second cliff far enough away so that a person reaching it must

stretch to make it onto that cliff. This distance will vary depending on your gym space and the length of the rope. Cover the floor area with tumbling mats. Place additional mats around the cliffs to reduce risk of injury should someone fall off. If a cliff is near a wall, be sure to place crash pads against the wall so that if students swing into the wall space, they will not be hurt. See figure 9.4.

▷ Rules and Sacrifices

1. If a group member touches the floor (Grand Canyon), that person and one successful person must return to the first cliff.

2. If a group member falls off a cliff onto the floor, that person and one successful person must go back to the first cliff.

3. No one may use last names or put-downs.

▷ Possible Solutions

Although groups follow one basic pattern in solving this task, each group finds a unique challenge. The group begins by trying to find one person who can make it across the canyon and safely land on the second cliff. This process often takes a while. The group must find an efficient method to swing group members. Those who make it to the second cliff should help their teammates as they land there. The group must also carefully choose the last person to swing across because that person will have to cross the canyon without benefit of a push or other help. Balance is important because the group works off both cliffs. Carelessness will cause people to step off the cliffs, thus requiring the group to make a sacrifice. In addition, group members must make good choices in their sacrifices. If possible, they

Figure 9.4   Grand Canyon II setup.

Adapted, by permission, from D. Midura and D. Glover, 1995, *More team building challenges* (Champaign, IL: Human Kinetics), 51.

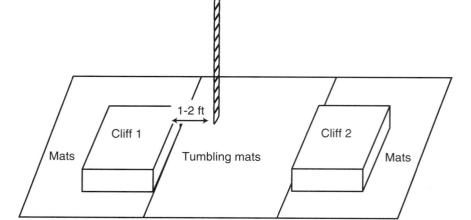

should not sacrifice people who were difficult to get across the canyon.

▷ Conclusion of the Task

The group completes the challenge when all the group members have successfully made it across the canyon. They must all be standing on the second cliff (and they will be cheering wildly).

▷ Additions and Variations

The placement of the first cliff and the distance to the second cliff determine the difficulty of this challenge. Make this task tough. The group should struggle. If you have a group member who needs a special adaptation, feel free to make an exception to the rules. A tire placed in the canyon could serve as a resting place or stepping-stone. Do not allow the entire group to use the adaptation.

▷ Safety Considerations

Participants need to take care while swinging on the rope. A person may possibly swing into a teammate. If a person jumps off the rope and lands poorly, he or she could twist an ankle or knee joint. Teammates who push people on the rope need to use good judgment and not swing the rope too hard or carelessly. They must not swing a teammate in a direction that could take the person into a wall.

Reprinted, by permission, from D. Midura and D. Glover, 1995, *More team building challenges* (Champaign, IL: Human Kinetics, 50-53).

Spider's Web

▷ Description

This challenge seems to have been around forever. Spider's Web can be done outside or indoors. You can make your own equipment or buy a commercially made frame with stretch (bungee) cords that snap in place to make the web design. The goal of this challenge is to get each team member through the spider's web without touching any part of it. An additional requirement is that each group member must pass through a different opening in the web.

The group begins on one side of the spider's web. The challenge is to get every group member through the web to the other side. Group members can help one another in a variety of ways. They must all pass through the web without touching it, and each must choose a different hole in the web to pass through. An exception is that a group member may use a space originally used by a teammate who had to start over because he or she broke a rule.

▷ Success Criteria

The group completes the challenge when all group members are standing on the opposite side of the spider's web from where they began the challenge.

▷ Equipment

You need either the commercially made spider's web (from Gopher Sport) or a web that you build using string, stretch cords, or sash cord material. The number of openings in the web should exceed the number of group members. You should cover the floor area with tumbling mats. You may wish to add small bells that ring if anyone touches the spider's web. Groups can do this challenge on a playground area that has pea gravel, wood chips, or deep sand as a safety base. Groups have also done the challenge outdoors in winter with a snow base.

▷ Setup

Create the spider's web so that group members can pass through a number of openings and shapes as they attempt to move from one side of the web to the other. The openings should be large enough so that participants have a reasonable chance of getting through the hole. Make sure that the support base is safe by using tumbling mats or crash pads or, for an outdoor web, be sure that the materials beneath the web are adequate to prevent anyone from getting hurt by a fall to the ground.

Photo courtesy of Gopher Sport.

▷ Rules and Sacrifices

1. Each group member must pass through a different opening in the spider's web.

2. No one may touch any part of the web with his or her body.

3. Group members may reach through the web to help a teammate, but they may not touch the web.

4. No one may dive through an opening.

5. The group may not toss anyone through an opening.

6. No one may call others by their last names or use put-downs.

7. If a group member breaks a rule, that person and a successful teammate must start the task again.

8. If bells are hung from the spider's web, a sacrifice will be necessary if the bell makes a sound.

▷ Possible Solutions

This challenge has a basic solution. Group members attempt to find the holes that are the easiest to pass through. Teammates should physically assist each other as they pass through the openings. As in the Black Hole challenge, no one may dive through the openings, and groups cannot toss anyone through. If the group lifts a group member off the ground to pass that person through an opening, those doing the lifting must make a commitment to that person's safety. If the spider's web is built outdoors or in a manner that would allow a group member to go under the web, you may wish to prohibit anyone from passing under the web or possibly allow only one person to use that path.

▷ Conclusion of the Task

The group completes the challenge when all group members are on the opposite side of the spider's web from where they started.

▷ Additions and Variations

We offer no additions or variations for this task.

▷ Safety Considerations

As with the Black Hole challenge, do not allow participants to dive through openings. If group members plan to lift and pass teammates through openings in the spider's web, those doing the lifting need to make a safety commitment to the people they are lifting. The group may not throw a teammate through an opening, even if that person suggests the idea or volunteers to be thrown.

Neutral Zone

▷ Description

The Neutral Zone is one of the few advanced challenges created in one of our graduate team-building classes. Although the concept for solving this challenge is simple, the execution of the solution is difficult. The students who helped create this challenge built their own equipment, although we have learned that the equipment is now commercially manufactured.

This challenge bears some similarities to the Stepping-Stones challenges in that group members must change places during the task. The added level of difficulty occurs because group members balance on a teeter-totter device. The board on which the group balances may not touch the floor (or tumbling mats) while the group performs the challenge.

▷ Success Criteria

The group completes the challenge when the group members on one side of the balance board cross the neutral zone and change sides with the group members on the other side of the balance board. Neither the team members nor the balance board may touch the ground during the course of the challenge.

▷ Equipment

The challenge requires a balance board, balanced on a fulcrum. Marked on the board should be numbered placements for group members. In addition, an area in the middle of the balance board should be identified as the neutral zone. Cover the floor with tumbling mats throughout the working area.

▷ Setup

Place tumbling mats around the neutral-zone equipment on tumbling mats. Surround the entire working area with tumbling mats.

▷ Rules and Sacrifices

1. No one may touch the ground (or mats) during the challenge.
2. The balance board may not touch the ground during the challenge.
3. No one may call others by their last names or use put-downs.
4. Group members may step on the fulcrum when changing positions.
5. If the group breaks a rule, it must start the challenge from the beginning.

▷ Possible Solutions

Teammates must constantly communicate and agree to all team movements. All movements should be done slowly and with assistance from teammates.

▷ Conclusion of the Task

The group completes the challenge when its members are balanced on opposite sides of the neutral-zone balance board.

▷ Additions and Variations

Because this challenge is so difficult to perform, we have not seen the need to create many variations. We have tried having group members change places so that they line up in exact reverse order from their starting positions. For example, when starting in the order 4-3-2-1-1-2-3-4, team members must trade places with the same numbered person. This variation adds difficulty to the challenge and may not warrant the extra time needed to work through the sacrifices. We have also experimented with the idea of not allowing team members to step on the neutral-zone fulcrum. This variation also adds significantly to the difficulty of attaining the solution. Because teams with advanced skills or teams that need a higher level of difficulty will be performing this challenge, allowing adaptations to make the challenge easier will probably not be necessary. One idea would be to allow a group a specified number of touches or errors (such as three) before it must make a sacrifice.

▷ Safety Considerations

If a group member loses his or her balance in this challenge, he or she may try to hang on to a teammate and cause both to fall. If group members fall quickly or carelessly, the neutral-zone board and fulcrum could slip out of position. The group should be aware that fast or impulsive movements could cause the balance board to crash down just as a teeter-totter does when a person at one end abandons his or her partner.

Marble Twist and Turn

▷ Description

This challenge should be a New Year's Eve party game. Our college and elementary education students really loved this challenge. We think that it will become a favorite of yours as well. This challenge is adaptable for all ages. You can make it easy or extremely difficult.

Students try to pass three marbles from one end of a tube to the other. Teammates must watch the marbles and communicate to others where they are at all times. Teammates can also physically assist each other.

▷ Success Criteria

The group completes the challenge when all three marbles have passed through the entire length of the tube and out the other end.

▷ Equipment

You need one twist and turn marble racetrack and three marbles. You can buy the marble twist and turn tube through sporting-goods catalogs such as Gopher Sport.

▷ Setup

Arrange the team of six students in a long straight line along the length of the tube, which should be lying on the floor, stretched out to its full length. Each student attaches a waist belt. After attaching the waist belts, students attach left arm straps and

the right leg straps. Now, all six teammates are connected to the tube by three straps with about 2 feet (60 centimeters) of tube between students. The teacher or a team member puts one marble into the tube, and the first team member attempts to pass it to the second team member. After the second team member has successfully passed the marble to the third team member, the first team member starts the second marble. This sequence continues until each team member has passed all three marbles and the marbles come out the other end of the tube.

▷ Rules and Sacrifices

1. Team members may not touch the tube with their hands.

2. The team must pass three marbles through the entire length of the tube without letting the marbles touch.

3. No one may call others by their last names or use put-downs.

4. The first team member may place the marble inside the tube and momentarily hold the tube to insert the marble.

5. Teammates may physically assist one another.

6. If the group breaks any rule, all three marbles must be returned to the first teammate and the challenge starts again from the beginning.

▷ Possible Solutions

The way the challenge is described, students must vary the height of their arms and legs to keep the marble moving. One teammate may have to get lower to receive the marble and then stand tall once in possession of the marble. The marble is difficult to see. Teammates must help one another by spotting the marble and communicating. Also, when a marble becomes stuck, team members may move the tube with their feet. They can touch the tube with any part of the body but the hands. Team members may physically assist one another as well as communicate directions orally.

▷ Conclusion of the Task

The group completes the challenge when all three marbles have passed through the tube without touching one another.

▷ Additions and Variations

- The easiest variation is to connect at the waist and both arms. Use your imagination and have students connect other parts of the body to the tube, for example, arm, waist, and knee, or knee, waist, and knee. To make the challenge more difficult, have students go completely around the waist.
- Time the challenge.

▷ Safety Considerations

This challenge does not present any dangerous physical risks. No group is likely to choose a solution that would create special safety issues.

Reprinted, by permission, from D. Glover and L. Anderson, 2003, *Character education* (Champaign, IL: Human Kinetics), 230.

Thinking Outside the Dots

▷ Description

Thinking Outside the Dots was the result of a couple of our students taking a children's brainteaser activity and turning it into a team-building challenge. When used in a classroom setting, this activity requires the student to connect nine dots using four straight lines without lifting the pencil off the paper.

The group attempts to connect ropes in a straight-line manner so that the ropes pass over all nine poly spots set on the floor.

▷ Success Criteria

The group is successful when it connects all nine dots with no more than four rope (line) segments.

▷ Equipment

- Nine poly spots or bases
- Four long jump ropes

▷ Setup

Create a three-by-three patterned square with the bases approximately 6 feet (180 centimeters) apart. Lay the ropes on the floor to one side of the square.

▷ Rules and Sacrifices

1. Team members may tie ropes together.
2. The team must suspend the ropes above the bases without touching the floor or bases during all attempts.
3. The rope may pass over a base more than once, but no part of the rope may overlap.
4. If any part of the rope touches the floor, the attempt fails and the team must begin the task again.
5. If the team creates more than four line segments, the attempt fails.

6. With each failed attempt, the team must start the task over with one fewer teammate being allowed to speak.

7. No one may call others by their last names or use put-downs.

▷ Possible Solutions

Although the common solution is similar to the paper-and-pencil solution, visualizing the solution while holding onto the ropes complicates the challenge. Keeping the ropes off the ground creates a much greater challenge than allowing the ropes to lie on the ground and poly spots.

▷ Conclusion of the Task

The ropes will be stretched in such a manner that they will go over (cover) each of the dots placed on the floor.

▷ Additions and Variations

- To simplify the challenge, allow the ropes to lie on the ground and touch the bases.
- To make the challenge more difficult, spread the bases farther apart. You will need longer ropes for this variation.
- If a group gets completely stuck, give them paper and pencils to help them discover the solution.

▷ Safety Considerations

This challenge presents no safety concerns.

Character Development and Community-Building Challenges

The challenges in this chapter give participants a chance to practice moral behavior and caring behavior. Caring is a character education concept that teachers should provide to all students by giving them examples of how people care about one another, such as giving to charities and helping neighbors. But team building gives students a chance to practice caring by supporting their teammates during a physical challenge. The process emphasizes and enhances tolerance and respect for teammates before and during a challenge. Students learn to listen to one another's ideas and to encourage and praise. The character education and community-building challenges in this chapter allow team members to practice these values.

Building Blocks

▷ Description

Building Blocks is a challenge that has numerous variations and solutions. It was created by Doug Hicks and Bobbie Bigwood during one of our Saint Mary's University classes. Refer to Additions and Variations before deciding which methods you might use. This task does not require a large space, and it uses a simple concept for the needed equipment. You can do this challenge in a classroom setting.

The group works together to build a tower of eight character education colored boxes using at least two different methods. In one method half of the team members are blindfolded. Each sighted team member works with a blindfolded teammate. In this part of the challenge, the sighted group member is able to speak only to his or her blindfolded partner. The sighted team member may not touch the character education block; only the blindfolded teammate may lift a block. No one block is designated as the first, or starting, block. During the second part of the challenge, group members still have partners, but no one is blindfolded. Each set of partners must stack its block or blocks using a completely different method for each block in the stack. The partners must lift the block together.

▷ Success Criteria

The team masters the challenge when the blocks are standing as a vertical tower, without the boxes falling. Groups do the challenge using two different methods.

▷ Equipment

The group needs eight 15-inch (38-centimeter) square boxes. Each box should have a character education term printed on its side. If possible, use colors on the boxes so that each block is different. If placing blindfolds on team members is part of the challenge, provide at least one blindfold for every pair of participants.

▷ Setup

Provide group members with boxes lying randomly on the floor. The working area does not need to be large, but the ceiling should be high enough that the boxes do not touch it when stacked vertically.

▷ Rules and Sacrifices

1. If the tower falls at any time, the group must start again with all boxes lying on the floor.

2. Only blindfolded team members may lift the building blocks as the group builds the tower during the first part of the challenge. Sighted group members may not touch a block.

3. Sighted team members may speak only to their blindfolded partners.

4. If a team member breaks rule #2 or #3, the group begins again with all blocks lying on the floor.

5. Once a block is placed on the tower, the sighted and blindfolded teammates that placed it there must give the correct definition of the character education term printed on it. If they cannot give the correct definition, the entire team must dismantle the tower and begin again.

6. In the second part of the challenge, team members must lift every block using a different method or by using different body parts. Partners must lift the block together. If any set of partners repeats a method, the team must rebuild the entire tower.

7. In the second part of the challenge, every group member may talk.

8. No one may call others by their last names or use put-downs.

▷ Possible Solutions

During the first part of the challenge, team members may try to throw blocks to the top of the tower. This difficult method will likely result in failure. Success will more likely come from building a few smaller towers and then adding these on top of one another. Groups will find it difficult to figure how to make orderly progress when group members can speak only to their partners and not to other group mem-

bers. Partners should also consult with other team members and agree on the definition of the character term they placed on the tower.

During the second part of the challenge, group members will need to figure out the best ways to lift the blocks as the challenge develops. If two partners lift the first block using both hands, no one will be able to use two hands again for the rest of the task. Therefore, saving this method for the very last move would be a good strategy. The best solution may be to make two stacks of four blocks each and then lift one stack using both hands of two partners onto another stack of four boxes.

▷ Conclusion of the Task

The group completes the task when it has successfully built a vertical tower of blocks using two different methods of construction, and all character education terms were defined correctly.

▷ Additions and Variations

- Have students stack the boxes without using their hands or otherwise limit the use of certain body parts.
- Have students stack the boxes using a specific color or character education word order.
- Allow only one sighted group member to give directions.
- Use letters or numbers on each box and create math or spelling games with the solutions.
- This challenge can be done without character education terms.

▷ Safety Considerations

As with all challenges using blindfolds, do not allow blindfolded team members to wander from the group or trip over the boxes. Because the boxes are light, it is unlikely that a falling box would injure anyone, but you should instruct blindfolded participants to cover their heads if the tower falls.

Lean on Me

▷ Description

Lean on Me is a unique challenge in that a very large group can attempt it. We have had groups as large as 36 do this task. The group holds onto a rope that is formed into a circle. The rope can be from 50 to 75 feet (15 to 23 meters) long. Tie the ends of the rope together so that the group can form the circle. The group lets go of the rope by twos until the fewest number of people remaining can support the rope off the ground without moving their feet or bending their elbows.

After someone has tied the ends of the rope together so that the group can make a circle with it, group member space themselves evenly around the rope. They then step backward until the rope is taut. Every group member holds onto the rope with two hands, elbows held straight. Each group member has memorized either a character education word or a character education definition. Group members have to decide which two should let go of the rope and when they should release it. Only matching group members may let go of the rope. For instance, a student with a character education word may not let go until the group comes up with the correct definition. After the group provides the definition, matching group members may let go. The group continues to release matching pairs until the remaining group members can no longer support the rope, the rope touches the ground, or someone moves his or her feet.

▷ Success Criteria

The group has a predetermined number of attempts to see how many matching pairs can let go of the rope until only two or four group members are left supporting it.

▷ Equipment

- You will need a very long rope, such as a tug-of-war rope or a long sash cord rope. The rope will need to have the ends tied together so that it can be formed into a circle.
- If possible, provide enough vinyl bases or poly spots so that each group member has a clearly defined standing space.
- Every team member needs a card with a character education word, such as *respect* or *honesty*, and a partner should have the definition for that word.

▷ Setup

Most likely, you will need a large open area, indoors or outdoors, in which to conduct this challenge. After group members hold onto the rope with their arms held straight, give each person a base on which to stand. Once they are on the bases, they cannot move off them until they have released the rope with their hands. Give each student a character education focus word or a character education definition. You should have an equal number of focus words and matching definitions.

▷ Rules and Sacrifices

1. Group members may not step off a base until they have released the rope with their hands.
2. Group members may not move their hands on the rope once they have started the task.
3. Group members must not bend their elbows while holding the rope.
4. The team must match a character education word and the definition before the team members with the focus word and the matching definition can step off. One set of team members steps off at a time.
5. No one may call others by their last names or use put-downs.

▷ Possible Solutions

Prior to the activity, the team should study the focus words and their definitions. The matching word and definition should be opposite one another so when they let go of the rope very slowly and carefully it will not throw others off balance.

▷ Conclusion of the Task

The challenge attempt is over when the rope hits the floor, when someone bends his or her elbows, when someone steps off a base before releasing the rope, or when the group feels that it has reached its limit. You may want to set a predetermined number of attempts at this challenge before the start of the task.

▷ Additions and Variations

We have not used any variations of this task other than to experiment with different numbers of participants.

▷ Safety Considerations

As with other challenges that use poly spots or vinyl bases, you should make sure that they stick to the floor so that participants cannot slip from their positions. Falling is a possibility if a group member loses his or her balance and cannot regain it.

Rainbow Swamp Trail DVD

▷ Description

This challenge uses minimal equipment but requires constant communication and physical support as the group attempts to solve the task.

Each member of the team must get to the other side of the swamp. Along the way each team member must retrieve a beanbag with a character education word and definition on it and take it with him or her to dry land. The group must plan a route through the bog on the stepping-stones. Some of the stepping-stones are slippery and can only hold one teammate. Students must be careful so that they don't fall into the swamp!

▷ Success Criteria

The team masters the challenge when all team members and all character education beanbags make it to the opposite shore.

▷ Equipment

- One dozen 12-inch (30-centimeter) poly spots (or bases)
- Six character education rainbow beanbags (beanbags of different colors), available through Gopher Sport

▷ Setup

Designate a starting line and a finish line. The swamp is the area between the two lines, which should be about 15 feet (4.5 meters) apart. Place the poly spots in a parallel line formation between the starting line and the finish line.

The poly spots (stepping-stones) should be about one giant step apart. The distance will vary with the age of your students, from up to 4 feet (120 centimeters) apart for middle school and down to 18 inches (45 centimeters) for first graders. Place the six beanbags near poly spots #2, #3, #5, #7, #9, and #10. The beanbags should be from 2 to 4 feet (60 to 120 centimeters) away from the poly spots, depending on the age and size of your students. A person 5 feet (150 centimeters) tall can get a beanbag 4 feet (120 centimeters) away without stepping off the spot but needs a lot of support to reach it. Here is a suggested list of distances for a group of sixth graders:

- Place a yellow character education beanbag 3 feet (90 centimeters) away from poly spot #2.
- Place a red character education beanbag 2 feet (60 centimeters) away from poly spot #3.

- Place a green character education beanbag 4 feet (120 centimeters) away from poly spot #5.
- Place an orange character education beanbag 3.5 feet (105 centimeters) away from poly spot #7.
- Place a blue character education beanbag 2 feet (60 centimeters) away from poly spot #9.
- Place a purple character education beanbag 4 feet (120 centimeters) away from poly spot #10.

▷ Rules and Sacrifices

1. The team must hold hands and stay connected throughout its trip through the swamp. A team member who is attempting to pick up a beanbag may let go of one other teammate's hand but must rejoin hands before moving to another base.

2. No one may touch the floor during the trip through the swamp. If a team member breaks either rule #1 or rule #2, the group must start the task from the beginning.

3. Each team member must collect one beanbag on the journey and take it across the swamp. The beanbag cannot be dropped. If it is dropped, the beanbag must be replaced to its original position and retrieved again.

4. Team members must read the character education word and give the definition after they retrieve the bag.

5. No one may call others by their last names or use put-downs.

▷ Possible Solutions

The team must discuss which team member should get which beanbag. The taller teammates should get the beanbags that are the farthest away. The team will also have to figure out how best to assist students who cannot easily reach their beanbags. Team members must move slowly and communicate constantly to avoid pulling a teammate off a stepping-stone.

▷ Conclusion of the Task

The team completes the challenge when all team members and all beanbags are on the shore beyond the finish line.

▷ Additions and Variations

- Make one base a slippery base. Only one foot at a time is allowed to touch this base.
- Require the team to be silent except for one person who will direct the team.
- Time the team to set a course record.

▷ Safety Considerations

Set down the poly spots or bases with tape backing so that they do not slide. If group members begin to fall and do not let go of one another's hands, a number of people could lose their balance. The group should discuss the difference between trying to hold someone up and allowing the group to break apart so that the whole group does not fall.

Reprinted, by permission, from D. Glover and L. Anderson, 2003, *Character education* (Champaign, IL: Human Kinetics), 133.

Integrity Tower

▷ Description

This brand new challenge further connects character education and team building. Students must work together to build a tower of bricks. The bricks are made of foam and are labeled *character, respect, sportsmanship, judgment, pride,* and *integrity*. The task will be extremely difficult for elementary-age children, but middle school students may find it easy to master.

The students must transport the foam blocks with a partner and build a tower at the designated site located 20 to 30 feet (6 to 9 meters) away. The bricks should be spread out on the floor with the team around the blocks. Team members must figure out how to transport the blocks to the building site and then figure out how they will work together to build the tower.

▷ Success Criteria

The team achieves success when it stacks the bricks to create the type of tower that the teacher requested.

▷ Equipment

Provide six foam bricks labeled *character, respect, sportsmanship, judgment, pride,* and *integrity*. These bricks are available from Gopher Sport.

▷ Setup

Place the bricks on the floor. Designate a building site 20 to 30 feet (6 to 9 meters) away. The students must figure out how to transport the bricks to the building site. Once they get the bricks to the site, they must figure out how they will work together in order to build the tower.

▷ Rules and Sacrifices

1. Two teammates must transport each brick. Each set of partners may transport only one brick at a time.

2. Group members may not touch the bricks with their hands, nor can the bricks ever touch the ground except for the character brick, which must be the first brick transported. All other bricks will be built on the character brick.

3. The group must transport each brick using a different combination of body parts. No set of partners can transport a brick in the same method that other teammates did. For example, the first set of partners may use the elbows, the second set of partners may use the knees, and so on.

4. One set of partners may not help another set during the transport phase of the challenge. Team members may, however, help teammates stack the bricks on the tower, as long as they don't use their hands. The teammates who transported the brick must still be the principal stackers. They cannot relinquish control of the brick, but teammates may assist them by steadying the tower or balancing a brick while it is being placed.

5. The group places the integrity brick last.

6. No one may use put-downs or call others by their last names.

7. If the group breaks any rule, it must take all bricks back to the starting point and start the challenge from the beginning.

▷ Possible Solutions

Team members first need to decide who will work together as partners and then discuss how they will transport the bricks so that each set of partners uses a different method. After moving the bricks to the building site, team members need to help one another stack the bricks. Teammates who are finished transporting should assist those who are attempting to stack a brick.

▷ Conclusion of the Task

The team masters the challenge when the tower is complete and stable within the building site.

▷ Additions and Variations

- Make the students go over and under an obstacle while transporting.
- Have students design and build different types of towers.
- Require the team to place the bricks so that the character education words are all facing the same direction.

▷ Safety Considerations

Generally, no safety considerations are associated with this challenge. If students walk backward, teammates should warn them if an object is placed where they could trip.

Reprinted, by permission, from D. Glover and L. Anderson, 2003, *Character education* (Champaign, IL: Human Kinetics), 138.

Appendix

CHALLENGE CARD DVD
The Great Communicator

Equipment

A pencil and one piece of paper per drawing for each group member, a picture to describe, and a clipboard on which to put the picture for the Great Communicator.

Starting Position

The group sits in a semicircle or random pattern in front of the Great Communicator.

Our Challenge

Each group member attempts to draw a picture from the descriptions given by the Great Communicator.

Rules and Sacrifices

This challenge has no sacrifices. Group members may not ask the Great Communicator any questions.

ORGANIZER CARD DVD
The Great Communicator

Questions

1. What equipment do we use?
2. What is our starting position?
3. What can we ask the Great Communicator?

From *Essentials of Team Building* by Daniel W. Midura and Donald R. Glover, 2005, Champaign, IL: Human Kinetics.

Reprinted, by permission, from D. Midura and D. Glover, 1995, *More team building challenges* (Champaign, IL: Human Kinetics), Appendix B.

CHALLENGE CARD

 DVD

Construction Zone

Equipment

One to four blindfolds and a construction puzzle or puzzles.

Starting Position

The sighted group members mix up the puzzle. The blindfolded group members sit in the construction zone.

Our Challenge

The blindfolded construction workers assemble the puzzle while receiving oral instructions from the sighted group members.

Rules and Sacrifices

1. Only the blindfolded team members may touch the puzzle pieces. If sighted members touch the puzzle pieces, the group must mix up the puzzle again and start from the beginning.

2. The sighted group members may not physically touch the blindfolded group members. If they do, the group must mix up the puzzle and start from the beginning.

3. Blindfolded group members may remove blindfolds when the puzzle has been completed.

4. No one may use put-downs or last names.

ORGANIZER CARD

 DVD

Construction Zone

Questions

1. What equipment do we use?

2. What happens if a sighted group member touches a blindfolded construction worker?

3. What happens if a sighted group member touches a puzzle piece?

4. When can the blindfolded construction workers remove their blindfolds?

5. Can you think of any safety issues that we should discuss?

From *Essentials of Team Building* by Daniel W. Midura and Donald R. Glover, 2005, Champaign, IL: Human Kinetics.

CHALLENGE CARD

 DVD

Geography Masters

Equipment

A map of the United States and a U.S. puzzle.

Starting Position

The group finds an open space where it can construct the puzzle.

Our Challenge

The group completes the task when it constructs the puzzle without using oral communication.

Rules and Sacrifices

1. No one may use oral communication (talking, throat noises, coughing, or any other sound coming from the mouth or throat).
2. If the group breaks rule #1, it must mix up the puzzle and start the task from the beginning.

ORGANIZER CARD

 DVD

Geography Masters

Questions

1. What equipment do we use?
2. What kinds of communication are we not allowed to use?
3. What kinds of communication may we use?
4. What happens if we break rule #1?
5. Can you think of any safety issues that we should discuss?

From *Essentials of Team Building* by Daniel W. Midura and Donald R. Glover, 2005, Champaign, IL: Human Kinetics.

CHALLENGE CARD DVD

General Hospital Emergency Room

Equipment

The challenge uses a Gopher Sport skeleton puzzle. Blindfolds are necessary to do the optional challenge.

Starting Position

The team gathers around the puzzle pieces. The puzzle will be stacked up randomly or mixed up in a box.

Our Challenge

The group constructs the puzzle so that all the pieces form a human skeleton.

Rules and Sacrifices

1. Sighted group members may not touch the puzzle pieces.
2. Sighted group members may not touch the blindfolded group members.
3. The group cannot use any form of oral communication.
4. If group members break any rule, they must mix up the puzzle pieces and start the task from the beginning.

ORGANIZER CARD DVD

General Hospital Emergency Room

Questions

1. What equipment do we get?
2. What are we constructing?
3. What happens if we break rule #1 or #2?
4. Can you think of any safety issues that we should discuss?

From *Essentials of Team Building* by Daniel W. Midura and Donald R. Glover, 2005, Champaign, IL: Human Kinetics.

CHALLENGE CARD

 DVD

Atom Transfer

Equipment

The Atom Transfer equipment shown on this page.

Starting Position

Group members stand around the Atom Transfer ring and post. Each group member holds at least one handle. The ring must be touching the base of the post.

Our Challenge

The group must lift the atom (ball) off its resting post, carry it to the second post, and set the ball on the second post without allowing the ball to touch the floor or fall off the transfer ring.

Rules and Sacrifices

1. Each group member must hold at least one rope handle.

2. The ball must not fall off the transfer ring or resting post.

3. The ball may not touch the floor or a person.

4. The ball may not fall off the post until after the group has placed the transfer ring on the floor.

5. No one may use last names or put-downs.

6. If the group breaks a rule, it must slip the transfer device over the first post and onto the floor, set the atom back on the post, and start again.

From *Essentials of Team Building* by Daniel W. Midura and Donald R. Glover, 2005, Champaign, IL: Human Kinetics.

175

ORGANIZER CARD

 DVD

Atom Transfer

Questions

1. What equipment do we get?

2. Where do we place the atom (ball)?

3. What happens if the ball touches the floor?

4. What happens if a group member holds any part of the rope other than the handle?

5. Can you think of any safety issues that we should discuss?

CHALLENGE CARD

 DVD

Riverboat

Equipment

Two folded tumbling mats, two small tires, and two jump ropes.

Starting Position

All group members begin at one end of the gym.

Our Challenge

Using the designated equipment, the group travels from one end of the gym to the other end without touching the floor (river).

Rules and Sacrifices

1. If a group member touches the floor, the entire group must go back to the starting position.
2. The group must take all equipment across the river.
3. The mats must remain folded. If the riverboat falls apart, the group starts over.
4. If the mat crashes to the floor (the riverboat explodes) and makes a loud noise, the group returns to the starting line.

ORGANIZER CARD

 DVD

Riverboat

Questions

1. Where are the beginning and end lines of the river?
2. What happens if someone touches the river?
3. What must we do with the equipment?
4. What happens if the mat crashes to the floor?
5. What happens if the mat falls apart while we are moving it?
6. Can you think of any safety issues that we should discuss?

From *Essentials of Team Building* by Daniel W. Midura and Donald R. Glover, 2005, Champaign, IL: Human Kinetics.

Reprinted, by permission, from D. Midura and D. Glover, 1995, *More team building challenges* (Champaign, IL: Human Kinetics), Appendix B.

CHALLENGE CARD

 DVD

Swamp Machine

Equipment

Four standard tumbling mats (two for each land space), one 6-foot-by-12-foot (1.8-meter-by-3.6-meter) UCS tumbling mat for the swamp machine, and a large open space for the swamp.

Starting Position

All group members begin on the first land space with the swamp machine.

Our Challenge

The group completes the challenge when all group members are standing on the second land space along with the swamp machine.

Rules and Sacrifices

1. If a group member touches the floor (swamp), that person and one successful person must go back to the first land space.

2. If the swamp machine falls apart, there is no sacrifice, but if the group members in the swamp cannot repair it, the entire group must return to the first land space.

3. No group member may take more than two consecutive trips across the swamp. If a group member does so, that person and a person from the second land space must return to the first land space.

4. Two, three, or four teammates must always be in the swamp machine as it crosses the swamp. If one or more than four members occupy the swamp machine, the entire group must begin the task again.

5. No one may use last names or put-downs.

ORGANIZER CARD

 DVD

Swamp Machine

Questions

1. What happens if a group member touches the floor?

2. What happens if the swamp machine falls apart?

3. What happens if we cannot repair the swamp machine while it is in the swamp?

4. What happens if a group member takes more than two consecutive trips across the swamp?

5. How many group members must travel in the swamp machine?

6. Can you think of any safety issues that we should discuss?

From *Essentials of Team Building* by Daniel W. Midura and Donald R. Glover, 2005, Champaign, IL: Human Kinetics.

Reprinted, by permission, from D. Midura and D. Glover, 1995, *More team building challenges* (Champaign, IL: Human Kinetics), Appendix B.

CHALLENGE CARD

 DVD

The Whole World in Their Hands

Equipment

Two tires and one cage ball (or earth ball) 48 inches (120 centimeters) in diameter or larger.

Starting Position

The group gathers around the cage ball while the ball sits on the first tire.

Our Challenge

The group completes the task when it has moved the ball from tire to tire a total of four times, without allowing the ball to touch the floor. The group must move the ball in a new manner each time.

Rules and Sacrifices

1. The cage ball cannot touch the floor.
2. The cage ball cannot touch the hands or arms of any group member.
3. If a group member breaks a rule, the group must return the ball to the tire where it was last sitting and start again.
4. The group must successfully move the ball four times.
5. No one may call others by their last names or use put-downs.

ORGANIZER CARD

 DVD

The Whole World in Their Hands

Questions

1. What is our starting position?
2. Where do we put the cage ball?
3. What body parts cannot touch the ball?
4. What happens if the ball touches the floor?
5. What happens if we touch the ball with our hands or arms?
6. How many times do we move the ball from one tire to the other?
7. Can you think of any safety issues that we should discuss?

From *Essentials of Team Building* by Daniel W. Midura and Donald R. Glover, 2005, Champaign, IL: Human Kinetics.

Reprinted, by permission, from D. Glover and D. Midura, 1992, *Team building through physical challenges* (Champaign, IL: Human Kinetics), Appendix.

CHALLENGE CARD

 DVD

The Snake

Equipment

One tug-of-war rope.

Starting Position

All group members begin near the center of the assigned working space with the tug-of-war rope.

Our Challenge

The group makes six to eight specific shapes (letters, numbers, and figures) using the tug-of-war rope. When they make the shape, group members must use their bodies to cover the entire rope. The teacher assigns the shapes or the group creates them.

Rules and Sacrifices

1. The group must use the rope as a guide to make the shapes.
2. All group members must lie on the rope.
3. Group members must completely cover the rope.
4. The teacher must approve each shape before the group creates the next one.
5. No one may call others by their last names or use put-downs.

ORGANIZER CARD

 DVD

The Snake

Questions

1. What equipment do we use?
2. How many shapes do we make?
3. What do we do with the rope?
4. Who has to be on the rope?
5. What do we do after the teacher approves the shape?
6. Can you think of any safety issues that we should discuss?

From *Essentials of Team Building* by Daniel W. Midura and Donald R. Glover, 2005, Champaign, IL: Human Kinetics.

Reprinted, by permission, from D. Glover and D. Midura, 1992, *Team building through physical challenges* (Champaign, IL: Human Kinetics), Appendix.

CHALLENGE CARD DVD

Tire Bridge

Equipment

One tire for each group member plus one extra tire.

Starting Position

The group starts on one side of the river (floor) with a stack of tires.

Our Challenge

The group completes the task by using the tire bridge to move from one side of the river to the other (across the river). The group must be on land with the tires stacked in a vertical stack.

Rules and Sacrifices

1. Only one person may be on a tire at a time.

2. If anyone touches the river with any body part, the group must move the bridge back behind the starting line.

3. If two people step on a tire at the same time, the group must start the task from the beginning.

4. The group does not complete the task until the tires are stacked in one vertical stack.

5. No one may call others by their last names or use put-downs.

ORGANIZER CARD DVD

Tire Bridge

Questions

1. Where are the river boundaries?

2. How many tires do we get?

3. What happens if someone touches the river (floor)?

4. What happens if two people step on a tire at the same time?

5. Where will we be when we are done with the task?

6. What will we do with the tires when we reach land?

7. Can you think of any safety issues that we should discuss?

From *Essentials of Team Building* by Daniel W. Midura and Donald R. Glover, 2005, Champaign, IL: Human Kinetics.

Reprinted, by permission, from D. Glover and D. Midura, 1992, *Team building through physical challenges* (Champaign, IL: Human Kinetics), Appendix.

CHALLENGE CARD

 DVD

Toxic Waste Transfer

Equipment

The challenge requires two containers—one with ropes attached and filled with small objects that represent toxic waste material and the other without ropes. (In addition, a box or backpack containing a work suit, boots, gloves, and a hat or helmet may be used.)

Starting Position

Group members stand around the first container, holding onto the ends of the ropes (some group members may have more than one rope).

Our Challenge

The group completes the task by transferring all the material from the first container into the second container without leaving any material on the floor.

Rules and Sacrifices

1. If the toxic waste container touches the floor, the entire group must start the task from the beginning.

2. If a group member touches any toxic waste from the first container without wearing the protective clothing, the group must start the task again.

3. If the toxic waste expert places the spilled contents into the wrong container, the group must go back to the starting place.

4. After a toxic waste cleanup, the group cannot continue the process until the expert has taken off all the protective clothing. The sacrifice is to start from the beginning.

5. The ropes may not touch the floor. If they do, the group must start from the beginning.

6. No one may touch the rope between the red tape mark and the container.

7. No one may use last names or put-downs.

ORGANIZER CARD

 DVD

Toxic Waste Transfer

Questions

1. What happens if the toxic waste container touches the floor?

2. What happens if someone touches toxic waste material without wearing the protective clothing?

3. In which container must we place any spilled material?

4. What happens if we touch a rope between the red line and the container?

5. What happens if the rope touches the floor?

6. Can you think of any safety issues that we should discuss?

From *Essentials of Team Building* by Daniel W. Midura and Donald R. Glover, 2005, Champaign, IL: Human Kinetics.

Reprinted, by permission, from D. Glover and D. Midura, 1992, *Team building through physical challenges* (Champaign, IL: Human Kinetics), Appendix.

CHALLENGE CARD
 DVD
The Rock

Equipment

Tumbling mats and one tire (the rock).

Starting Position

Group members stand on the tumbling mats next to the tire.

Our Challenge

The group completes the challenge when all group members balance on the rock (off the floor) for a slow count of "one-and-two-and-three-and-four-and-five."

Rules and Sacrifices

1. All group members must be off the floor.

2. All group members do not have to be touching the rock as long as they are off the floor.

3. Stepping on the rock and then touching the floor for even an instant means that the group must start over with no one touching the rock.

4. When group members have practiced a successful solution, they call the teacher to the working area to witness the solution.

5. No one may call others by their last names or use put-downs.

ORGANIZER CARD
 DVD
The Rock

Questions

1. What equipment do we use?

2. What happens if someone touches the floor after being on the rock?

3. How long do we have to stay on the rock?

4. Do we all have to be touching the rock?

5. Who does the counting for the task?

6. Can you think of any safety issues that we should discuss?

From *Essentials of Team Building* by Daniel W. Midura and Donald R. Glover, 2005, Champaign, IL: Human Kinetics.

Reprinted, by permission, from D. Glover and D. Midura, 1992, *Team building through physical challenges* (Champaign, IL: Human Kinetics), Appendix.

CHALLENGE CARD

 DVD

River Crossing

Equipment

Two scooters, one long jump rope, and two deck tennis rings.

Starting Position

All group members start on one side of the river. Place all equipment there.

Our Challenge

The group completes the task when all group members have crossed the river without touching the floor with any part of their bodies. They must take all equipment across the river.

Rules and Sacrifices

1. The river is the area between the end line and midcourt line of the basketball court.

2. If any part of a person's body touches the river (the floor), that person and one successful person (or the team member who has advanced the farthest) must start again.

3. If a person enters the river to retrieve equipment, the group must make a sacrifice.

4. The first person across the river cannot be sacrificed during the challenge; however, he or she cannot touch the river.

5. No one may use last names or put-downs.

ORGANIZER CARD

 DVD

River Crossing

Questions

1. What equipment do we use?

2. Where is the river?

3. What happens if a person touches the river?

4. Who cannot be sacrificed?

5. How will we know when we have completed the challenge?

6. Where must the equipment be at the end of the task?

7. Can you think of any safety issues that we should discuss?

From *Essentials of Team Building* by Daniel W. Midura and Donald R. Glover, 2005, Champaign, IL: Human Kinetics.

Reprinted, by permission, from D. Glover and D. Midura, 1992, *Team building through physical challenges* (Champaign, IL: Human Kinetics), Appendix.

CHALLENGE CARD

 DVD

Lifeline

Equipment

One tire, one tug-of-war rope, and two scooters.

Starting Position

The group starts on one side of the swamp with only one scooter. One scooter is upside down on the tire. The tug-of-war rope is across the swamp.

Our Challenge

The group completes the task when all group members cross the swamp without touching the swamp (floor).

Rules and Sacrifices

1. No one may touch the floor with any part of his or her body or clothes.

2. No one may stand on a scooter.

3. No one may call others by their last names or use put-downs.

4. If a group member breaks a rule, that person and one successful person (or the person who has advanced the farthest) must go back to the starting line. They may not take a scooter back with them unless it was the first scooter that the group used.

ORGANIZER CARD

 DVD

Lifeline

Questions

1. What are the boundaries of the swamp?

2. What equipment do we get?

3. What happens if a group member touches the swamp?

4. Where will we be when we complete the task?

5. Can you think of any safety issues that we should discuss?

From *Essentials of Team Building* by Daniel W. Midura and Donald R. Glover, 2005, Champaign, IL: Human Kinetics.

CHALLENGE CARD

 DVD

The Wall I

Equipment

A large crash pad or tall stack of tumbling mats with unfolded mats covering the floor under the wall.

Starting Position

All group members start on one side of the wall.

Our Challenge

The group completes the task when all group members cross over the wall and are on the other side.

Rules and Sacrifices

1. The wall (crash pad) must not fall over.
2. When group members climb over the wall, they may not hold the crash pad handles or ropes tied around the wall for support (group members who are not climbing may hold these objects to support the wall).
3. No one may step over the dividing line between the two sides.
4. If the wall falls over, the entire group must start over.
5. If a group member breaks rule #2 or #3, the person making the mistake and one successful person (across the wall) must start the task from the beginning.
6. No one may call others by their last names or use put-downs, or the entire group must start over.

ORGANIZER CARD

 DVD

The Wall I

Questions

1. What is our challenge?
2. What happens if someone steps over the dividing line?
3. What happens if the wall falls over?
4. What happens if someone holds onto the crash pad handles or ropes while climbing?
5. Where will we be when we have completed the task?
6. Can you think of any safety issues that we should discuss?

From *Essentials of Team Building* by Daniel W. Midura and Donald R. Glover, 2005, Champaign, IL: Human Kinetics.

Reprinted, by permission, from D. Glover and D. Midura, 1992, *Team building through physical challenges* (Champaign, IL: Human Kinetics), Appendix.

CHALLENGE CARD DVD
Magic Bases

Equipment

At least one 12-inch (30-centimeter-diameter) poly spot or base for each team member.

Starting Position

Group members all join hands before the lead person steps on the entry base.

Our Challenge

The group must successfully go through the figure-eight path without letting go of hands or touching the floor between the entry base and the exit base.

Rules and Sacrifices

1. The team must travel the figure-eight pattern holding hands. Hands may not come apart.

2. Team members may not touch the floor between the entry base and the exit base.

3. No more than four feet may be on one poly spot at a time.

4. No one may call others by their last names or use put-downs.

5. If a rule is broken, the entire group must start the task from the beginning.

ORGANIZER CARD DVD
Magic Bases

Questions

1. What equipment do we get?
2. Where is the entry base?
3. Where is the exit base?
4. What happens if our hands come apart?
5. What happens if a group member touches the floor between the entry base and the exit base?
6. When can we touch the floor?
7. Can we talk during the challenge?
8. Can you think of any safety issues that we should discuss?

From *Essentials of Team Building* by Daniel W. Midura and Donald R. Glover, 2005, Champaign, IL: Human Kinetics.

Reprinted, by permission, from D. Glover and L. Anderson, 2003, *Character education* (Champaign, IL: Human Kinetics), Appendix p. 226-227.

CHALLENGE CARD

 DVD

Geo Sphere

Equipment

One geo sphere and a holding container.

Starting Position

The geo sphere lies on the ground along with the container. The group must set up and balance the geo sphere in the container.

Our Challenge

Group members create paths to enter and exit the geo sphere. Each teammate must pass through the geo sphere without causing it to fall down or collapse. Each group member must create a unique (different) path to enter and exit the geo sphere.

Rules and Sacrifices

1. Team members travel through the geo sphere one at a time.

2. The geo sphere may not fall down or collapse, or the group starts over.

3. Teammates may help one another verbally and physically.

4. No one may hold onto the geo sphere.

5. No one may jump or dive through the geo sphere headfirst.

6. After a group member goes through a pathway, a second group member may not use that same sequence. Every path must be different.

7. No one may call others by their last names or use put-downs.

8. If any group member breaks a rule, the group must start over from the beginning.

ORGANIZER CARD

 DVD

Geo Sphere

Questions

1. What equipment do we get?
2. What path must we take?
3. Can we touch the geo sphere?
4. What happens if the geo sphere falls down?

5. Can we touch our teammates?
6. Are there any safety issues that we should discuss?

From *Essentials of Team Building* by Daniel W. Midura and Donald R. Glover, 2005, Champaign, IL: Human Kinetics.

Reprinted, by permission, from D. Glover and L. Anderson, 2003, *Character education* (Champaign, IL: Human Kinetics), Appendix p. 227-228.

CHALLENGE CARD

 DVD

Island Escape

Equipment

Five hula hoops or tires (to remain stationary), five balloons or 18-inch (45-centimeter) cones, six scooters, and five long jump ropes.

Starting Position

All group members begin at one end of the gym.

Our Challenge

The group must travel from island to island until all group members make it across the ocean. The group must leave one scooter, one balloon (or cone), and one jump rope at each island after the last person leaves that island.

Rules and Sacrifices

1. If a group member touches the floor, that person and the person who has advanced the farthest must return to the beginning.

2. If a sacrifice occurs after people are across the ocean, group members may take a scooter back to the start.

3. The group may not move the hula hoops.

4. The group may not skip an island. No group member may go two islands ahead (the group may not leave an empty island between group members). No one may touch the floor (ocean).

5. No one may call others by their last names or use put-downs.

ORGANIZER CARD

 DVD

Island Escape

Questions

1. What happens if someone touches the floor?

2. Can we move the hula hoops?

3. Can we skip islands?

4. What must we leave at each island as the last group member leaves that island?

5. Can you think of any safety issues that we should discuss?

From *Essentials of Team Building* by Daniel W. Midura and Donald R. Glover, 2005, Champaign, IL: Human Kinetics.

Reprinted, by permission, from D. Midura and D. Glover, 1995, *More team building challenges* (Champaign, IL: Human Kinetics), Appendix B.

CHALLENGE CARD DVD

Plunger Ball

Equipment

Five sets of tinikling poles, three basketballs, three deck tennis rings, four plungers (bathroom plungers), one plunger mounted on a 5- to 6-foot (150- to 180-centimeter) pole (such as a mop handle), and a large container (such as a custodial cart).

Starting Position

The group starts near the place where the basketballs are lying.

Our Challenge

The group must transfer each basketball across the five sets of poles to the basket at the far end of the basketball court. The group then must transfer the ball onto the tall plunger and into the basket. The ball must then fall into the custodial cart (or large container). While transferring the ball across the poles, the ball must be over the heads of the people manipulating the poles.

Rules and Sacrifices

1. If the ball touches the floor, the group must start again at the beginning.
2. If the ball touches any part of a group member's body, the ball must go back to the starting position. One exception is that the ball may roll over the hands of the people holding the poles.
3. Group members may hold onto only one plunger at a time. If a group member holds onto two plungers, the group must return the ball to the beginning position.
4. When the ball goes through the basket, it must fall into the large container. If it misses, the group must start again.
5. No one may use last names or put-downs.

ORGANIZER CARD DVD

Plunger Ball

Questions

1. Where is our starting position?
2. To which basket do we transfer the basketballs?
3. What do we use to lift the basketballs?
4. What happens if the basketballs touch the floor?
5. What happens if the basketballs touch any part of our bodies?
6. What is the exception to question #5?
7. What do we use to lift the ball into the basket?
8. Do we have to use the poles above our heads?
9. How many plungers can each group member hold at a time?
10. Can you think of any safety issues that we should discuss?

From *Essentials of Team Building* by Daniel W. Midura and Donald R. Glover, 2005, Champaign, IL: Human Kinetics.

Reprinted, by permission, from D. Midura and D. Glover, 1995, *More team building challenges* (Champaign, IL: Human Kinetics), Appendix B.

CHALLENGE CARD
 DVD

The Maze

Equipment

Sixteen or 25 poly spots or bases to set up into a square grid with an equal number in each row.

Starting Position

Group members begin at a designated poly spot or base, usually at one corner of the grid. The instructor has a copy of the correct route through the maze.

Our Challenge

The group must learn the path through the maze from the beginning spot to the exit position. Moves will be forward, sideways, or diagonal. Group members cannot move backward (meaning that they cannot move back to a previous spot). They must step on each spot or base that is part of the path. All group members must go through the maze after the group has discovered the path. In the second maze, group members may not use any form of oral communication while trying to discover the path.

Rules and Sacrifices

1. If a group member steps on the wrong base, that person's turn ends, he or she goes back to the line, and the next group member begins.

2. Once a person steps off a base, it is considered a move.

3. No one may step back to a previous base.

4. After making it successfully through the path, a group member does not have to repeat the path if a teammate makes a mistake. Upon successful completion of the maze, that group member is done.

5. When attempting the second maze, no one may use any form of oral communication. If this happens, the person moving through the maze must step off the path and let the next person begin.

6. No one may use last names or put-downs. If this happens, the person traveling through the maze must step off the path and let the next person begin.

ORGANIZER CARD
 DVD

The Maze

Questions

1. What happens if a group member makes an incorrect move?

2. What happens if a group member moves back to a previous spot (a backward move)?

3. What is it considered if a group member steps off a base or spot?

4. Do all group members have to go successfully through the maze?

5. When working on the second maze, what happens if a group member uses any form of oral communication?

6. Can you think of any safety issues that we should discuss?

From *Essentials of Team Building* by Daniel W. Midura and Donald R. Glover, 2005, Champaign, IL: Human Kinetics.

Reprinted, by permission, from D. Glover and L. Anderson, 2003, *Character education* (Champaign, IL: Human Kinetics), Appendix p. 224-225.

CHALLENGE CARD
Stepping-Stones I

Equipment

One base for each group member and one extra base.

Starting Position

All group members stand on one base, leaving an open base at one end of the line. Group members number off so that each person knows where to begin and where to end the challenge.

Our Challenge

The group completes the task when group members are in exact reverse order from the starting order, as in the following example.
Starting position: 1, 2, 3, 4, 5, 6, 7, 8
Ending position: 8, 7, 6, 5, 4, 3, 2, 1

Rules and Sacrifices

1. Only one person may touch a base at a time.
2. A person may move in either direction to a neighboring base.
3. Group members may touch a new base only if it is empty.
4. The bases may not be moved.
5. Group members must wear shoes.
6. If more than one person touches a base, the entire group must start over.
7. No one may call others by their last names or use put-downs.
8. If anyone touches the floor, the group must start over.

	(Seth)	(Ann)	(Ericka)	(Matt)	(Megan)	(Tasha)	(Luke)	(Sally)	
Starting position:	1	2	3	4	5	6	7	8	

	(Sally)	(Luke)	(Tasha)	(Megan)	(Matt)	(Ericka)	(Ann)	(Seth)	
Finishing position:	8	7	6	5	4	3	2	1	

ORGANIZER CARD

DVD

Stepping-Stones I

Questions

1. What are we trying to accomplish?
2. How many bases do we get?
3. What happens if someone touches the floor?
4. What happens if two people touch a base at the same time?
5. What are some ways that we can help each other?
6. Can you think of any safety issues that we should discuss?

From *Essentials of Team Building* by Daniel W. Midura and Donald R. Glover, 2005, Champaign, IL: Human Kinetics.

Reprinted, by permission, from D. Glover and D. Midura, 1992, *Team building through physical challenges* (Champaign, IL: Human Kinetics), Appendix.

CHALLENGE CARD

 DVD

Bridge Over the Raging River

Equipment

Four tires, two long jump ropes, and two eight-foot (2.5-meter) two-by-fours.

Starting Position

All group members begin at the starting line at one end of the river with their equipment.

Our Challenge

The group completes the task when all group members have crossed the river without touching the floor. They take all the equipment with them.

Rules and Sacrifices

1. Group members may not touch the river (floor).

2. Group members may not step on a two-by-four if the board is in the river.

3. If a group member breaks a rule, the group must take all the equipment back to the starting line and begin again.

4. If the two-by-four touches the river under the weight of the team stepping on it, no sacrifice is required.

5. No one may call others by their last names or use put-downs.

Safety note: Be sure that no one steps on the end of a two-by-four so that the board flips up. Also, be careful that the board does not drop on anyone.

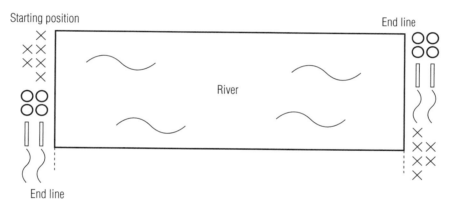

ORGANIZER CARD

 DVD

Bridge Over the Raging River

Questions

1. What equipment do we use?

2. Where are the river boundaries?

3. What happens if a person touches the river (floor)?

4. What happens if the two-by-four is in the river and someone steps on it?

5. Where will we be when we complete the task?

6. Do we need to take all the equipment?

7. What is the special safety note?

8. Can you think of any other safety issues that we should discuss?

From *Essentials of Team Building* by Daniel W. Midura and Donald R. Glover, 2005, Champaign, IL: Human Kinetics.

Reprinted, by permission, from D. Glover and D. Midura, 1992, *Team building through physical challenges* (Champaign, IL: Human Kinetics), Appendix.

CHALLENGE CARD DVD
Skywriters

Equipment

A hanging cargo net, tumbling mats or crash pads under the net for safety, a checklist of shapes to be constructed, and paper and pencils for drawing plans.

Starting Position

All group members stand on the mats next to the cargo net and on the same side of the net.

Our Challenge

Using all group members, the team constructs the number of shapes assigned by the teacher.

Rules and Sacrifices

1. All group members must be on the cargo net and off the floor.
2. All group members must be on the same side of the cargo net.
3. All group members must get off the cargo net before they construct a new shape.
4. This task has no sacrifices, but the teacher must approve a shape before the group builds another one.

ORGANIZER CARD DVD
Skywriters

Questions

1. What equipment do we use?
2. Do we all have to be on the cargo net?
3. How many people have to be part of each shape that we make?
4. How many shapes do we build?
5. What do we do after the teacher approves our shape?
6. What are the sacrifices in this challenge?
7. Can you think of any safety issues that we should discuss?

From *Essentials of Team Building* by Daniel W. Midura and Donald R. Glover, 2005, Champaign, IL: Human Kinetics.

Reprinted, by permission, from D. Midura and D. Glover, 1995, *More team building challenges* (Champaign, IL: Human Kinetics), Appendix B.

CHALLENGE CARD DVD
Human Billboard

Equipment

A hanging cargo net, tumbling mats or crash pads under the net for safety, a checklist of letters to be constructed, and paper and pencils for drawing plans.

Starting Position

All the group members stand on the mats next to the cargo net and on the same side of the net.

Our Challenge

Using all group members, the team must construct the number of letters assigned by the teacher. The group chooses letters from the checklist that the teacher gives to the group.

Rules and Sacrifices

1. All group members must be on the cargo net and off the floor.
2. All group members must be on the same side of the cargo net.
3. All group members must get off the cargo net before they construct a new letter.
4. No one may call others by their last names or use put-downs.
5. This task has no sacrifices, but the teacher must approve a shape before the group builds another one.

ORGANIZER CARD DVD
Human Billboard

Questions

1. What equipment do we use?
2. Do we all have to be on the cargo net?
3. How many people have to be part of each letter that we make?
4. How many letters will we build?
5. What do we do after the teacher approves our letter?
6. What are the sacrifices in this challenge?
7. Are there any safety issues that we should discuss?

From *Essentials of Team Building* by Daniel W. Midura and Donald R. Glover, 2005, Champaign, IL: Human Kinetics.

Reprinted, by permission, from D. Glover and D. Midura, 1992, *Team building through physical challenges* (Champaign, IL: Human Kinetics), Appendix.

CHALLENGE CARD

Jumping Machine

Equipment

One long rope approximately 30 feet (9 meters) long.

Starting Position

All group members stand next to the long rope as it lies on the floor.

Our Challenge

The group masters the task when all group members have completed 10 consecutive jumps without a miss. For a jump to count, all jumpers must jump at the same time. The turners must turn the rope in normal rope-jumping fashion.

Rules and Sacrifices

1. Only one group member may be at each end of the rope as a rope turner.
2. The 10 jumps must be consecutive. If a miss occurs, the task begins again.
3. The turners must turn the rope so that it goes over the heads and below the feet of the jumpers.
4. Counting does not begin until all jumpers are jumping.
5. The group should count aloud.
6. No one should call others by their last names or use put-downs.

ORGANIZER CARD

Jumping Machine

Questions

1. What equipment do we use?
2. How many jumps must we accomplish?
3. Do our jumps have to be consecutive?
4. What do we do if we miss?
5. Must the rope pass over our heads?
6. Do we count our jumps aloud?
7. When do we start counting our jumps?
8. Do we actually have to jump the rope?
9. Can you think of any safety issues that we should discuss?

From *Essentials of Team Building* by Daniel W. Midura and Donald R. Glover, 2005, Champaign, IL: Human Kinetics.

Reprinted, by permission, from D. Glover and D. Midura, 1992, *Team building through physical challenges* (Champaign, IL: Human Kinetics), Appendix.

CHALLENGE CARD

 DVD

Human Pegs

Equipment

Ten bases set up in a triangle and large cones to take the place of group members if the group does not have nine members.

Starting Position

Each group member stands on a base. The group places a cone on an empty base to take the place of a person if necessary. One base must be left open.

Our Challenge

Group members jump one another, one at a time, to eliminate teammates until only one person is left on a base.

Rules and Sacrifices

1. Group members may not touch the floor before being eliminated.

2. Team members may go over one another to a new base. They cannot walk around one another to a new base.

3. Only one person at a time may touch a base.

4. Group members can make all moves by jumping or stepping over teammates. They may not just step to a new base.

5. No one may use last names or put-downs.

6. If a group member breaks a rule, all group members get back onto a base, but they must start with a different base as the open base.

ORGANIZER CARD

 DVD

Human Pegs

Questions

1. What equipment do we get?

2. What are we trying to accomplish?

3. How do we make a move in this challenge?

4. What happens if we break a rule?

5. What do we do if we cannot make another move and we have more than one teammate left?

6. Can you think of any safety issues that we should discuss?

From *Essentials of Team Building* by Daniel W. Midura and Donald R. Glover, 2005, Champaign, IL: Human Kinetics.

CHALLENGE CARD

 DVD

The Wall II

Equipment

Three large crash pads stacked on top of one another with unfolded tumbling mats covering the floor beneath the wall and surrounding area.

Starting Position

All group members start on one side of the wall.

Our Challenge

The group completes the challenge when all group members have climbed over the wall and are standing safely on the other side.

Rules and Sacrifices

1. Group members may not hold onto the crash pad handles when climbing the wall (they may hold them if they are helping to support the wall).

2. Group members may not step over the dividing line between the two sides of the working area.

3. After a team member gets off the top of the wall, he or she may not climb back up to help a teammate.

4. Team members may not step off the floor mats onto the floor.

5. No one may call others by their last names or use put-downs.

6. If a group member breaks a rule, that person and a successful teammate (over the walll) must start the task again.

ORGANIZER CARD

 DVD

The Wall II

Questions

1. What is our challenge?
2. What happens if someone steps over the dividing line?
3. What happens if someone steps off the floor mats?
4. What happens if someone holds the crash pad handles while climbing?
5. What happens when someone gets off the top of the wall?
6. Where will we be when we complete the task?
7. Can you think of any safety issues that we should discuss?

From *Essentials of Team Building* by Daniel W. Midura and Donald R. Glover, 2005, Champaign, IL: Human Kinetics.

Reprinted, by permission, from D. Glover and D. Midura, 1992, *Team building through physical challenges* (Champaign, IL: Human Kinetics), Appendix.

CHALLENGE CARD

 DVD

Indiana's Challenge

Equipment

Four long jump ropes, one basketball, and one 18-inch (45-centimeter) cone.

Starting Position

The group stands outside a 10-foot (3-meter) circle (basketball jump circle). The cone is in the middle of the circle with the ball on top of it.

Our Challenge

The group must remove the ball from the cone without allowing the ball to touch the floor inside or outside the circle. The group must find three different ways to remove the ball. At least one method requires group members to fling the ball so that they have to catch it in the air. They must use the ropes to retrieve the ball from the cone.

Rules and Sacrifices

1. If the ball touches the floor, either inside or outside of the circle, one group member may cross the circle line to place the ball on the cone.
2. Group members may not cross the line with any part of their body.
3. The cone may not be moved.
4. The teammate replacing the ball on the cone may not manipulate the ropes while in the circle.
5. No one may use last names or put-downs.
6. Anytime the group breaks a rule, it must stop, replace the ball, and begin again.

ORGANIZER CARD

 DVD

Indiana's Challenge

Questions

1. What equipment do we use?
2. Can the ball touch the floor either inside or outside the circle?
3. Can we move the cone?
4. How many times do we remove the ball from the cone?
5. Can we remove the ball from the cone the same way each time?
6. How many times do we have to fling the ball to our team?
7. Can you think of any safety issues that we should discuss?

From *Essentials of Team Building* by Daniel W. Midura and Donald R. Glover, 2005, Champaign, IL: Human Kinetics.

CHALLENGE CARD

 DVD

Teamwork Walk

Equipment

One set of team skis, rope or sash cord, and a designated path.

Starting Position

Group members stand on the team skis behind the starting line, holding onto the rope handles.

Our Challenge

The group completes the task when it has walked through the course on the skis without anyone having touched the floor, a wall, or any other stationary object with any part of his or her body.

Rules and Sacrifices

1. All group members must be standing on the skis.
2. No one may touch the floor, a wall, or any other stationary object in the path of the designated course.
3. Group members must all travel the path from start to finish.
4. No one may call others by their last names or use put-downs.
5. If the team breaks a rule, it must start the task again from the beginning.

ORGANIZER CARD

 DVD

Teamwork Walk

Questions

1. Where is our starting point?
2. Where is our ending point?
3. What happens if someone touches the floor while we are walking?
4. What happens if someone touches a wall or any other object while we are walking?
5. Can you think of any safety issues that we should discuss?

From *Essentials of Team Building* by Daniel W. Midura and Donald R. Glover, 2005, Champaign, IL: Human Kinetics.

Reprinted, by permission, from D. Glover and D. Midura, 1992, *Team building through physical challenges* (Champaign, IL: Human Kinetics), Appendix.

CHALLENGE CARD
 DVD

Great Pearl Caper

Equipment

Two pearl track transports, one 22-inch (56-centimeter) or larger ball, and two crates (or tires).

Starting Position

The pearl transports and the pearl (the ball) are placed at the beginning crate.

Our Challenge

The group must move the pearl from the first crate to the second crate using only the pearl transports to move the ball.

Rules and Sacrifices

1. No part of a team member's body may touch the pearl.

2. The team can move the pearl only with the pearl track transports.

3. After part of the team has the pearl in a track transport, those teammates cannot move toward the pearl stand. They can move anywhere if they are not in possession of the pearl.

4. The pearl may never touch the ground.

5. No one may call others by their last names or use put-downs.

6. If the team breaks any rule, it must return to the starting line, replace the pearl on the first crate, and attempt the challenge from the beginning.

ORGANIZER CARD
 DVD

Great Pearl Caper

Questions

1. What equipment do we use in this challenge?

2. Can the ball touch the floor?

3. Can we touch the ball (pearl) with any part of our bodies?

4. What can we use to move the pearl?

5. Can the group members holding the pearl on their transport move their feet?

6. When can we move our feet?

7. Where must we set the pearl?

8. What happens if we break a rule?

9. Are there any safety issues that we should discuss?

From *Essentials of Team Building* by Daniel W. Midura and Donald R. Glover, 2005, Champaign, IL: Human Kinetics.

Reprinted, by permission, from D. Glover and L. Anderson, 2003, *Character education* (Champaign, IL: Human Kinetics), Appendix p. 232-233.

CHALLENGE CARD

 DVD

Stomp It

Equipment

A stomp-it ball launcher, five colored balls, and at least one poly spot or base per group member.

Starting Position

One group member stands by the ball launcher. The other group members stand on poly spots near the ball launcher.

Our Challenge

The group must complete two stages of this challenge. In the first stage, group members must catch all five balls before they touch the ground. In the second stage, each group member must catch a specific colored ball before the ball touches the ground.

Rules and Sacrifices

1. In the first stage, any group member may catch a ball.
2. If a ball touches the floor, the group rotates, a new stomper takes a turn, and the group tries again.
3. In the second stage, group members must each catch an assigned colored ball. If a ball touches the floor, or if a group member catches the wrong ball, group members rotate positions, a new stomper takes a turn, each group member gets a new assigned colored ball, and the group tries again.

ORGANIZER CARD

 DVD

Stomp It

Questions

1. What equipment do we get?
2. What happens if a ball touches the floor?
3. How do we know if we finish the first stage?
4. In the second stage, what happens if a ball touches the floor?
5. In the second stage, what happens if someone catches the wrong ball?
6. Can you think of any safety issues that we should discuss?

From *Essentials of Team Building* by Daniel W. Midura and Donald R. Glover, 2005, Champaign, IL: Human Kinetics.

Adapted, by permission, from D. Glover and L. Anderson, 2003, *Character education* (Champaign, IL: Human Kinetics), Appendix p. 233-234.

CHALLENGE CARD

 DVD

Missing Bucket

Equipment

One 5-gallon (20-liter) bucket of water, empty cups for carrying water, a 1-gallon (4-liter) jug to receive water, eight to twelve flat bases or poly spots to use as obstacles, blindfolds for half of the group, and jump ropes to mark the boundary lines of the walking course.

Starting Position

All blindfolded group members start behind the starting line. All sighted group members stand outside or near the out-of-bounds lines.

Our Challenge

Sighted team members orally direct blindfolded group members through the course. Blindfolded teammates carry cups of water through the course and fill up the empty receiving container. Blindfolded group members may not step on any of the obstacles lying on the ground. The group completes the task when it fills the empty container. After a blindfolded teammate pours a cup of water into the empty container, a sighted teammate will guide him or her back to the starting line on a route on either side of the maze area.

Rules and Sacrifices

1. Blindfolded group members may not step on a mine (flat obstacle).
2. Blindfolded group members may not cross the side boundary lines.
3. Sighted group members may not touch a blindfolded teammate.
4. Sighted group members may not touch either the bucket or the water-carrying cups.
5. No one may call others by their last names or use put-downs.
6. If the group breaks a rule, a blindfolded group member loses the water in his or her cup and returns to the starting line.

ORGANIZER CARD

 DVD

Missing Bucket

Questions

1. What happens if a blindfolded team member steps on a land mine?
2. What happens if a blindfolded team member crosses the boundary line?
3. Can a sighted team member touch a blindfolded teammate?
4. Can a sighted team member touch the water-source bucket, the receiving container, or a carrying cup?
5. What happens if the group breaks a rule?
6. How will we know when we have completed the challenge?
7. Can you think of any safety issues that we should discuss?

From *Essentials of Team Building* by Daniel W. Midura and Donald R. Glover, 2005, Champaign, IL: Human Kinetics.

CHALLENGE CARD

 DVD

Great Balls of Color

Equipment

A sheet or tarp with five holes cut out, five colored balls, a catching container, and two scoops.

Starting Position

Group members spread out around the sheet. They hold onto the sheet with their hands. The container is placed beneath the sheet. One or two group members may be designated as scoopers. When the group is ready, the instructor or a designated person places the balls onto the sheet.

Our Challenge

All balls placed on the sheet must go through the corresponding holes in the sheet and land in the catching container.

Rules and Sacrifices

1. The hands of the group members must remain on the edges of the sheet or tarp.

2. No hands or other body parts may touch a ball.

3. The group may not move the container.

4. If a ball goes through the wrong hole, the group must start the task again (unless a scooper catches the ball).

5. If a ball touches the ground, the group must start the task over.

6. Scoopers may catch a ball that falls off the sheet or passes through the wrong hole. If they make the catch, they place the ball back onto the sheet.

7. Scoopers may not touch the sheet with their bodies or the scoop.

8. No one may use last names or put-downs.

ORGANIZER CARD

 DVD

Great Balls of Color

Questions

1. Do our hands have to remain holding onto the sheet?

2. Can other parts of our bodies touch a ball?

3. Can we move the catching container?

4. What happens if a ball goes through the wrong hole?

5. What happens if a ball touches the ground?

6. Can a scooper catch a ball before it hits the ground?

7. Can the scoopers touch the sheet?

8. Are there any safety issues that we should discuss?

From *Essentials of Team Building* by Daniel W. Midura and Donald R. Glover, 2005, Champaign, IL: Human Kinetics.

CHALLENGE CARD

 DVD

Juggler's Carry

Equipment

Four large balls, a rope, and materials to make a barrier.

Starting Position

Group members start at the designated starting line, which will also serve as the finish line. Two large balls are placed at the starting (ending) line, and two large balls are placed at the mid-line.

Our Challenge

The team must transfer four large balls across the barrier. The group makes four trips, and on each trip the group adds one ball.

Rules and Sacrifices

1. No ball may touch the floor between the starting and ending line.

2. Team members may not touch the balls with their hands.

3. A different person or different group of people must pick up a ball on each trip.

4. When traveling across the gym, all team members must be connected to one another and must be touching a ball.

5. No one may use last names or put-downs.

6. If a team member breaks a rule, the team must start over from the line where it completed the last successful trip.

ORGANIZER CARD

 DVD

Juggler's Carry

Questions

1. What equipment do we use?
2. Where is the starting line?
3. Where is the ending line?
4. What happens if a ball touches the floor?
5. Do we all have to be connected in some way when moving a ball?
6. Do we all have to be touching a ball?
7. Are there any safety issues that we should discuss?

From *Essentials of Team Building* by Daniel W. Midura and Donald R. Glover, 2005, Champaign, IL: Human Kinetics.

Reprinted, by permission, from D. Glover and L. Anderson, 2003, *Character education* (Champaign, IL: Human Kinetics), Appendix p. 218-219.

CHALLENGE CARD

 DVD

Frankenstein

Equipment

One skeleton puzzle, five bases, one container, and one deck tennis ring.

Starting Position

One team member stands on each of the five bases. The medic and doctors stand in the lab. The container with the bones of Frankenstein will be about 15 feet (4.5 meters) from base #5.

Our Challenge

The group arranges the bones of Frankenstein in the correct order in the fastest time possible following the rules of the relay sequence.

Rules and Sacrifices

1. A group member must toss the deck tennis ring from base #1 to base #2. The person on base #2 must catch the ring and turn and toss to the person on base #3. This process continues until the ring has traveled all the way to base #5 and back to base #1. If a group member drops the ring, it must be sent back to the group member who last tossed it.

2. Once the ring gets back to base #1, the medic runs to the storage crate at the opposite end of the gym and brings back three bones. The medic cannot leave the building area (the lab) until the ring gets back to base #1.

3. When the medic returns, he or she must give the bones to the doctors, who begin assembling the puzzle. When the doctors receive the bones, all players rotate positions. The medic goes to base #1, the person on base #1 goes to base #2, the person on base #2 goes to base #3, the person on base #3 moves to base #4, and the person on base #4 moves to base #5. The person on base #5 becomes a new doctor, and one of the doctors becomes the new medic. Team members cannot rotate positions until the medic returns to the building area with three bones.

4. The ring must make seven successful round trips to get all the puzzle pieces to the building area. After the last medic has delivered the last three puzzle pieces, team members can hustle to the lab and confer about any changes they need to make to Frankenstein to make him complete. When they think that they have put Frankenstein together correctly, the last medic yells, "Lightning." This is the signal to stop the clock. The instructor then checks the puzzle for accuracy. If the puzzle is correct, the time stands. If it is incorrect, the clock starts again as the team rearranges the bones. This process continues until the team assembles Frankenstein correctly.

From *Essentials of Team Building* by Daniel W. Midura and Donald R. Glover, 2005, Champaign, IL: Human Kinetics.

Reprinted, by permission, from D. Glover and L. Anderson, 2003, *Character education* (Champaign, IL: Human Kinetics), Appendix p. 222-223.

ORGANIZER CARD

 DVD

Frankenstein

Questions

1. What equipment will we use in this challenge?
2. What is the order or sequence of events we must follow in this challenge?
3. How do we rotate positions in this task?
4. What happens if we drop the ring?
5. How many bones can the medic carry at one time?
6. Who becomes the next medic?
7. Who becomes the next doctor?
8. When do we yell, "Lightning"?
9. What happens if we make a mistake assembling Frankenstein?
10. Are there any safety issues that we should discuss?

From *Essentials of Team Building* by Daniel W. Midura and Donald R. Glover, 2005, Champaign, IL: Human Kinetics.

Reprinted, by permission, from D. Glover and L. Anderson, 2003, *Character education* (Champaign, IL: Human Kinetics), Appendix p. 224.

CHALLENGE CARD

 DVD

Dynamic Barrier

Equipment

One long jump rope, one large 22- to 34-inch (56- to 86-centimeter) ball, three deck tennis rings, one hula hoop, and one gym scooter.

Starting Position

All group members and all equipment start on one side of the turning rope. Two group members begin by turning the rope toward the remaining team members.

Our Challenge

The team must get all team members and all equipment through the turning rope in the methods described in the rules.

Rules and Sacrifices

1. All group members and all equipment must pass through the barrier without touching it.

2. Group members must roll the large ball through the barrier, and a group member must accompany it. In other words, a team member and the ball must pass through the barrier together, but the ball must be rolling.

3. Team members must toss the deck tennis rings through the barrier, and a team member on the opposite side must catch them. If a team member drops a ring, the team must start the challenge over from the beginning.

4. The scooter must carry a team member through. The team must decide who will sit on the scooter and then push that person through the barrier. Caution: Teammates may assist and push the scooter and their teammate through, but they must be aware of their proximity to the walls. As soon as the scooter gets through the barrier, the rider should stop it and not coast into teammates or equipment.

5. Two teammates must pass through at the same time while holding the hula hoop.

6. All remaining students on the team must pass through the barrier together. Although they do not have to be connected, they must pass through at the same time.

7. If any teammate or any equipment touches the barrier, then that person or that piece of equipment and all team members who have already successfully passed through the barrier must go back to the start.

8. No one may call others by their last names or use put-downs.

From *Essentials of Team Building* by Daniel W. Midura and Donald R. Glover, 2005, Champaign, IL: Human Kinetics.

Reprinted, by permission, from D. Glover and L. Anderson, 2003, *Character education* (Champaign, IL: Human Kinetics), Appendix p. 219-220.

ORGANIZER CARD

 DVD

Dynamic Barrier

Questions

1. What equipment do we use?
2. What will be our order of traveling through the rope?
3. What happens if the turning rope touches a team member?
4. What happens if the rope touches a piece of our equipment?
5. Are there any safety issues that we should discuss?

From *Essentials of Team Building* by Daniel W. Midura and Donald R. Glover, 2005, Champaign, IL: Human Kinetics.

Reprinted, by permission, from D. Glover and L. Anderson, 2003, *Character education* (Champaign, IL: Human Kinetics), Appendix p. 221.

CHALLENGE CARD

 DVD

Tower of Tires

Equipment

Five tires (different sizes) numbered 1 through 5 from top to bottom and three large cones.

Starting Position

The tires are stacked in order of size, from largest on the bottom to smallest on top. The tires are stacked on the middle cone, between two other large cones.

Our Challenge

The group completes the task when it has restacked the five tires onto one of the other cones in the exact order of the starting position.

Rules and Sacrifices

1. The group may move only one tire at a time.

2. A tire may not be stacked on top of a smaller tire.

3. Two teammates must move each tire, with each person using two hands.

4. Each time the team moves a tire, a different combination of teammates must move it.

5. When team members move a tire, they must move it onto a cone (the cone may be empty or have another tire on it). A move is considered to have occurred when one or both teammates let go of the tire.

6. No tire may touch the floor, unless it is on the cone.

7. No one may use put-downs or last names.

8. If a team breaks a rule, team members must restack all tires in the original position.

ORGANIZER CARD

 DVD

Tower of Tires

Questions

1. What equipment do we use?

2. How many tires can we move at a time?

3. How many people must move each tire on each turn?

4. How many hands must be on the tires?

5. When is a move completed?

6. Can we place a tire on a smaller tire?

7. What happens if we break a rule?

8. How will we know when we have completed the challenge?

From *Essentials of Team Building* by Daniel W. Midura and Donald R. Glover, 2005, Champaign, IL: Human Kinetics.

CHALLENGE CARD

 DVD

Factor In

Equipment

Twelve round bases with numbers written or taped on top.

Starting Position

The team should be at the entrance to the maze, connected, and ready to enter.

Our Challenge

The team must remain connected and move through a maze of numbered bases. The team members must stand on various bases in the maze, but the bases they are using must have a total number that can be factored by three.

The task is mastered when all group members move from the entrance of the maze to the exit while remaining connected, and they must keep the sum total of the bases a factor of three.

Rules and Sacrifices

1. Team members must stay connected during travel.

2. Team members may only move one base at a time.

3. Team members may move only in either a straight or diagonal path.

4. Teammates may not be two bases away from the immediate person they are connected to.

5. Only one team member may enter the maze at a time. When teammates get to the last row of the maze, they must stay connected, but they may step out of the maze.

6. After each team member enters or exits the maze, the total-sum number (of the bases team members are standing on) must be a factor of three. Otherwise, the team must start again.

7. Only one person on a base at a time.

8. No one should call others by their last names or use put-downs.

9. If any rule is broken, the team must go back to the entrance and start again.

ORGANIZER CARD

 DVD

Factor In

Questions

1. Do teammates have to stay connected during travel?

2. How many bases can one person move at a time?

3. The sum total of all the bases that the teammates are standing on must be a factor of what number?

4. Can teams have more than one person on a base at a time?

5. What happens if a team member breaks a rule?

From *Essentials of Team Building* by Daniel W. Midura and Donald R. Glover, 2005, Champaign, IL: Human Kinetics.

Created by Marc Bachman and Jay Ehlers.

CHALLENGE CARD
Black Hole

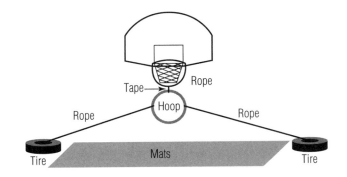

Equipment

Two tires, one hula hoop, a rope and tape to suspend the hoop between the tires and basket, and mats and crash pads on the floor for safety.

Starting Position

All group members stand on one side of the suspended hula hoop (black hole). Group members must remain on the tumbling mats.

Our Challenge

The group masters the task when all group members have passed from one side of the hoop (outer space) through the hoop (black hole) to the other side (earth) without touching the hoop.

Rules and Sacrifices

1. All group members must pass through the hoop.
2. Group members may not touch the hoop or the ropes connected to the hoop.
3. No one may step over the dividing line.

4. All group members must remain on the mats or crash pads during the task.
5. Group members may not reach under, around, or over the hula hoop to help. They may reach through the hoop to help.
6. No one may call others by their last names or use put-downs.
7. No one may dive through the hoop.
8. If a group member breaks a rule, that person and one successful person (who passed through the hoop) must start over.

ORGANIZER CARD
Black Hole

Questions

1. What is our starting position?
2. What is our ending position?
3. What happens if someone touches the black hole (hoop)?
4. What happens if someone steps over the dividing line?

5. What happens if someone dives through the hoop?
6. Can you think of any safety issues that we should discuss?

CHALLENGE CARD

 DVD

Stepping-Stones II

Equipment

Nine indoor bases or carpet squares set in a straight line and, if desired, different colored jerseys to identify the two halves of the team.

Starting Position

Each group member stands on a base with the empty base in the middle of the line. Each group member gets a letter or a number, for example, 4, 3, 2, 1, empty base, A, B, C, D. The team divides itself into two equal groups, and the groups face the empty base.

Our Challenge

The group completes the task when it ends up like this: A, B, C, D, empty base, 4, 3, 2, 1, compared with the starting position of 4, 3, 2, 1, empty base, A, B, C, D.

Rules and Sacrifices

1. Only one person may move to a base at a time.
2. Team members may not move backward.
3. Only one person may be on a base at a time.
4. Group members may move to an empty base directly in front of them or go around one other person to an empty base. Group members may not go around two other people to an empty base.
5. No one should call others by their last names or use put-downs.
6. If a team member breaks a rule, all group members must go back to their original bases.

ORGANIZER CARD

 DVD

Stepping-Stones II

Questions

1. How do we line up to start the challenge?
2. How will we be lined up when we complete the challenge?
3. Where is the extra base?
4. When can we move off our bases?
5. Can we move backward?
6. Can two people move at the same time?
7. Can we move two or more bases at a time?
8. How many people may touch a base at one time?
9. Can you think of any safety issues that we should discuss?

From *Essentials of Team Building* by Daniel W. Midura and Donald R. Glover, 2005, Champaign, IL: Human Kinetics.

Reprinted, by permission, from D. Glover and D. Midura, 1992, *Team building through physical challenges* (Champaign, IL: Human Kinetics), Appendix.

CHALLENGE CARD

Alphabet Balance Beam

Equipment

A high balance beam, plenty of mats for safety, and at least two crash pads.

Starting Position

Group members sit on the balance beam in random order. The instructor may assign the group to arrange itself alphabetically by first name, middle name, last name, or other scheme.

Our Challenge

The group completes the challenge when all group members are standing on the beam in the assigned alphabetical order.

Rules and Sacrifices

1. All group members must stay on the beam during the task.

2. If any person touches the floor or mats, the entire group must start the task from the beginning.

3. If any group member touches the support legs of the beam, the group must start over.

4. No one may call others by their last names or use put-downs.

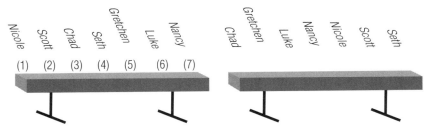

Starting position (example): First names

Nicole (1) Scott (2) Chad (3) Seth (4) Gretchen (5) Luke (6) Nancy (7)

Finish position

Chad Gretchen Luke Nancy Nicole Scott Seth

ORGANIZER CARD

Alphabet Balance Beam

Questions

1. By which names are we alphabetizing ourselves?

2. In which direction are we getting into alphabetical order?

3. What happens if a person touches the floor during the task?

4. What happens if a person touches the support legs of the beam?

5. What will we be doing when we have completed the challenge?

6. Can you think of any safety issues that we should discuss?

From *Essentials of Team Building* by Daniel W. Midura and Donald R. Glover, 2005, Champaign, IL: Human Kinetics.

Reprinted, by permission, from D. Glover and D. Midura, 1992, *Team building through physical challenges* (Champaign, IL: Human Kinetics), Appendix.

CHALLENGE CARD

 DVD

Knights of the Around Table

Equipment

A sturdy table big enough—5 to 6 feet (150 to 180 centimeters) long—to crawl under without brushing the table legs, two tape strips to mark starting and finishing lines, and mats under the table for safety.

Starting Positions

All group members start behind the starting line, located about 3 feet (one meter) from one side of the table.

Our Challenge

With the help of group members, all team members must cross over the top of the table, climb under it, and again cross over the top of it without touching the floor. All group members must finish behind the finish line. The finish line is located about 3 feet (one meter) from the other end of the table.

Rules and Sacrifices

1. Group members may not touch the floor between the starting line and finish line.
2. Group members standing behind either tape line may assist a team member on the table but may not touch the table. Or, allow three people to touch the table (instructor's discretion).
3. After a group member gets off the table and crosses the finish line, he or she may not get back on top of the table.
4. No one may call others by their last names or use put-downs.
5. If a group member breaks a rule, that person and one successful person (or the person who has advanced the farthest) must start the task again.

ORGANIZER CARD

 DVD

Knights of the Around Table

Questions

1. What equipment do we use?
2. What happens if a group member touches the floor between the starting and finishing lines?
3. What happens if a group member standing behind the starting or finishing line touches the table?
4. If a group member gets off the top of the table and makes to the finish line, can he or she get back on top of the table?
5. What happens if a group member uses last names or put-downs?
6. Can you think of any safety issues that we should discuss?

From *Essentials of Team Building* by Daniel W. Midura and Donald R. Glover, 2005, Champaign, IL: Human Kinetics.

Reprinted, by permission, from D. Midura and D. Glover, 1995, *More team building challenges* (Champaign, IL: Human Kinetics), Appendix B.

CHALLENGE CARD

 DVD

Electric Fence

Equipment

A high balance beam, tumbling mats for safety, a volleyball net, and two volleyball net standards.

Starting Position

All group members stand on the entry mat at one end of the balance beam.

Our Challenge

The group completes the task when all group members have advanced from the entry mat to the exit mat without touching the electric fence (net). All group members must pass under the net.

Rules and Sacrifices

1. Group members must begin the task by getting on the top of the balance beam.
2. Group members must go under the electric fence (net) without touching the net.
3. Group members may not touch the floor or mats between the entry and exit mats.
4. Group members must get back on top of the beam before getting off the beam.
5. After group members get off the beam and onto the exit mat, they may not get back onto the beam to help.
6. Teammates must be on the ledge in order to help teammates on top of the beam. Teammates on the ledge may not assist those hanging under the beam.
7. Only the team members on top of the beam may assist teammates hanging under the beam.
8. No one may call others by their last names or use put-downs.
9. If a group member breaks a rule, that person and one successful person must start at the beginning.

ORGANIZER CARD

 DVD

Electric Fence

Questions

1. Where is the entry mat?
2. Where is the exit mat?
3. What happens if we touch the floor between the entry and exit mats?
4. Must we go under the electric fence (net)?
5. What happens if we touch the electric fence?
6. What do we have to do before we get off the beam?
7. Where will we be when we finish the challenge?
8. Can you think of any safety issues that we should discuss?

From *Essentials of Team Building* by Daniel W. Midura and Donald R. Glover, 2005, Champaign, IL: Human Kinetics.

Reprinted, by permission, from D. Glover and D. Midura, 1992, *Team building through physical challenges* (Champaign, IL: Human Kinetics), Appendix.

CHALLENGE CARD

 DVD

Grand Canyon I

Equipment

One climbing rope, one vaulting box (or vertical stack of mats), tumbling mats to cover the working space, and a distinct starting line.

Starting Position

All group members stand behind the starting line, facing the vaulting box. A tape line marks the starting line. The group has the rope to start the task.

Our Challenge

The group completes the task when all group members have crossed the Grand Canyon and are standing on top of the vaulting box.

Rules and Sacrifices

1. The Grand Canyon is all the area beyond the starting line, except for the cliff (vaulting box).

2. If a group member touches the Grand Canyon, that person and a successful teammate (who crossed the canyon) must start again at the beginning.

3. If a group member falls off the vaulting box, that person and a successful teammate must start again at the beginning.

4. No one may call others by their last names or use put-downs.

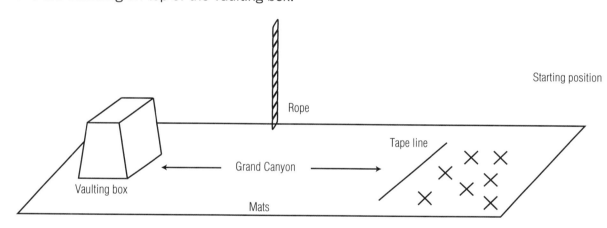

ORGANIZER CARD

 DVD

Grand Canyon I

Questions

1. Where is the Grand Canyon?

2. What happens if a team member touches the Grand Canyon?

3. What happens if a team member falls off the cliff (vaulting box)?

4. What happens if a team member steps over the starting line?

5. What will we be doing when we complete the task?

6. Can you think of safety issues that we should discuss?

From *Essentials of Team Building* by Daniel W. Midura and Donald R. Glover, 2005, Champaign, IL: Human Kinetics.

Reprinted, by permission, from D. Glover and D. Midura, 1992, *Team building through physical challenges* (Champaign, IL: Human Kinetics), Appendix.

CHALLENGE CARD

 DVD

Grand Canyon II

Equipment

One climbing rope for swinging, crash pads for cliffs, mats to cover the floor space.

Starting Position

Group members begin by standing on the first cliff.

Our Challenge

The group completes the task when all group members have crossed the Grand Canyon and are standing on the second cliff.

Rules and Sacrifices

1. If a group member touches the floor (Grand Canyon), that person and a successful teammate must return to the first cliff.

2. If a group member falls off a cliff and touches the floor, that person and a successful teammate must go back to the first cliff.

3. No one may use last names or putdowns.

ORGANIZER CARD

 DVD

Grand Canyon II

Questions

1. Where is the Grand Canyon?
2. What happens if a team member touches the Grand Canyon?
3. What happens if a team member falls off a cliff?
4. Where will we be when we are done?
5. What will we be doing when we complete the challenge?
6. Can you think of any safety issues that we should discuss?

From *Essentials of Team Building* by Daniel W. Midura and Donald R. Glover, 2005, Champaign, IL: Human Kinetics.

Reprinted, by permission, from D. Glover and D. Midura, 1992, *Team building through physical challenges* (Champaign, IL: Human Kinetics), Appendix.

CHALLENGE CARD

 DVD

Spider's Web

Equipment

A spider's web and a safe base of mats beneath the web.

Starting Position

All group members start on one side of the spider's web.

Our Challenge

All the group members must pass through the spider's web to the other side without touching any part of the web with their bodies. If bells are hung from the web, the group must not cause them to make a sound.

Rules and Sacrifices

1. Each group member must pass through a different opening in the web.

2. No one may touch any part of the web with his or her body.

3. Group members may reach through the web to help a teammate, but they may not touch the web while helping.

4. No one may dive through the web.

5. The group may not toss anyone through the web.

6. If bells are hung from the spider's web, a sacrifice will be necessary if the bell makes a sound.

7. No one may call others by their last names or use put-downs.

8. If a group member breaks a rule, that person and a successful teammate (who passed through the web) must start the task again.

ORGANIZER CARD

 DVD

Spider's Web

Questions

1. Do we each have to go through a different opening?

2. Can we touch the spider's web?

3. Can we reach through the web to help teammates?

4. Can anyone dive through the spider's web?

5. Can we throw teammates through an opening?

6. What happens if we break a rule?

7. If a bell hanging from the spider's web makes a sound, what happens?

8. Can you think of any safety issues that we should discuss?

From *Essentials of Team Building* by Daniel W. Midura and Donald R. Glover, 2005, Champaign, IL: Human Kinetics.

CHALLENGE CARD

 DVD

Neutral Zone

Equipment

A neutral-zone balance board and fulcrum set up on tumbling mats that cover the entire working area.

Starting Position

Group members start by balancing themselves with half of the group on each side of the neutral-zone balance board.

Our Challenge

The group completes the challenge when group members all switch sides of the balance board and end up on the opposite side of the neutral zone.

Rules and Sacrifices

1. No group member may touch the floor (or tumbling mats).
2. The neutral-zone balance board may not touch the floor.
3. Group members may step on the neutral-zone fulcrum when attempting to change positions.
4. No one may call others by their last names or use put-downs.
5. If the group breaks a rule, it must begin the challenge from the beginning.

ORGANIZER CARD

 DVD

Neutral Zone

Questions

1. What equipment do we use?
2. What happens if a group member touches the floor?
3. What happens if the balance board touches the floor?
4. Can we step on the neutral-zone fulcrum?
5. How will we know when we have completed the task?
6. Can you think of any safety issues that we should discuss?

From *Essentials of Team Building* by Daniel W. Midura and Donald R. Glover, 2005, Champaign, IL: Human Kinetics.

CHALLENGE CARD

 DVD

Marble Twist and Turn

Equipment

One twist and turn marble racetrack and three marbles.

Starting Position

Six group members attach themselves to the twist and turn racetrack tubing using the waist band, arm band, and leg band. One group member is designated as the person to put the marbles into one end of the tube.

Our Challenge

The group completes the task when it gets the three marbles to travel from one end of the tube through the racetrack and out the other end. The marbles may not touch each other while inside the tube.

Rules and Sacrifices

1. Team members may not touch the tube with their hands.
2. The team must pass three marbles through the entire length of the tube without letting the marbles touch.
3. The first team member may place the marble inside the tube and momentarily hold the tube to insert the marble.
4. Teammates may physically assist one another.
5. No one may call others by their last names or use put-downs.
6. If the group breaks any rule, all three marbles must be returned to the first teammate and the challenge starts again from the beginning.

ORGANIZER CARD

 DVD

Marble Twist and Turn

Questions

1. What equipment do we use in this challenge?
2. How many marbles must pass completely through the tube?
3. How many group members must be attached to the racetrack tube?
4. What parts of our bodies may not touch the tube?
5. What happens if any marbles touch each other while inside the tube?
6. Can we help each other?
7. Are there any safety issues that we should discuss?

From *Essentials of Team Building* by Daniel W. Midura and Donald R. Glover, 2005, Champaign, IL: Human Kinetics.

Adapted, by permission, from D. Glover and L. Anderson, 2003, *Character education* (Champaign, IL: Human Kinetics), Appendix p. 230-231.

CHALLENGE CARD
 DVD

Thinking Outside the Dots

Equipment

Nine poly spots set up in a grid and four long jump ropes.

Starting Position

The ropes are lying next to the grid. The group begins the challenge by lifting the ropes off the ground and starting.

Our Challenge

The group must find a way to suspend the ropes over the dots so that the ropes cross above all nine dots. The group may not double up the ropes.

Rules and Sacrifices

1. The group may tie ropes together.
2. The group must suspend the ropes above the bases without touching the floor or bases during all attempts.

3. The rope may pass over a base more than once but no part of the rope may overlap.
4. If any part of the rope touches the floor, the attempt fails and the group must begin the task again.
5. If the group creates more than four line segments, the attempt fails.
6. With each failed attempt, the team must start the task over with one fewer teammate being allowed to speak.
7. No one may call others by their last names or use put-downs.

ORGANIZER CARD
 DVD

Thinking Outside the Dots

Questions

1. What equipment do we get?
2. What happens if the ropes touch the floor?
3. What happens if we double up the ropes?
4. How many line segments must we create?
5. Are there any safety issues that we should discuss?

From *Essentials of Team Building* by Daniel W. Midura and Donald R. Glover, 2005, Champaign, IL: Human Kinetics.

CHALLENGE CARD

 DVD

Building Blocks

Equipment

Eight 15-inch (38-centimeter) cardboard boxes (building blocks), and blindfolds are necessary for the first part of the challenge.

Starting Position

All the blocks are lying randomly on the floor. The team gathers around the building blocks. Each team member works with a partner.

Our Challenge

In each part of this two-part challenge, the group builds a vertical tower of building blocks. During the first part, one team member of each set of partners wears a blindfold. Only the blindfolded teammate may touch the building blocks. Only the sighted teammate may speak to the blindfolded teammate.

During the second part, all group members may speak and no one wears a blindfold. Partners must pick up blocks together, but each set of partners must stack its block in a different manner.

Rules and Sacrifices

1. If the tower falls, the group must start over.
2. In the first part, sighted group members may not touch the building blocks.
3. In the first part, sighted group members may speak only to their partners.
4. In the second part, each block must be stacked using a different method.
5. In the second part, partners must pick up the block together.
6. If character education terms are used, students must give the proper definition after placing the blocks.
7. No one may call others by their last names or use put-downs.
8. If the group breaks any rule, it must rebuild the tower from the beginning.

ORGANIZER CARD

 DVD

Building Blocks

Questions

1. What happens if the tower falls over?
2. What happens if a sighted team member touches a building block or blindfolded teammate in the first part?
3. What happens if a sighted team member speaks to anyone other than his or her partner in the first part?
4. What happens if both partners do not stack a building block together in the second part?
5. What happens if our team repeats a method of stacking the blocks in the second part?
6. How will we know when we have completed the task?
7. Can you think of any safety issues that we should discuss?

From *Essentials of Team Building* by Daniel W. Midura and Donald R. Glover, 2005, Champaign, IL: Human Kinetics.

CHALLENGE CARD DVD

Lean on Me

Equipment

A very long rope with the ends tied together to create a large circle and one base or poly spot for each group member.

Starting Position

Group members stand evenly spaced around the rope. The group backs up so that the rope is taut. Group members each stand on a base. Their arms should be straight. After group members begin the challenge, they may not move their hands on the rope.

Our Challenge

The group decides which group members let go of the rope so that eventually as few teammates as possible are holding the rope.

Rules and Sacrifices

1. Group members may not step off a base until they have released the rope with their hands.
2. Group members may not move their hands on the rope after they have started doing the task.
3. Group members may not bend their elbows while holding onto the rope.
4. The rope may not touch the floor.
5. No one may call others by their last names or use put-downs.

ORGANIZER CARD DVD

Lean on Me

Questions

1. What equipment do we use?
2. What shape will the group form with the rope?
3. What happens if the rope touches the floor?
4. What happens if we step off the base before we let go of the rope?
5. Can we move our hands on the rope?
6. Can we bend our elbows?
7. How will we know when we have completed the task?
8. Can you think of any safety issues that we should discuss?

From *Essentials of Team Building* by Daniel W. Midura and Donald R. Glover, 2005, Champaign, IL: Human Kinetics.

CHALLENGE CARD

 DVD

Rainbow Swamp Trail

Equipment

One dozen 12-inch (30-centimeter) poly spots (or bases) and six character education rainbow beanbags (beanbags of different colors).

Starting Position

Group members join hands before stepping onto the first base. The bases are marked so that the group knows the order in which to travel.

Our Challenge

Group members all step onto each of the bases marking the trail. Each group member picks up one beanbag and carries it to the end of the swamp trail.

Rules and Sacrifices

1. Team members must hold hands and stay connected throughout their trip through the swamp. A team member attempting to pick up a beanbag may let go of one teammate's hand but must rejoin hands before moving to another base.

2. No one may touch the floor during the trip through the swamp. If a team member breaks either rule #1 or rule #2, the group must start the task from the beginning.

3. Each team member must collect one beanbag on the journey and take it across the swamp. The beanbag cannot be dropped. If it is dropped, the beanbag must be replaced to its original position and retrieved again.

4. Team members must read the character education word and definition after they retrieve the bag.

5. No one may call others by their last names or use put-downs.

ORGANIZER CARD

 DVD

Rainbow Swamp Trail

Questions

1. What equipment do we use?
2. What happens if one of us touches the floor (swamp)?
3. What happens if our group falls apart?
4. When can we let go of our teammates' hands?
5. What happens if we drop a beanbag?
6. How many beanbags can a group member pick up and hold?
7. When will we finish the challenge?
8. Are there any safety issues that we should discuss?

From *Essentials of Team Building* by Daniel W. Midura and Donald R. Glover, 2005, Champaign, IL: Human Kinetics.

Reprinted, by permission, from D. Glover and L. Anderson, 2003, *Character education* (Champaign, IL: Human Kinetics), Appendix p. 228.

CHALLENGE CARD

 DVD

Integrity Tower

Equipment

Six foam bricks labeled with the words: *character, respect, sportsmanship, judgment, pride,* and *integrity.*

Starting Position

The group begins at a designated starting area with the six character building blocks. The starting area is 20 to 30 feet (6 to 9 meters) away from the construction site.

Our Challenge

The group constructs a tower with the blocks. The character block will be the base, and the integrity block will be placed last, on the top of the tower.

Rules and Sacrifices

1. Two teammates must transport each block. Each set of partners may transport only one block at a time.

2. Group members may not touch the blocks with their hands, nor can the blocks ever touch the ground, except for the character block, which must be the first block transported. The group places all other blocks on the character block.

3. The group must transport each block using a different combination of body parts. No set of partners can transport a block in the same method that other teammates used. For example, the first set of partners may use the elbows, the second set of partners may use the knees, and so on, but the partners cannot repeat the use of any method.

4. Teammates may not help other partners during the transport phase of the challenge. They may, however, help teammates stack the blocks on the tower, as long as they don't use their hands. The teammates who transported the block must still be the principal stackers. They cannot relinquish control of the block, but teammates may assist by steadying the tower or by balancing a block while it is being placed.

5. The group places the integrity block last.

6. No one may use put-downs or call others by their last names.

7. If group members break any rule, the group must take all blocks to the starting point and start the challenge from the beginning.

From *Essentials of Team Building* by Daniel W. Midura and Donald R. Glover, 2005, Champaign, IL: Human Kinetics.

Reprinted, by permission, from D. Glover and L. Anderson, 2003, *Character education* (Champaign, IL: Human Kinetics), Appendix p. 229.

ORGANIZER CARD

 DVD

Integrity Tower

Questions

1. What equipment do we use?
2. Where do we build the tower?
3. Can our hands touch the blocks?
4. Who can move the blocks?
5. Can we help a set of partners?
6. Which block will be the base of the tower?
7. Which block must be on the top?
8. If one set of partners moves its block in a certain way, can we duplicate that method?
9. Are there any safety issues that we should discuss?

From *Essentials of Team Building* by Daniel W. Midura and Donald R. Glover, 2005, Champaign, IL: Human Kinetics.

Reprinted, by permission, from D. Glover and L. Anderson, 2003, *Character education* (Champaign, IL: Human Kinetics), Appendix p. 230.

References

Bloom, B.S. 1956. *Taxonomy of educational objectives: The classification of educational goals.* New York, NY: Longmans, Green.

Ebbeck, V. and S. Gibbons. 1998. The effect of a team building program on the self-conceptions of grade 6 and 7 physical education students. *Journal of Sport and Exercise Physiology.* 20:300-310.

Glasser, W. 1998. *Choice theory: A new psychological freedom.* New York: Harper-Perennial.

Glover, D. and D. Midura. 1992. *Team building through physical challenges.* Champaign, IL: Human Kinetics.

Glover, D. and L. Anderson. 2003. *Character education.* Champaign, IL: Human Kinetics.

Hattie, J., Marsh, H., Neill, J., and G. Richards. 1997. *Adventure education and outward bound: Out-of-class experiences that make a lasting difference. Review of Educational Research,* 67, 43-87.

Heck, T. Teach Me Teamwork. Web site: www.teachmeteamwork.com [April 26, 2005]

Katz, L. 1993. All about me. *American Educator.* 17(2) 18-23.

Lickona, T., E. Schaps, and C. Lewis. 2003. *Eleven principles of effective character education.* The Character Education Partner (CEP). Web site: www.character.org/principles [April 26, 2005]

Melograno, V. 1998. *Professional and student portfolios for physical education.* Champaign, IL: Human Kinetics.

Metcalfe, J. 2002. USOC looks to build on success. *Arizona Republic.* February 26, 2002.

Midura, D. and D. Glover. 1995. *More team building challenges.* Champaign, IL: Human Kinetics.

North Carolina Outward Bound School. Web site: www.ncoutwardbound.org/courses [April 26, 2005]

Odyssey of the Mind. Fall 1995:5. Web site: www.odysseyofthemind.com [April 26, 2005]

Orlick, T. 1978. *The cooperative sports and games book.* New York: Pantheon Books.

Orlick, T. 1982. *The second cooperative sports and games book: Over two hundred noncompetitive games for kids and adults both.* New York, NY: Pantheon Books.

Priest, S. and M. Gass. 1997. *Effective Leadership in Adventure Programming.* Champaign, IL: Human Kinetics.

Schoel, J., Prouty, D., and P. Radcliffe. 1988. Islands of healing: *A guide to adventure based counseling.* Dubuque, IA: Kendal/Hunt.

The Community Toolbox. Web site: http://ctb.ku.edu [April 26, 2005]

The Odyssey School. Web site: www.odysseydenver.org [April 26, 2005]

Vindero, D. 1997. Adventure programs found to have lasting, positive impact. *Education Week* on the Web. Web site: www.edweek.org [April 26, 2005]

About the Authors

Daniel W. Midura, MEd, is a physical education specialist and coordinator at Falcon Heights Elementary School in Falcon Heights, Minnesota. He has been a physical education specialist for 35 years; in that time he has presented at more than 100 conferences and workshops. In addition, he has coauthored three books and was named the Minnesota Physical Education Teacher of the Year in 1994. He was awarded the 1995 NASPE (National Association for Sport and Physical Education) Teacher of the Year for Minnesota and has received other awards and honors in connection with his teaching. He has served as president of the Minnesota AAHPERD (American Alliance for Health, Physical Education, Recreation and Dance) and is an adjunct faculty member at Bethel University and Saint Mary's University.

Donald R. Glover has taught physical education, including adapted physical education, since 1967 at the preschool, elementary, secondary, and postsecondary levels. He currently teaches elementary physical education methods at the University of Wisconsin at River Falls.

In 1981, Glover was recognized as Minnesota's Teacher of the Year and was named the Minnesota Adapted Physical Education Teacher of the Year in 1989. He has written four books, published numerous magazine and journal articles on physical education and sport, and has been a clinician at more than 100 workshops and clinics.

Glover earned his master's degree in physical education from Winona State University in 1970. A former president of MAHPERD, he is also a member of AAHPERD, NASPE, COPEC, and the Minnesota Education Association.